D1450029

Cram101 Textbook Outlines to accompany:

Strategic Management Competitiveness and Globalization

Hitt, Ireland, Hoskisson, 6th Edition

An Academic Internet Publishers (AIPI) publication (c) 2007.

You have a discounted membership at www.Cram101.com with this book.

Get all of the practice tests for the chapters of this textbook, and access in-depth reference material for writing essays and papers. Here is an example from a Cram101 Biology text:

When you need problem solving help with math, stats, and other disciplines, www.Cram101.com will walk through the formulas and solutions step by step.

With Cram101.com online, you also have access to extensive reference material.

You will nail those essays and papers. Here is an example from a Cram101 Biology text:

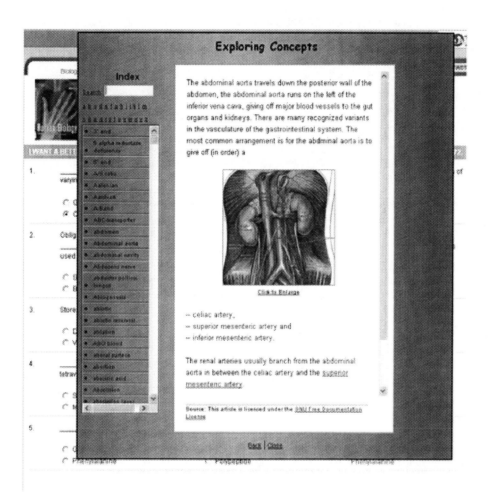

Visit **www.Cram101.com**, click Sign Up at the top of the screen, and enter DK73DW in the promo code box on the registration screen. Access to www.Cram101.com is normally $9.95, but because you have purchased this book, your access fee is only $4.95. Sign up and stop highlighting textbooks forever.

Learning System

Cram101 Textbook Outlines is a learning system. The notes in this book are the highlights of your textbook, you will never have to highlight a book again.

How to use this book. Take this book to class, it is your notebook for the lecture. The notes and highlights on the left hand side of the pages follow the outline and order of the textbook. All you have to do is follow along while your intructor presents the lecture. Circle the items emphasized in class and add other important information on the right side. With Cram101 Textbook Outlines you'll spend less time writing and more time listening. Learning becomes more efficient.

Cram101.com Online

Increase your studying efficiency by using Cram101.com's practice tests and online reference material. It is the perfect complement to Cram101 Textbook Outlines. Use self-teaching matching tests or simulate in-class testing with comprehensive multiple choice tests, or simply use Cram's true and false tests for quick review. Cram101.com even allows you to enter your in-class notes for an integrated studying format combining the textbook notes with your class notes.

Visit **www.Cram101.com**, click Sign Up at the top of the screen, and enter **DK73DW2987** in the promo code box on the registration screen. Access to www.Cram101.com is normally $9.95, but because you have purchased this book, your access fee is only $4.95. Sign up and stop highlighting textbooks forever.

Strategic Management Competitiveness and Globalization
Hitt, Ireland, Hoskisson, 6th

CONTENTS

1. Strategic Management and Strategic Competitiveness 2
2. The External Environment 24
3. Resources, Capabilities, and Core Competencies 50
4. Business-Level Strategy 68
5. Competitive Rivalry and Competitive Dynamics 94
6. Corporate-Level Strategy 112
7. Acquisition and Restructuring Strategies 142
8. International Strategy 170
9. Cooperative Strategy 186
10. Corporate Governance 208
11. Organizational Structure and Controls 234
12. Strategic Leadership 258
13. Strategic Entrepreneurship 270

Strategic intent	Strategic intent is when a firm relentlessly pursues a difficult strategic goa and concentrates its competitive actions and energies on achieving that goal.
Stakeholder	A stakeholder is an individual or group with a vested interest in or expectation for organizational performance. Usually stakeholders can either have an effect on or are affected by an organization.
Research and development	The use of resources for the deliberate discovery of new information and ways of doing things, together with the application of that information in inventing new products or processes is referred to as research and development.
Samsung	On November 30, 2005 Samsung pleaded guilty to a charge it participated in a worldwide DRAM price fixing conspiracy during 1999-2002 that damaged competition and raized PC prices.
Verizon	Verizon a Dow 30 company, is a broadband and telecommunications provider. The acquisition of GTE by Bell Atlantic, on June 30, 2000, which formed Verizon, was among the largest mergers in United States business history. Verizon, with MCI, is currently the second largest telecommunications company in the United States.
Sony	Sony is a multinational corporation and one of the world's largest media conglomerates founded in Tokyo, Japan. One of its divisions Sony Electronics is one of the leading manufacturers of electronics, video, communications, and information technology products for the consumer and professional markets.
Competitiveness	Competitiveness usually refers to characteristics that permit a firm to compete effectively with other firms due to low cost or superior technology, perhaps internationally.
Novation	A mutual agreement, between all parties concerned, for the discharge of a valid existing obligation by the substitution of a new valid obligation on the part of the debtor or another, or a like agreement for the discharge of a debtor to his creditor by the substitution of a new creditor is referred to as novation.
Innovation	Innovation refers to the first commercially successful introduction of a new product, the use of a new method of production, or the creation of a new form of business organization.
Industry	A group of firms that produce identical or similar products is an industry. It is also used specifically to refer to an area of economic production focused on manufacturing which involves large amounts of capital investment before any profit can be realized, also called "heavy industry".
Consultant	A professional that provides expert advice in a particular field or area in which customers occassionaly require this type of knowledge is a consultant.
Management	Management characterizes the process of leading and directing all or part of an organization, often a business, through the deployment and manipulation of resources. Early twentieth-century management writer Mary Parker Follett defined management as "the art of getting things done through people."
Firm	An organization that employs resources to produce a good or service for profit and owns and operates one or more plants is referred to as a firm.
DuPont	DuPont was the inventor of CFCs (along with General Motors) and the largest producer of these ozone depleting chemicals (used primarily in aerosol sprays and refrigerants) in the world, with a 25% market share in the late 1980s.
Productivity	Productivity refers to the total output of goods and services in a given period of time divided by work hours.
Analyst	Analyst refers to a person or tool with a primary function of information analysis, generally with a more limited, practical and short term set of goals than a researcher.
Accounting	A system that collects and processes financial information about an organization and reports that information to decision makers is referred to as accounting.
Market	A market is, as defined in economics, a social arrangement that allows buyers and sellers to discover

	information and carry out a voluntary exchange of goods or services.
Gain	In finance, gain is a profit or an increase in value of an investment such as a stock or bond. Gain is calculated by fair market value or the proceeds from the sale of the investment minus the sum of the purchase price and all costs associated with it.
Market leader	The market leader is dominant in its industry. It has substantial market share and often extensive distribution arrangements with retailers. It typically is the industry leader in developing innovative new business models and new products (although not always).
Service	Service refers to a "non tangible product" that is not embodied in a physical good and that typically effects some change in another product, person, or institution. Contrasts with good.
Product line	A group of products that are physically similar or are intended for a similar market are called the product line.
Competitor	Other organizations in the same industry or type of business that provide a good or service to the same set of customers is referred to as a competitor.
Nintendo	Nintendo has the reputation of historically being both the oldest intact company in the video game console market and one of the most influential and well-known console manufacturers, as well as being the most dominant entity in the handheld console market.
Acquisition	A company's purchase of the property and obligations of another company is an acquisition.
Budget	Budget refers to an account, usually for a year, of the planned expenditures and the expected receipts of an entity. For a government, the receipts are tax revenues.
Compaq	Compaq was founded in February 1982 by Rod Canion, Jim Harris and Bill Murto, three senior managers from semiconductor manufacturer Texas Instruments. Each invested $1,000 to form the company. Their first venture capital came from Ben Rosen and Sevin-Rosen partners. It is often told that the architecture of the original PC was first sketched out on a placemat by the founders while dining in the Houston restaurant, House of Pies.
Strategy formulation	The process of deciding on a strategic direction by defining a company's mission and goals, its external opportunities and threats, and its internal strengths and weaknesses is referred to as a strategy formulation.
Competitive Strategy	An outline of how a business intends to compete with other firms in the same industry is called competitive strategy.
Competitive advantage	A business is said to have a competitive advantage when its unique strengths, often based on cost, quality, time, and innovation, offer consumers a greater percieved value and there by differtiating it from its competitors.
Investment	Investment refers to spending for the production and accumulation of capital and additions to inventories. In a financial sense, buying an asset with the expectation of making a return.
Return on equity	Net profit after taxes per dollar of equity capital is referred to as return on equity.
Return on Assets	The Return on Assets percentage shows how profitable a company's assets are in generating revenue.
Return on sales	Return on sales refers to the percent of net income generated by each dollar of sales; computed by dividing net income before taxes by sales revenue.
Equity	Equity is the name given to the set of legal principles, in countries following the English common law tradition, which supplement strict rules of law where their application would operate harshly, so as to achieve what is sometimes referred to as "natural justice."
Asset	An item of property, such as land, capital, money, a share in ownership, or a claim on others for future payment, such as a bond or a bank deposit is an asset.

Stock market	An organized marketplace in which common stocks are traded. In the United States, the largest stock market is the New York Stock Exchange, on which are traded the stocks of the largest U.S. companies.
Stock	In financial terminology, stock is the capital raized by a corporation, through the issuance and sale of shares.
Long run	In economic models, the long run time frame assumes no fixed factors of production. Firms can enter or leave the marketplace, and the cost (and availability) of land, labor, raw materials, and capital goods can be assumed to vary.
Strategic management	A philosophy of management that links strategic planning with dayto-day decision making. Strategic management seeks a fit between an organization's external and internal environments.
Inputs	The inputs used by a firm or an economy are the labor, raw materials, electricity and other resources it uses to produce its outputs.
Cisco Systems	While Cisco Systems was not the first company to develop and sell a router (a device that forwards computer traffic from one network to another), it did create the first commercially successful multi-protocol router to allow previously incompatible computers to communicate using different network protocols.
Profit	Profit refers to the return to the resource entrepreneurial ability; total revenue minus total cost.
Corporation	A legal entity chartered by a state or the Federal government that is distinct and separate from the individuals who own it is a corporation. This separation gives the corporation unique powers which other legal entities lack.
Bankruptcy	Bankruptcy is a legally declared inability or impairment of ability of an individual or organization to pay their creditors.
Loyalty	Marketers tend to define customer loyalty as making repeat purchases. Some argue that it should be defined attitudinally as a strongly positive feeling about the brand.
Customer satisfaction	Customer satisfaction is a business term which is used to capture the idea of measuring how satisfied an enterprise's customers are with the organization's efforts in a marketplace.
Leadership	Management merely consists of leadership applied to business situations; or in other words: management forms a sub-set of the broader process of leadership.
Business Week	Business Week is a business magazine published by McGraw-Hill. It was first published in 1929 under the direction of Malcolm Muir, who was serving as president of the McGraw-Hill Publishing company at the time. It is considered to be the standard both in industry and among students.
Economy	The income, expenditures, and resources that affect the cost of running a business and household are called an economy.
Intel	Intel Corporation, founded in 1968 and based in Santa Clara, California, USA, is the world's largest semiconductor company. Intel is best known for its PC microprocessors, where it maintains roughly 80% market share.
Core competency	A company's core competency are things that a firm can (alsosns) do well and that meet the following three conditions. 1. It provides customer benefits, 2. It is hard for competitors to imitate, and 3. it can be leveraged widely to many products and market. A core competency can take various forms, including technical/subject matter knowhow, a reliable process, and/or close relationships with customers and suppliers. It may also include product development or culture such as employee dedication. Modern business theories suggest that most activities that are not part of a company's core competency should be outsourced.
Core	A core is the set of feasible allocations in an economy that cannot be improved upon by subset of the set of the economy's consumers (a coalition). In construction, when the force in an element is within a certain center section, the core, the element will only be under compression.

Portfolio	In finance, a portfolio is a collection of investments held by an institution or a private individual. Holding but not always a portfolio is part of an investment and risk-limiting strategy called diversification. By owning several assets, certain types of risk (in particular specific risk) can be reduced.
Microsoft	Microsoft is a multinational computer technology corporation with 2004 global annual sales of US$39.79 billion and 71,553 employees in 102 countries and regions as of July 2006. It develops, manufactures, licenses, and supports a wide range of software products for computing devices.
Economies of scale	In economics, returns to scale and economies of scale are related terms that describe what happens as the scale of production increases. They are different terms and not to be used interchangeably.
Advertising	Advertising refers to paid, nonpersonal communication through various media by organizations and individuals who are in some way identified in the advertising message.
Business unit	The lowest level of the company which contains the set of functions that carry a product through its life span from concept through manufacture, distribution, sales and service is a business unit.
Technological change	The introduction of new methods of production or new products intended to increase the productivity of existing inputs or to raise marginal products is a technological change.
Technology	The body of knowledge and techniques that can be used to combine economic resources to produce goods and services is called technology.
Ford	Ford is an American company that manufactures and sells automobiles worldwide. Ford introduced methods for large-scale manufacturing of cars, and large-scale management of an industrial workforce, especially elaborately engineered manufacturing sequences typified by the moving assembly lines.
BMW	BMW is an independent German company and manufacturer of automobiles and motorcycles. BMW is the world's largest premium carmaker and is the parent company of the BMW MINI and Rolls-Royce car brands, and, formerly, Rover.
Market segments	Market segments refer to the groups that result from the process of market segmentation; these groups ideally have common needs and will respond similarly to a marketing action.
Manufacturing	Production of goods primarily by the application of labor and capital to raw materials and other intermediate inputs, in contrast to agriculture, mining, forestry, fishing, and services a manufacturing.
Targeting	In advertizing, targeting is to select a demographic or other group of people to advertise to, and create advertisements appropriately.
Product development	In business and engineering, new product development is the complete process of bringing a new product to market. There are two parallel aspects to this process : one involves product engineering ; the other marketing analysis. Marketers see new product development as the first stage in product life cycle management, engineers as part of Product Lifecycle Management.
Tactic	A short-term immediate decision that, in its totality, leads to the achievement of strategic goals is called a tactic.
New product development	New product development is the complete process of bringing a new product to market. There are two parallel aspects to this process : one involves product engineering ; the other marketing analysis.
Consumer Reports	Consumer Reports is known for publishing reviews and comparisons of consumer products and services based on reporting and results from its in-house testing laboratory. Consumer Reports does not accept advertizing nor permit the commercial use of its reviews for selling products.
Pension	A pension is a steady income given to a person (usually after retirement). Pensions are typically payments made in the form of a guaranteed annuity to a retired or disabled employee.
Management team	A management team is directly responsible for managing the day-to-day operations (and profitability) of

a company.

Turnover	Turnover in a financial context refers to the rate at which a provider of goods cycles through its average inventory. Turnover in a human resources context refers to the characteristic of a given company or industry, relative to rate at which an employer gains and loses staff.
Marketing	Promoting and selling products or services to customers, or prospective customers, is referred to as marketing.
Strategic plan	The formal document that presents the ways and means by which a strategic goal will be achieved is a strategic plan. A long-term flexible plan that does not regulate activities but rather outlines the means to achieve certain results, and provides the means to alter the course of action should the desired ends change.
Standard of living	Standard of living refers to the level of consumption that people enjoy, on the average, and is measured by average income per person.
Financial capital	Common stock, preferred stock, bonds, and retained earnings are financial capital. Financial capital appears on the corporate balance sheet under long-term liabilities and equity.
Raw material	Raw material refers to a good that has not been transformed by production; a primary product.
Capital	Capital generally refers to financial wealth, especially that used to start or maintain a business. In classical economics, capital is one of four factors of production, the others being land and labor and entrepreneurship.
Logistics	Those activities that focus on getting the right amount of the right products to the right place at the right time at the lowest possible cost is referred to as logistics.
Retailing	All activities involved in selling, renting, and providing goods and services to ultimate consumers for personal, family, or household use is referred to as retailing.
Internationa-ization	Internationalization refers to another term for fragmentation. Used by Grossman and Helpman.
Domestic	From or in one's own country. A domestic producer is one that produces inside the home country. A domestic price is the price inside the home country. Opposite of 'foreign' or 'world.'.
DaimlerChrysler	In 2002, the merged company, DaimlerChrysler, appeared to run two independent product lines, with few signs of corporate integration. In 2003, however, it was alleged by the Detroit News that the "merger of equals" was, in fact, a takeover.
Operation	A standardized method or technique that is performed repetitively, often on different materials resulting in different finished goods is called an operation.
Brand	A name, symbol, or design that identifies the goods or services of one seller or group of sellers and distinguishes them from the goods and services of competitors is a brand.
Integration	Economic integration refers to reducing barriers among countries to transactions and to movements of goods, capital, and labor, including harmonization of laws, regulations, and standards. Integrated markets theoretically function as a unified market.
Chrysler	The Chrysler Corporation was an American automobile manufacturer that existed independently from 1925–1998. The company was formed by Walter Percy Chrysler on June 6, 1925, with the remaining assets of Maxwell Motor Company.
Globalization	The increasing world-wide integration of markets for goods, services and capital that attracted special attention in the late 1990s is called globalization.
Manufactured good	A manufactured good refers to goods that have been processed in any way.

11

Aggregate output	The total production of final goods and services in the economy is called aggregate output.
Free trade	Free trade refers to a situation in which there are no artificial barriers to trade, such as tariffs and quotas. Usually used, often only implicitly, with frictionless trade, so that it implies that there are no barriers to trade of any kind.
Global competition	Global competition exists when competitive conditions across national markets are linked strongly enough to form a true international market and when leading competitors compete head to head in many different countries.
Cemex	Although it is not a monopoly, Cemex, along with Holcim-Apasco, controls the Mexican cement market. This has given rise to allegations that because of the oligopolistic structure in the Mexican cement market (as in many other markets in Mexico) consumers pay a higher price for cement than in other countries. However given the peculiarities of the Mexican cement market, the fact that it is sold mostly in bags, and the fact that cement is not an easily transported commodity make this accuzation difficult, if not impossible to prove.
Emerging market	The term emerging market is commonly used to describe business and market activity in industrializing or emerging regions of the world.
Option	A contract that gives the purchaser the option to buy or sell the underlying financial instrument at a specified price, called the exercise price or strike price, within a specific period of time.
Homogeneous	In the context of procurement/purchasing, homogeneous is used to describe goods that do not vary in their essential characteristic irrespective of the source of supply.
Strategic choice	Strategic choice refers to an organization's strategy; the ways an organization will attempt to fulfill its mission and achieve its long-term goals.
Trend	Trend refers to the long-term movement of an economic variable, such as its average rate of increase or decrease over enough years to encompass several business cycles.
Product life cycle	Product life cycle refers to a series of phases in a product's sales and cash flows over time; these phases, in order of occurrence, are introductory, growth, maturity, and decline.
Diffusion	Diffusion is the process by which a new idea or new product is accepted by the market. The rate of diffusion is the speed that the new idea spreads from one consumer to the next.
Premium	Premium refers to the fee charged by an insurance company for an insurance policy. The rate of losses must be relatively predictable: In order to set the premium (prices) insurers must be able to estimate them accurately.
Patent	The legal right to the proceeds from and control over the use of an invented product or process, granted for a fixed period of time, usually 20 years. Patent is one form of intellectual property that is subject of the TRIPS agreement.
Proprietary	Proprietary indicates that a party, or proprietor, exercises private ownership, control or use over an item of property, usually to the exclusion of other parties. Where a party, holds or claims proprietary interests in relation to certain types of property (eg. a creative literary work, or software), that property may also be the subject of intellectual property law (eg. copyright or patents).
Vendor	A person who sells property to a vendee is a vendor. The words vendor and vendee are more commonly applied to the seller and purchaser of real estate, and the words seller and buyer are more commonly applied to the seller and purchaser of personal property.
Information technology	Information technology refers to technology that helps companies change business by allowing them to use new methods.
Yield	The interest rate that equates a future value or an annuity to a given present value is a yield.

Privilege	Generally, a legal right to engage in conduct that would otherwise result in legal liability is a privilege. Privileges are commonly classified as absolute or conditional. Occasionally, privilege is also used to denote a legal right to refrain from particular behavior.
Electronic commerce	Electronic commerce or e-commerce, refers to any activity that uses some form of electronic communication in the inventory, exchange, advertisement, distribution, and payment of goods and services.
Commerce	Commerce is the exchange of something of value between two entities. It is the central mechanism from which capitalism is derived.
Cost of capital	Cost of capital refers to the percentage cost of funds used for acquiring resources for an organization, typically a weighted average of the firms cost of equity and cost of debt.
Rate of return	A rate of return is a comparison of the money earned (or lost) on an investment to the amount of money invested.
Buyer	A buyer refers to a role in the buying center with formal authority and responsibility to select the supplier and negotiate the terms of the contract.
Consolidation	The combination of two or more firms, generally of equal size and market power, to form an entirely new entity is a consolidation.
Southwest airlines	Southwest Airlines is a low-fare airline in the United States. It is the third-largest airline in the world, by number of passengers carried, and the largest in the United States by number of passengers carried domestically.
Economic environment	The economic environment represents the external conditions under which people are engaged in, and benefit from, economic activity. It includes aspects of economic status, paid employment, and finances.
Depression	Depression refers to a prolonged period characterized by high unemployment, low output and investment, depressed business confidence, falling prices, and widespread business failures. A milder form of business downturn is a recession.
Cost structure	The relative proportion of an organization's fixed, variable, and mixed costs is referred to as cost structure.
Regulation	Regulation refers to restrictions state and federal laws place on business with regard to the conduct of its activities.
Human capital	Human capital refers to the stock of knowledge and skill, embodied in an individual as a result of education, training, and experience that makes them more productive. The stock of knowledge and skill embodied in the population of an economy.
Downturn	A decline in a stock market or economic cycle is a downturn.
Fund	Independent accounting entity with a self-balancing set of accounts segregated for the purposes of carrying on specific activities is referred to as a fund.
Evaluation	The consumer's appraisal of the product or brand on important attributes is called evaluation.
Production	The creation of finished goods and services using the factors of production: land, labor, capital, entrepreneurship, and knowledge.
Tangible	Having a physical existence is referred to as the tangible. Personal property other than real estate, such as cars, boats, stocks, or other assets.
Accumulation	The acquisition of an increasing quantity of something. The accumulation of factors, especially capital, is a primary mechanism for economic growth.
Shill	A shill is an associate of a person selling goods or services, who pretends no association to the

14

Go to **Cram101.com** for the Practice Tests for this Chapter.

seller and assumes the air of an enthusiastic customer.

Philip Morris	Philip Morris, is the world's largest commercial tobacco company by sales. Philip Morris was begun by a London tobacconist of the same name. He was one of the first people to sell hand-rolled cigarettes in the 1860s, selling them under the brand names Oxford and Cambridge Blues, following the adoption of cigarette smoking by British soldiers returning from the Crimean War.
Apple Computer	Apple Computer has been a major player in the evolution of personal computing since its founding in 1976. The Apple II microcomputer, introduced in 1977, was a hit with home users.
Market share	That fraction of an industry's output accounted for by an individual firm or group of firms is called market share.
Scope	Scope of a project is the sum total of all projects products and their requirements or features.
Mission statement	Mission statement refers to an outline of the fundamental purposes of an organization.
Net worth	Net worth is the total assets minus total liabilities of an individual or company
Interest	In finance and economics, interest is the price paid by a borrower for the use of a lender's money. In other words, interest is the amount of paid to "rent" money for a period of time.
Holder	A person in possession of a document of title or an instrument payable or indorsed to him, his order, or to bearer is a holder.
Controlling	A management function that involves determining whether or not an organization is progressing toward its goals and objectives, and taking corrective action if it is not is called controlling.
Inventory	Tangible property held for sale in the normal course of business or used in producing goods or services for sale is an inventory.
Layoff	A layoff is the termination of an employee or (more commonly) a group of employees for business reasons, such as the decision that certain positions are no longer necessary.
Shareholder	A shareholder is an individual or company (including a corporation) that legally owns one or more shares of stock in a joined stock company.
Supply	Supply is the aggregate amount of any material good that can be called into being at a certain price point; it comprises one half of the equation of supply and demand. In classical economic theory, a curve representing supply is one of the factors that produce price.
Slowdown	A slowdown is an industrial action in which employees perform their duties but seek to reduce productivity or efficiency in their performance of these duties. A slowdown may be used as either a prelude or an alternative to a strike, as it is seen as less disruptive as well as less risky and costly for workers and their union.
Contribution	In business organization law, the cash or property contributed to a business by its owners is referred to as contribution.
Revenue	Revenue is a U.S. business term for the amount of money that a company receives from its activities, mostly from sales of products and/or services to customers.
Net loss	Net loss refers to the amount by which expenses exceed revenues. The difference between income received and expenses, when expenses are greater.
Net profit	Net profit is an accounting term which is commonly used in business. It is equal to the gross revenue for a given time period minus associated expenses.
Injunction	Injunction refers to a court order directing a person or organization not to perform a certain act because the act would do irreparable damage to some other person or persons; a restraining order.
Exporting	Selling products to another country is called exporting.

Expense	In accounting, an expense represents an event in which an asset is used up or a liability is incurred. In terms of the accounting equation, expenses reduce owners' equity.
Capital market	A financial market in which long-term debt and equity instruments are traded is referred to as a capital market. The capital market includes the stock market and the bond market.
Lender	Suppliers and financial institutions that lend money to companies is referred to as a lender.
Covenant	A covenant is a signed written agreement between two or more parties. Also referred to as a contract.
Stockholder	A stockholder is an individual or company (including a corporation) that legally owns one or more shares of stock in a joined stock company. The shareholders are the owners of a corporation. Companies listed at the stock market strive to enhance shareholder value.
Union	A worker association that bargains with employers over wages and working conditions is called a union.
Consumer demand	Consumer demand or consumption is also known as personal consumption expenditure. It is the largest part of aggregate demand or effective demand at the macroeconomic level. There are two variants of consumption in the aggregate demand model, including induced consumption and autonomous consumption.
Contract	A contract is a "promise" or an "agreement" that is enforced or recognized by the law. In the civil law, a contract is considered to be part of the general law of obligations.
Strategy implementation	Strategy implementation refers to the process of devising structures and allocating resources to enact the strategy a company has chosen.
Chief operating officer	A chief operating officer is a corporate officer responsible for managing the day-to-day activities of the corporation. The chief operating officer is one of the highest ranking members of an organization, monitoring the daily operations of the company and reporting to the chief executive officer directly.
Chief financial officer	Chief financial officer refers to executive responsible for overseeing the financial operations of an organization.
Mistake	In contract law a mistake is incorrect understanding by one or more parties to a contract and may be used as grounds to invalidate the agreement. Common law has identified three different types of mistake in contract: unilateral mistake, mutual mistake, and common mistake.
Organizational culture	The mindset of employees, including their shared beliefs, values, and goals is called the organizational culture.
Heir	In common law jurisdictions an heir is a person who is entitled to receive a share of the decedent's property via the rules of inheritance in the jurisdiction where the decedent died or owned property at the time of his death.
EBay	eBay manages an online auction and shopping website, where people buy and sell goods and services worldwide.
Foundation	A Foundation is a type of philanthropic organization set up by either individuals or institutions as a legal entity (either as a corporation or trust) with the purpose of distributing grants to support causes in line with the goals of the foundation.
Utility	Utility refers to the want-satisfying power of a good or service; the satisfaction or pleasure a consumer obtains from the consumption of a good or service.
Points	Loan origination fees that may be deductible as interest by a buyer of property. A seller of property who pays points reduces the selling price by the amount of the points paid for the buyer.
Value chain	The sequence of business functions in which usefulness is added to the products or services of a company is a value chain.
General Motors	General Motors is the world's largest automaker. Founded in 1908, today it employs about 327,000 people around the world. With global headquarters in Detroit, it manufactures its cars and trucks in 33

Go to **Cram101.com** for the Practice Tests for this Chapter.

countries.

Organization structure	The system of task, reporting, and authority relationships within which the organization does its work is referred to as the organization structure.
Primary factor	Primary factor refers to an input that exists as a stock, providing services that contribute to production. The stock is not used up in production, although it may deteriorate with use, providing a smaller flow of services later.
Value chain activities	Value chain activities refer to Porter's chain of activities, including inbound logistics, production, and outbound logistics.
Enabling	Enabling refers to giving workers the education and tools they need to assume their new decision-making powers.
Pfizer	Pfizer is the world's largest pharmaceutical company based in New York City. It produces the number-one selling drug Lipitor (atorvastatin, used to lower blood cholesterol).
Corporate culture	The whole collection of beliefs, values, and behaviors of a firm that send messages to those within and outside the company about how business is done is the corporate culture.
International diversification	Achieving diversification through many different foreign investments that are influenced by a variety of factors is referred to as international diversification. By diversifying across nations whose economic cycles are not perfectly correlated, investors can typically reduce the variability of their returns.
International management	International management refers to the management of business operations conducted in more than one country.
Strategic alliance	Strategic alliance refers to a long-term partnership between two or more companies established to help each company build competitive market advantages.
Business strategy	Business strategy, which refers to the aggregated operational strategies of single business firm or that of an SBU in a diversified corporation refers to the way in which a firm competes in its chosen arenas.
Diversification	Investing in a collection of assets whose returns do not always move together, with the result that overall risk is lower than for individual assets is referred to as diversification.
Distribution	Distribution in economics, the manner in which total output and income is distributed among individuals or factors.
Liability	A liability is a present obligation of the enterprise arizing from past events, the settlement of which is expected to result in an outflow from the enterprise of resources embodying economic benefits.
Petition	A petition is a request to an authority, most commonly a government official or public entity. In the colloquial sense, a petition is a document addressed to some official and signed by numerous individuals.
Journal	Book of original entry, in which transactions are recorded in a general ledger system, is referred to as a journal.
Harvard Business Review	Harvard Business Review is a research-based magazine written for business practitioners, it claims a high ranking business readership and enjoys the reverence of academics, executives, and management consultants. It has been the frequent publishing home for well known scholars and management thinkers.
Context	The effect of the background under which a message often takes on more and richer meaning is a context. Context is especially important in cross-cultural interactions because some cultures are said to be high context or low context.
Entrepreneurship	The assembling of resources to produce new or improved products and technologies is referred to as entrepreneurship.

Go to **Cram101.com** for the Practice Tests for this Chapter.

Privatization	A process in which investment bankers take companies that were previously owned by the government to the public markets is referred to as privatization.
Social responsibility	Social responsibility is a doctrine that claims that an entity whether it is state, government, corporation, organization or individual has a responsibility to society.
Employee stock option	An employee stock option is a stock option for the company's own stock that is often offered to upper-level employees as part of the executive compenzation package, especially by American corporations. An employee stock option is identical to a call option on the company's stock, with some extra restrictions.
Theory of the firm	The theory of the firm consists of a number of economic theories which describe the nature of the firm (company or corporation), including its behavior and its relationship with the market.
Stock option	A stock option is a specific type of option that uses the stock itself as an underlying instrument to determine the option's pay-off and therefore its value.

Industry	A group of firms that produce identical or similar products is an industry. It is also used specifically to refer to an area of economic production focused on manufacturing which involves large amounts of capital investment before any profit can be realized, also called "heavy industry".
Strategic group	A strategic group is a concept used in strategic management that groups companies within an industry that have similar business models or similar combinations of strategies.
Firm	An organization that employs resources to produce a good or service for profit and owns and operates one or more plants is referred to as a firm.
Competitor	Other organizations in the same industry or type of business that provide a good or service to the same set of customers is referred to as a competitor.
Service	Service refers to a "non tangible product" that is not embodied in a physical good and that typically effects some change in another product, person, or institution. Contrasts with good.
Technology	The body of knowledge and techniques that can be used to combine economic resources to produce goods and services is called technology.
Analyst	Analyst refers to a person or tool with a primary function of information analysis, generally with a more limited, practical and short term set of goals than a researcher.
Commodity	Could refer to any good, but in trade a commodity is usually a raw material or primary product that enters into international trade, such as metals or basic agricultural products.
Economy	The income, expenditures, and resources that affect the cost of running a business and household are called an economy.
Capital	Capital generally refers to financial wealth, especially that used to start or maintain a business. In classical economics, capital is one of four factors of production, the others being land and labor and entrepreneurship.
Sun Microsystems	Sun Microsystems is most well known for its Unix systems, which have a reputation for system stability and a consistent design philosophy.
A share	In finance the term A share has two distinct meanings, both relating to securities. The first is a designation for a 'class' of common or preferred stock. A share of common or preferred stock typically has enhanced voting rights or other benefits compared to the other forms of shares that may have been created. The equity structure, or how many types of shares are offered, is determined by the corporate charter.
Stock	In financial terminology, stock is the capital raized by a corporation, through the issuance and sale of shares.
Innovation	Innovation refers to the first commercially successful introduction of a new product, the use of a new method of production, or the creation of a new form of business organization.
Revenue	Revenue is a U.S. business term for the amount of money that a company receives from its activities, mostly from sales of products and/or services to customers.
Product line	A group of products that are physically similar or are intended for a similar market are called the product line.
Specialist	A specialist is a trader who makes a market in one or several stocks and holds the limit order book for those stocks.
Microsoft	Microsoft is a multinational computer technology corporation with 2004 global annual sales of US$39.79 billion and 71,553 employees in 102 countries and regions as of July 2006. It develops, manufactures, licenses, and supports a wide range of software products for

Go to **Cram101.com** for the Practice Tests for this Chapter.

	computing devices.
Intel	Intel Corporation, founded in 1968 and based in Santa Clara, California, USA, is the world's largest semiconductor company. Intel is best known for its PC microprocessors, where it maintains roughly 80% market share.
Business Week	Business Week is a business magazine published by McGraw-Hill. It was first published in 1929 under the direction of Malcolm Muir, who was serving as president of the McGraw-Hill Publishing company at the time. It is considered to be the standard both in industry and among students.
Option	A contract that gives the purchaser the option to buy or sell the underlying financial instrument at a specified price, called the exercise price or strike price, within a specific period of time.
Technological change	The introduction of new methods of production or new products intended to increase the productivity of existing inputs or to raise marginal products is a technological change.
Labor	People's physical and mental talents and efforts that are used to help produce goods and services are called labor.
Deregulation	The lessening or complete removal of government regulations on an industry, especially concerning the price that firms are allowed to charge and leaving price to be determined by market forces a deregulation.
Utility	Utility refers to the want-satisfying power of a good or service; the satisfaction or pleasure a consumer obtains from the consumption of a good or service.
Policy	Similar to a script in that a policy can be a less than completely rational decision-making method. Involves the use of a pre-existing set of decision steps for any problem that presents itself.
Competitiveness	Competitiveness usually refers to characteristics that permit a firm to compete effectively with other firms due to low cost or superior technology, perhaps internationally.
Competitive advantage	A business is said to have a competitive advantage when its unique strengths, often based on cost, quality, time, and innovation, offer consumers a greater percieved value and there by differtiating it from its competitors.
Stakeholder	A stakeholder is an individual or group with a vested interest in or expectation for organizational performance. Usually stakeholders can either have an effect on or are affected by an organization.
Internal environment	Variables that are under some degree of control by organizational members is the internal enviroment. Internal environment scans are conducted to identify an organization's internal capabilities, performance levels, strengths, and weaknesses.
Demographic	A demographic is a term used in marketing and broadcasting, to describe a demographic grouping or a market segment.
Buyer	A buyer refers to a role in the buying center with formal authority and responsibility to select the supplier and negotiate the terms of the contract.
Controlling	A management function that involves determining whether or not an organization is progressing toward its goals and objectives, and taking corrective action if it is not is called controlling.
Profit	Profit refers to the return to the resource entrepreneurial ability; total revenue minus total cost.
Complement	A good that is used in conjunction with another good is a complement. For example, cameras

Go to **Cram101.com** for the Practice Tests for this Chapter.

and film would complement eachother.

Strategic intent	Strategic intent is when a firm relentlessly pursues a difficult strategic goa and concentrates its competitive actions and energies on achieving that goal.
Polaroid	The Polaroid Corporation was founded in 1937 by Edwin H. Land. It is most famous for its instant film cameras, which reached the market in 1948, and continue to be the company's flagship product line.
Attest	To bear witness to is called attest. To affirm, certify by oath or signature. It is an official act establishing authenticity.
Digital technology	Technology characterized by use of the Internet and other digital processes to conduct or support business operations is referred to as digital technology.
Bankruptcy	Bankruptcy is a legally declared inability or impairment of ability of an individual or organization to pay their creditors.
Bank One	On January 15, 2004, the Bank One announced that it was being acquired by J.P. Morgan Chase in a $58 billion merger. This merger was announced a few months after the proposed merger of Bank of America and FleetBoston banks. This awoke concerns about too much consolidation of the banking industry.
Trend	Trend refers to the long-term movement of an economic variable, such as its average rate of increase or decrease over enough years to encompass several business cycles.
Management	Management characterizes the process of leading and directing all or part of an organization, often a business, through the deployment and manipulation of resources. Early twentieth-century management writer Mary Parker Follett defined management as "the art of getting things done through people."
Trade show	A type of exhibition or forum where manufacturers can display their products to current as well as prospective buyers is referred to as trade show.
Testimony	In some contexts, the word bears the same import as the word evidence, but in most connections it has a much narrower meaning. Testimony are the words heard from the witness in court, and evidence is what the jury considers it worth.
Context	The effect of the background under which a message often takes on more and richer meaning is a context. Context is especially important in cross-cultural interactions because some cultures are said to be high context or low context.
Social Security	Social security primarily refers to a field of social welfare concerned with social protection, or protection against socially recognized conditions, including poverty, old age, disability, unemployment, families with children and others.
Contribution	In business organization law, the cash or property contributed to a business by its owners is referred to as contribution.
Security	Security refers to a claim on the borrower future income that is sold by the borrower to the lender. A security is a type of transferable interest representing financial value.
Pension	A pension is a steady income given to a person (usually after retirement). Pensions are typically payments made in the form of a guaranteed annuity to a retired or disabled employee.
Preference	The act of a debtor in paying or securing one or more of his creditors in a manner more favorable to them than to other creditors or to the exclusion of such other creditors is a preference. In the absence of statute, a preference is perfectly good, but to be legal it must be bona fide, and not a mere subterfuge of the debtor to secure a future benefit to himself or to prevent the application of his property to his debts.

Users	Users refer to people in the organization who actually use the product or service purchased by the buying center.
Business opportunity	A business opportunity involves the sale or lease of any product, service, equipment, etc. that will enable the purchaser-licensee to begin a business
Investment	Investment refers to spending for the production and accumulation of capital and additions to inventories. In a financial sense, buying an asset with the expectation of making a return.
Market	A market is, as defined in economics, a social arrangement that allows buyers and sellers to discover information and carry out a voluntary exchange of goods or services.
Composition	An out-of-court settlement in which creditors agree to accept a fractional settlement on their original claim is referred to as composition.
Purchasing	Purchasing refers to the function in a firm that searches for quality material resources, finds the best suppliers, and negotiates the best price for goods and services.
Strategic management	A philosophy of management that links strategic planning with dayto-day decision making. Strategic management seeks a fit between an organization's external and internal environments.
Assessment	Collecting information and providing feedback to employees about their behavior, communication style, or skills is an assessment.
Starbucks	Although it has endured much criticism for its purported monopoly on the global coffee-bean market, Starbucks purchases only 3% of the coffee beans grown worldwide. In 2000 the company introduced a line of fair trade products and now offers three options for socially conscious coffee drinkers. According to Starbucks, they purchased 4.8 million pounds of Certified Fair Trade coffee in fiscal year 2004 and 11.5 million pounds in 2005.
Franchise	A contractual right to sell certain products or services, use certain trademarks, or perform activities in a geographical region is called a franchise.
Franchising	Franchising is a method of doing business wherein a franchisor licenses trademarks and tried and proven methods of doing business to a franchisee in exchange for a recurring payment, and usually a percentage piece of gross sales or gross profits as well as the annual fees. The term " franchising " is used to describe a wide variety of business systems which may or may not fall into the legal definition provided above.
Income distribution	A description of the fractions of a population that are at various levels of income. The larger these differences in income, the 'worse' the income distribution is usually said to be, the smaller the 'better.'
Distribution	Distribution in economics, the manner in which total output and income is distributed among individuals or factors.
Developed country	A developed country is one that enjoys a relatively high standard of living derived through an industrialized, diversified economy. Countries with a very high Human Development Index are generally considered developed countries.
Labor force	In economics the labor force is the group of people who have a potential for being employed.
Shares	Shares refer to an equity security, representing a shareholder's ownership of a corporation. Shares are one of a finite number of equal portions in the capital of a company, entitling the owner to a proportion of distributed, non-reinvested profits known as dividends and to a portion of the value of the company in case of liquidation.
Workforce diversity	The similarities and differences in such characteristics as age, gender, ethnic heritage, physical abilities and disabilities, race, and sexual orientation among the employees of organizations is called workforce diversity.

Go to **Cram101.com** for the Practice Tests for this Chapter.

Household	An economic unit that provides the economy with resources and uses the income received to purchase goods and services that satisfy economic wants is called household.
Interest	In finance and economics, interest is the price paid by a borrower for the use of a lender's money. In other words, interest is the amount of paid to "rent" money for a period of time.
Real income	Real income refers to the amount of goods and services that can be purchased with nominal income during some period of time; nominal income adjusted for inflation.
Economic environment	The economic environment represents the external conditions under which people are engaged in, and benefit from, economic activity. It includes aspects of economic status, paid employment, and finances.
Recession	A significant decline in economic activity. In the U.S., recession is approximately defined as two successive quarters of falling GDP, as judged by NBER.
Interest rate	The rate of return on bonds, loans, or deposits. When one speaks of 'the' interest rate, it is usually in a model where there is only one.
Capital market	A financial market in which long-term debt and equity instruments are traded is referred to as a capital market. The capital market includes the stock market and the bond market.
Globalization	The increasing world-wide integration of markets for goods, services and capital that attracted special attention in the late 1990s is called globalization.
Bilateral trade	Bilateral trade refers to the trade between two countries; that is, the value or quantity of one country's exports to the other, or the sum of exports and imports between them.
Regulation	Regulation refers to restrictions state and federal laws place on business with regard to the conduct of its activities.
Administration	Administration refers to the management and direction of the affairs of governments and institutions; a collective term for all policymaking officials of a government; the execution and implementation of public policy.
Antitrust laws	Legislation that prohibits anticompetitive business activities such as price fixing, bid rigging, monopolization, and tying contracts is referred to as antitrust laws.
Operation	A standardized method or technique that is performed repetitively, often on different materials resulting in different finished goods is called an operation.
Antitrust	Government intervention to alter market structure or prevent abuse of market power is called antitrust.
Forming	The first stage of team development, where the team is formed and the objectives for the team are set is referred to as forming.
Trade barrier	An artificial disincentive to export and/or import, such as a tariff, quota, or other NTB is called a trade barrier.
International Monetary Fund	The International Monetary Fund is the international organization entrusted with overseeing the global financial system by monitoring exchange rates and balance of payments, as well as offering technical and financial assistance when asked.
Tariff	A tax imposed by a nation on an imported good is called a tariff.
Fund	Independent accounting entity with a self-balancing set of accounts segregated for the purposes of carrying on specific activities is referred to as a fund.
Food and Drug Administration	The Food and Drug Administration is an agency of the United States Department of Health and Human Services and is responsible for regulating food (human and animal), dietary supplements, drugs (human and animal), cosmetics, medical devices (human and animal) and

Go to **Cram101.com** for the Practice Tests for this Chapter.

radiation emitting devices (including non-medical devices), biologics, and blood products in the United States.

Advertising	Advertising refers to paid, nonpersonal communication through various media by organizations and individuals who are in some way identified in the advertising message.
Litigation	The process of bringing, maintaining, and defending a lawsuit is litigation.
Cultural values	The values that employees need to have and act on for the organization to act on the strategic values are called cultural values.
Variance	Variance refers to a measure of how much an economic or statistical variable varies across values or observations. Its calculation is the same as that of the covariance, being the covariance of the variable with itself.
Allocate	Allocate refers to the assignment of income for various tax purposes. A multistate corporation's nonbusiness income usually is distributed to the state where the nonbusiness assets are located; it is not apportioned with the rest of the entity's income.
Retailing	All activities involved in selling, renting, and providing goods and services to ultimate consumers for personal, family, or household use is referred to as retailing.
Leadership	Management merely consists of leadership applied to business situations; or in other words: management forms a sub-set of the broader process of leadership.
Organizational structure	Organizational structure is the way in which the interrelated groups of an organization are constructed. From a managerial point of view the main concerns are ensuring effective communication and coordination.
Domestic	From or in one's own country. A domestic producer is one that produces inside the home country. A domestic price is the price inside the home country. Opposite of 'foreign' or 'world.'.
Contract	A contract is a "promise" or an "agreement" that is enforced or recognized by the law. In the civil law, a contract is considered to be part of the general law of obligations.
Restructuring	Restructuring is the corporate management term for the act of partially dismantling and reorganizing a company for the purpose of making it more efficient and therefore more profitable.
Downsizing	The process of eliminating managerial and non-managerial positions are called downsizing.
Early adopters	Early adopters refers to the 13.5 percent of the population who are leaders in their social setting and act as an information source on new products for other people.
Market share	That fraction of an industry's output accounted for by an individual firm or group of firms is called market share.
Manufacturing	Production of goods primarily by the application of labor and capital to raw materials and other intermediate inputs, in contrast to agriculture, mining, forestry, fishing, and services a manufacturing.
Commerce	Commerce is the exchange of something of value between two entities. It is the central mechanism from which capitalism is derived.
Wireless communication	Wireless communication refers to a method of communication that uses low-powered radio waves to transmit data between devices. The term refers to communication without cables or cords, chiefly using radio frequency and infrared waves. Common uses include the various communications defined by the IrDA, the wireless networking of computers and cellular mobile phones.
Diffusion	Diffusion is the process by which a new idea or new product is accepted by the market. The

	rate of diffusion is the speed that the new idea spreads from one consumer to the next.
Disruptive technology	A disruptive technology is a new technological innovation, product, or service that eventually overturns the existing dominant technology in the market, despite the fact that the disruptive technology is both radically different from the leading technology and that it often initially performs worse than the leading technology according to existing measures of performance.
Acquisition	A company's purchase of the property and obligations of another company is an acquisition.
Licensing	Licensing is a form of strategic alliance which involves the sale of a right to use certain proprietary knowledge (so called intellectual property) in a defined way.
International firm	International firm refers to those firms who have responded to stiff competition domestically by expanding their sales abroad. They may start a production facility overseas and send some of their managers, who report to a global division, to that country.
World Trade Organization	The World Trade Organization is an international, multilateral organization, which sets the rules for the global trading system and resolves disputes between its member states, all of whom are signatories to its approximately 30 agreements.
Back office	A back office is a part of most corporations where tasks dedicated to running the company itself take place.
Accenture	In October 2002, the Congressional General Accounting Office (GAO) identified Accenture as one of four publicly-traded federal contractors that were incorporated in a tax haven country. Accenture is a global management consulting, technology services and outsourcing company. Its organizational structure includes divisions based on client industry types and employee workforces.
Toyota	Toyota is a Japanese multinational corporation that manufactures automobiles, trucks and buses. Toyota is the world's second largest automaker by sales. Toyota also provides financial services through its subsidiary, Toyota Financial Services, and participates in other lines of business.
Nokia	Nokia Corporation is the world's largest manufacturer of mobile telephones (as of June 2006), with a global market share of approximately 34% in Q2 of 2006. It produces mobile phones for every major market and protocol, including GSM, CDMA, and W-CDMA (UMTS).
Authority	Authority in agency law, refers to an agent's ability to affect his principal's legal relations with third parties. Also used to refer to an actor's legal power or ability to do something. In addition, sometimes used to refer to a statute, case, or other legal source that justifies a particular result.
Incentive	An incentive is any factor (financial or non-financial) that provides a motive for a particular course of action, or counts as a reason for preferring one choice to the alternatives.
Downturn	A decline in a stock market or economic cycle is a downturn.
Sociocultural dimension	The dimension of the general environment representing the demographic characteristics, norms, customs, and values of the population within which the organization operates is called sociocultural dimension.
Union	A worker association that bargains with employers over wages and working conditions is called a union.
United airlines	United Airlines is a major airline of the United States headquartered in unincorporated Elk Grove Township, Illinois, near Chicago's O'Hare International Airport, the airline's largest traffic hub, with 650 daily departures. On February 1, 2006, it emerged from Chapter 11

Go to **Cram101.com** for the Practice Tests for this Chapter.

bankruptcy protection under which it had operated since December 9, 2002, the largest and longest airline bankruptcy case in history.

Concession
A concession is a business operated under a contract or license associated with a degree of exclusivity in exploiting a business within a certain geographical area. For example, sports arenas or public parks may have concession stands; and public services such as water supply may be operated as concessions.

US airways
US Airways is an airline based in Tempe, Arizona, owned by US Airways Group, Inc.. As of May 2006, the combined airline is the fifth largest airline in the United States and has a fleet of 358 mainline jet aircraft and 295 express aircraft connecting 237 destinations in North America, Central America, the Caribbean, Hawaii, and Europe.

American Airlines
American Airlines developed from a conglomeration of about 82 small airlines through a series of corporate acquisitions and reorganizations: initially, the name American Airways was used as a common brand by a number of independent air carriers. American Airlines is the largest airline in the world in terms of total passengers transported and fleet size, and the second-largest airline in the world.

Wage
The payment for the service of a unit of labor, per unit time. In trade theory, it is the only payment to labor, usually unskilled labor. In empirical work, wage data may exclude other compenzation, which must be added to get the total cost of employment.

Market niche
A market niche or niche market is a focused, targetable portion of a market. By definition, then, a business that focuses on a niche market is addressing a need for a product or service that is not being addressed by mainstream providers.

Niche
In industry, a niche is a situation or an activity perfectly suited to a person. A niche can imply a working position or an area suited to a person who occupies it. Basically, a job where a person is able to succeed and thrive.

Consolidation
The combination of two or more firms, generally of equal size and market power, to form an entirely new entity is a consolidation.

Financial crisis
A loss of confidence in a country's currency or other financial assets causing international investors to withdraw their funds from the country is referred to as a financial crisis.

Recovery
Characterized by rizing output, falling unemployment, rizing profits, and increasing economic activity following a decline is a recovery.

Competitive Strategy
An outline of how a business intends to compete with other firms in the same industry is called competitive strategy.

Production
The creation of finished goods and services using the factors of production: land, labor, capital, entrepreneurship, and knowledge.

Competitive disadvantage
A situation in which a firm is not implementing using strategies that are being used by competing organizations is competitive disadvantage.

Entry barrier
An entry barrier or barrier to entry is an obstacle in the path of a potential firm which wants to enter a given market.

Economic problem
Economic problem refers to how to determine the use of scarce resources among competing uses. Because resources are scarce, the economy must choose what products to produce; how these products are to be produced: and for whom.

Barriers to entry
In economics and especially in the theory of competition, barriers to entry are obstacles in the path of a firm which wants to enter a given market.

Economies of scale
In economics, returns to scale and economies of scale are related terms that describe what happens as the scale of production increases. They are different terms and not to be used

Go to **Cram101.com** for the Practice Tests for this Chapter.

interchangeably.

Research and development	The use of resources for the deliberate discovery of new information and ways of doing things, together with the application of that information in inventing new products or processes is referred to as research and development.
Marketing	Promoting and selling products or services to customers, or prospective customers, is referred to as marketing.
Free cash flow	Cash provided by operating activities adjusted for capital expenditures and dividends paid is referred to as free cash flow.
Cash flow	In finance, cash flow refers to the amounts of cash being received and spent by a business during a defined period of time, sometimes tied to a specific project. Most of the time they are being used to determine gaps in the liquid position of a company.
Retaliation	The use of an increased trade barrier in response to another country increasing its trade barrier, either as a way of undoing the adverse effects of the latter's action or of punishing it is retaliation.
Gain	In finance, gain is a profit or an increase in value of an investment such as a stock or bond. Gain is calculated by fair market value or the proceeds from the sale of the investment minus the sum of the purchase price and all costs associated with it.
Mass customization	A manufacturing environment in which many standardized components are combined to produce custommade products to customer order is referred to as mass customization.
PepsiCo	In many ways, PepsiCo differs from its main competitor, having three times as many employees, larger revenues, but a smaller net profit.
Loyalty	Marketers tend to define customer loyalty as making repeat purchases. Some argue that it should be defined attitudinally as a strongly positive feeling about the brand.
Inventory	Tangible property held for sale in the normal course of business or used in producing goods or services for sale is an inventory.
Switching costs	Switching costs is a term used in microeconomics, strategic management, and marketing to describe any impediment to a customer's changing of suppliers. In many markets, consumers are forced to incur costs when switching from one supplier to another. These costs are called switching costs and can come in many different shapes.
Ancillary	An ancillary receiver is a receiver who has been appointed in aid of, and in subordination to, the primary receiver.
Loyalty programs	Loyalty programs refers to targeted marketing programs designed to encourage customers to purchase more.
Distribution channel	A distribution channel is a chain of intermediaries, each passing a product down the chain to the next organization, before it finally reaches the consumer or end-user.
Nondurable good	A consumer good with an expected life of less than 3 years is referred to as a nondurable good.
Channel	Channel, in communications (sometimes called communications channel), refers to the medium used to convey information from a sender (or transmitter) to a receiver.
Cooperative	A business owned and controlled by the people who use it, producers, consumers, or workers with similar needs who pool their resources for mutual gain is called cooperative.
Allowance	Reduction in the selling price of goods extended to the buyer because the goods are defective or of lower quality than the buyer ordered and to encourage a buyer to keep merchandise that would otherwise be returned is the allowance.

Go to **Cram101.com** for the Practice Tests for this Chapter.

Cooperative advertising	Advertising programs by which a manufacturer pays a percentage of the retailer's local advertising expense for advertising the manufacturer's products are called cooperative advertising.
Cost advantage	Possession of a lower cost of production or operation than a competing firm or country is cost advantage.
Final settlement	Final settlement occurs when the payor bank pays the check in cash, settles for the check without having a right to revoke the settlement, or fails to dishonor the check within certain statutory time periods.
Fixed asset	Fixed asset, also known as property, plant, and equipment (PP&E), is a term used in accountancy for assets and property which cannot easily be converted into cash. This can be compared with current assets such as cash or bank accounts, which are described as liquid assets. In most cases, only tangible assets are referred to as fixed.
Asset	An item of property, such as land, capital, money, a share in ownership, or a claim on others for future payment, such as a bond or a bank deposit is an asset.
Market segments	Market segments refer to the groups that result from the process of market segmentation; these groups ideally have common needs and will respond similarly to a marketing action.
Honda	With more than 14 million internal combustion engines built each year, Honda is the largest engine-maker in the world. In 2004, the company began to produce diesel motors, which were both very quiet whilst not requiring particulate filters to pass pollution standards. It is arguable, however, that the foundation of their success is the motorcycle division.
Targeting	In advertizing, targeting is to select a demographic or other group of people to advertise to, and create advertisements appropriately.
Bargaining power	Bargaining power refers to the ability to influence the setting of prices or wages, usually arising from some sort of monopoly or monopsony position
Substitute product	Any product viewed by a consumer as an alternative for other products is a substitute product. The substitution is rarely perfect, and varies from time to time depending on price, availability, etc.
Differentiated product	A firm's product that is not identical to products of other firms in the same industry is a differentiated product.
Airbus	In 2003, for the first time in its 33-year history, Airbus delivered more jet-powered airliners than Boeing. Boeing states that the Boeing 777 has outsold its Airbus counterparts, which include the A340 family as well as the A330-300. The smaller A330-200 competes with the 767, outselling its Boeing counterpart.
Boeing	Boeing is the world's largest aircraft manufacturer by revenue. Headquartered in Chicago, Illinois, Boeing is the second-largest defense contractor in the world. In 2005, the company was the world's largest civil aircraft manufacturer in terms of value.
Rate of return	A rate of return is a comparison of the money earned (or lost) on an investment to the amount of money invested.
Dealer	People who link buyers with sellers by buying and selling securities at stated prices are referred to as a dealer.
Market position	Market position is a measure of the position of a company or product on a market.
Homogeneous	In the context of procurement/purchasing, homogeneous is used to describe goods that do not vary in their essential characteristic irrespective of the source of supply.
Fixed cost	The cost that a firm bears if it does not produce at all and that is independent of its

Go to **Cram101.com** for the Practice Tests for this Chapter.

	output. The presence of a fixed cost tends to imply increasing returns to scale. Contrasts with variable cost.
Total cost	The sum of fixed cost and variable cost is referred to as total cost.
Discount	The difference between the face value of a bond and its selling price, when a bond is sold for less than its face value it's referred to as a discount.
Rebate	Rebate refers to a sales promotion in which money is returned to the consumer based on proof of purchase.
Excess capacity	Excess capacity refers to plant resources that are underused when imperfectly competitive firms produce less output than that associated with purely competitive firms, who by definiation, are achieving minimum average total cost.
Pricing strategy	The process in which the price of a product can be determined and is decided upon is a pricing strategy.
Single market	A single market is a customs union with common policies on product regulation, and freedom of movement of all the four factors of production (goods, services, capital and labor).
Time Warner	Time Warner is the world's largest media company with major Internet, publishing, film, telecommunications and television divisions.
Bertelsmann	Bertelsmann is a transnational media corporation founded in 1835, based in Gütersloh, Germany. Bertelsmann made headlines on May 17, 2002, when it announced it would acquire the assets of Napster for $8 million.
Evaluation	The consumer's appraisal of the product or brand on important attributes is called evaluation.
Merger	Merger refers to the combination of two firms into a single firm.
Sony	Sony is a multinational corporation and one of the world's largest media conglomerates founded in Tokyo, Japan. One of its divisions Sony Electronics is one of the leading manufacturers of electronics, video, communications, and information technology products for the consumer and professional markets.
Steve Case	Steve Case is a businessman best known as the co-founder and former chief executive officer and chairman of America Online (AOL). He reached his highest profile when he played an instrumental role in AOL's merger with Time Warner in 2000.
Conglomerate	A conglomerate is a large company that consists of divisions of often seemingly unrelated businesses.
Synergy	Corporate synergy occurs when corporations interact congruently. A corporate synergy refers to a financial benefit that a corporation expects to realize when it merges with or acquires another corporation.
Comcast	Comcast Corporation based in Philadelphia, Pennsylvania, is the largest cable company and the largest broadband (second overall) Internet service provider in the United States. They develop broadband cable networks and are involved in electronic retailing and television programming content.
Appeal	Appeal refers to the act of asking an appellate court to overturn a decision after the trial court's final judgment has been entered.
Home Depot	Home Depot has recently added self checkout registers at most of its stores in North America. These automated kiosks allow the customer to scan the barcode of the item they wish to purchase, then insert money to pay for the items, and receive any change automatically. The customer no longer needs to interact with a store employee during checkout.

Fragmented industry	An industry facing many opportunities for differentiation, such as restaurants is a fragmented industry.
Clear Channel	Clear Channel Communications is a media company based in the United States of America. Clear Channel, founded in 1972 by Lowry Mays and Red McCombs, wields considerable influence in radio broadcasting, concert promotion and hosting, and fixed advertizing in the United States through its subsidiaries.
Billboard	The most common form of outdoor advertising is called a billboard.
Tactic	A short-term immediate decision that, in its totality, leads to the achievement of strategic goals is called a tactic.
Premium	Premium refers to the fee charged by an insurance company for an insurance policy. The rate of losses must be relatively predictable: In order to set the premium (prices) insurers must be able to estimate them accurately.
Volkswagen	Volkswagen or VW is an automobile manufacturer based in Wolfsburg, Germany in the state of Lower Saxony. It forms the core of this Group, one of the world's four largest car producers. Its German tagline is "Aus Liebe zum Automobil", which is translated as "For the love of the car" - or, For Love of the People's Cars,".
Competitor analysis	Competitor analysis in marketing and strategic management is an assessment of the strengths and weaknesses of current and potential competitors.
Public policy	Decision making by government. Governments are constantly concerned about what they should or should not do. And whatever they do or do not do is public policy. public program All those activities designed to implement a public policy; often this calls for the creation of organizations, public agencies, and bureaus.
Knowledge management	Sharing, organizing and disseminating information in the simplest and most relevant way possible for the users of the information is a knowledge management.
Insurance	Insurance refers to a system by which individuals can reduce their exposure to risk of large losses by spreading the risks among a large number of persons.
Fraud	Tax fraud falls into two categories: civil and criminal. Under civil fraud, the IRS may impose as a penalty of an amount equal to as much as 75 percent of the underpayment.
Competitive intelligence	Competitive Intelligence is defined as business intelligence focusing on the external competitive environment.
Yield	The interest rate that equates a future value or an annuity to a given present value is a yield.
End user	End user refers to the ultimate user of a product or service.
Channel of distribution	A whole set of marketing intermediaries, such as wholesalers and retailers, who join together to transport and store goods in their path from producers to consumers is referred to as channel of distribution.
Inputs	The inputs used by a firm or an economy are the labor, raw materials, electricity and other resources it uses to produce its outputs.
Strategy formulation	The process of deciding on a strategic direction by defining a company's mission and goals, its external opportunities and threats, and its internal strengths and weaknesses is referred to as a strategy formulation.
Foundation	A Foundation is a type of philanthropic organization set up by either individuals or institutions as a legal entity (either as a corporation or trust) with the purpose of distributing grants to support causes in line with the goals of the foundation.

Journal	Book of original entry, in which transactions are recorded in a general ledger system, is referred to as a journal.
International diversification	Achieving diversification through many different foreign investments that are influenced by a variety of factors is referred to as international diversification. By diversifying across nations whose economic cycles are not perfectly correlated, investors can typically reduce the variability of their returns.
Multinational corporations	Firms that own production facilities in two or more countries and produce and sell their products globally are referred to as multinational corporations.
Multinational corporation	An organization that manufactures and markets products in many different countries and has multinational stock ownership and multinational management is referred to as multinational corporation.
Diversification strategy	Diversification strategy is a corporate strategy that takes the organization away from both its current markets and products, as opposed to either market or product development.
Venture capital	Venture capital is capital provided by outside investors for financing of new, growing or struggling businesses. Venture capital investments generally are high risk investments but offer the potential for above average returns.
Scope	Scope of a project is the sum total of all projects products and their requirements or features.
Diversification	Investing in a collection of assets whose returns do not always move together, with the result that overall risk is lower than for individual assets is referred to as diversification.
Privatization	A process in which investment bankers take companies that were previously owned by the government to the public markets is referred to as privatization.
Corporation	A legal entity chartered by a state or the Federal government that is distinct and separate from the individuals who own it is a corporation. This separation gives the corporation unique powers which other legal entities lack.
Agglomeration	The phenomenon of economic activity congregating in or close to a single location, rather than being spread out uniformly over space is an agglomeration.
Balance	In banking and accountancy, the outstanding balance is the amount of money owned, (or due), that remains in a deposit account (or a loan account) at a given date, after all past remittances, payments and withdrawal have been accounted for. It can be positive (then, in the balance sheet of a firm, it is an asset) or negative (a liability).
Entrepreneurial team	Entrepreneurial team refers to a group of experienced people from different areas of business that join together to form a managerial team with the skills needed to develop, make, and market a new product.
Complexity	The technical sophistication of the product and hence the amount of understanding required to use it is referred to as complexity. It is the opposite of simplicity.
Adoption	In corporation law, a corporation's acceptance of a pre-incorporation contract by action of its board of directors, by which the corporation becomes liable on the contract, is referred to as adoption.
Core	A core is the set of feasible allocations in an economy that cannot be improved upon by subset of the set of the economy's consumers (a coalition). In construction, when the force in an element is within a certain center section, the core, the element will only be under compression.

Tangible	Having a physical existence is referred to as the tangible. Personal property other than real estate, such as cars, boats, stocks, or other assets.
Core competency	A company's core competency are things that a firm can (alsosns) do well and that meet the following three conditions. 1. It provides customer benefits, 2. It is hard for competitors to imitate, and 3. it can be leveraged widely to many products and market. A core competency can take various forms, including technical/subject matter knowhow, a reliable process, and/or close relationships with customers and suppliers. It may also include product development or culture such as employee dedication. Modern business theories suggest that most activities that are not part of a company's core competency should be outsourced.
Core	A core is the set of feasible allocations in an economy that cannot be improved upon by subset of the set of the economy's consumers (a coalition). In construction, when the force in an element is within a certain center section, the core, the element will only be under compression.
Outsourcing	Outsourcing refers to a production activity that was previously done inside a firm or plant that is now conducted outside that firm or plant.
Internal environment	Variables that are under some degree of control by organizational members is the internal enviroment. Internal environment scans are conducted to identify an organization's internal capabilities, performance levels, strengths, and weaknesses.
Caterpillar	Caterpillar is a United States based corporation headquartered in Peoria, Illinois. Caterpillar is "the world's largest manufacturer of construction and mining equipment, diesel and natural gas engines, and industrial gas turbines."
Competitive advantage	A business is said to have a competitive advantage when its unique strengths, often based on cost, quality, time, and innovation, offer consumers a greater percieved value and there by diffetiating it from its competitors.
Technology	The body of knowledge and techniques that can be used to combine economic resources to produce goods and services is called technology.
Manufacturing	Production of goods primarily by the application of labor and capital to raw materials and other intermediate inputs, in contrast to agriculture, mining, forestry, fishing, and services a manufacturing.
Shareholder	A shareholder is an individual or company (including a corporation) that legally owns one or more shares of stock in a joined stock company.
Revenue	Revenue is a U.S. business term for the amount of money that a company receives from its activities, mostly from sales of products and/or services to customers.
Firm	An organization that employs resources to produce a good or service for profit and owns and operates one or more plants is referred to as a firm.
Economy	The income, expenditures, and resources that affect the cost of running a business and household are called an economy.
Industry	A group of firms that produce identical or similar products is an industry. It is also used specifically to refer to an area of economic production focused on manufacturing which involves large amounts of capital investment before any profit can be realized, also called "heavy industry".
Forbes	David Churbuck founded online Forbes in 1996. The site drew attention when it uncovered Stephen Glass' journalistic fraud in The New Republic in 1998, a scoop that gave credibility to internet journalism.
Strategic intent	Strategic intent is when a firm relentlessly pursues a difficult strategic goa and

Go to **Cram101.com** for the Practice Tests for this Chapter.

concentrates its competitive actions and energies on achieving that goal.

Customer value	Customer value refers to the unique combination of benefits received by targeted buyers that includes quality, price, convenience, on-time delivery, and both before-sale and after-sale service.
Service	Service refers to a "non tangible product" that is not embodied in a physical good and that typically effects some change in another product, person, or institution. Contrasts with good.
Patent	The legal right to the proceeds from and control over the use of an invented product or process, granted for a fixed period of time, usually 20 years. Patent is one form of intellectual property that is subject of the TRIPS agreement.
Raw material	Raw material refers to a good that has not been transformed by production; a primary product.
Dealer	People who link buyers with sellers by buying and selling securities at stated prices are referred to as a dealer.
Trust	An arrangement in which shareholders of independent firms agree to give up their stock in exchange for trust certificates that entitle them to a share of the trust's common profits.
Continuous improvement	The constant effort to eliminate waste, reduce response time, simplify the design of both products and processes, and improve quality and customer service is referred to as continuous improvement.
Distribution channel	A distribution channel is a chain of intermediaries, each passing a product down the chain to the next organization, before it finally reaches the consumer or end-user.
Distribution	Distribution in economics, the manner in which total output and income is distributed among individuals or factors.
Channel	Channel, in communications (sometimes called communications channel), refers to the medium used to convey information from a sender (or transmitter) to a receiver.
Success factor	The term success factor refers to the characteristics necessary for high performance; knowledge, skills, abilities, behaviors.
Market	A market is, as defined in economics, a social arrangement that allows buyers and sellers to discover information and carry out a voluntary exchange of goods or services.
Critical success factor	Critical Success Factor is a business term for an element which is necessary for an organization or project to achieve its mission.
Intellectual capital	Intellectual capital makes an organization worth more than its balance sheet value. For many years, intellectual capital and goodwill meant the same thing. Today, intellectual capital management is far broader. It seeks to explain how knowledge, collaboration, and process-engagement create decisions and actions that lead to cost allocations, productivity, and finally financial performance.
Entrepreneur	The owner/operator. The person who organizes, manages, and assumes the risks of a firm, taking a new idea or a new product and turning it into a successful business is an entrepreneur.
Competitor	Other organizations in the same industry or type of business that provide a good or service to the same set of customers is referred to as a competitor.
Capital	Capital generally refers to financial wealth, especially that used to start or maintain a business. In classical economics, capital is one of four factors of production, the others being land and labor and entrepreneurship.
Michael Dell	Michael Dell is the founder of Dell, Inc., the world's largest computer manufacturer which

	revolutionized the home computer industry.
Competitiveness	Competitiveness usually refers to characteristics that permit a firm to compete effectively with other firms due to low cost or superior technology, perhaps internationally.
Matching	Matching refers to an accounting concept that establishes when expenses are recognized. Expenses are matched with the revenues they helped to generate and are recognized when those revenues are recognized.
Enterprise	Enterprise refers to another name for a business organization. Other similar terms are business firm, sometimes simply business, sometimes simply firm, as well as company, and entity.
Brand	A name, symbol, or design that identifies the goods or services of one seller or group of sellers and distinguishes them from the goods and services of competitors is a brand.
Context	The effect of the background under which a message often takes on more and richer meaning is a context. Context is especially important in cross-cultural interactions because some cultures are said to be high context or low context.
Market position	Market position is a measure of the position of a company or product on a market.
Leverage	Leverage is using given resources in such a way that the potential positive or negative outcome is magnified. In finance, this generally refers to borrowing.
Internal analysis	A self analysis of the strengths and weaknesses of a company is an internal analysis. Includes an analysis of the company's manufacturing, marketing, technological, financial and human resources.
Sears	Before the Sears catalog, farmers typically bought supplies (often at very high prices) from local general stores. Sears took advantage of this by publishing his catalog with clearly stated prices, so that consumers could know what he was selling and at what price, and order and obtain them conveniently. The catalog business soon grew quickly.
Marketing	Promoting and selling products or services to customers, or prospective customers, is referred to as marketing.
Operation	A standardized method or technique that is performed repetitively, often on different materials resulting in different finished goods is called an operation.
Credit	Credit refers to a recording as positive in the balance of payments, any transaction that gives rise to a payment into the country, such as an export, the sale of an asset, or borrowing from abroad.
Home Depot	Home Depot has recently added self checkout registers at most of its stores in North America. These automated kiosks allow the customer to scan the barcode of the item they wish to purchase, then insert money to pay for the items, and receive any change automatically. The customer no longer needs to interact with a store employee during checkout.
Asset	An item of property, such as land, capital, money, a share in ownership, or a claim on others for future payment, such as a bond or a bank deposit is an asset.
Organizational structure	Organizational structure is the way in which the interrelated groups of an organization are constructed. From a managerial point of view the main concerns are ensuring effective communication and coordination.
Value creation	Value creation refers to performing activities that increase the value of goods or services to consumers.
Strategic partnership	Strategic partnership refers to an association between two firms by which they agree to work together to achieve a strategic goal. This is often associated with long-term supplier-

Go to **Cram101.com** for the Practice Tests for this Chapter.

	customer relationships.
Partnership	In the common law, a partnership is a type of business entity in which partners share with each other the profits or losses of the business undertaking in which they have all invested.
Mistake	In contract law a mistake is incorrect understanding by one or more parties to a contract and may be used as grounds to invalidate the agreement. Common law has identified three different types of mistake in contract: unilateral mistake, mutual mistake, and common mistake.
Forming	The first stage of team development, where the team is formed and the objectives for the team are set is referred to as forming.
Analyst	Analyst refers to a person or tool with a primary function of information analysis, generally with a more limited, practical and short term set of goals than a researcher.
Complexity	The technical sophistication of the product and hence the amount of understanding required to use it is referred to as complexity. It is the opposite of simplicity.
Loyalty	Marketers tend to define customer loyalty as making repeat purchases. Some argue that it should be defined attitudinally as a strongly positive feeling about the brand.
Stakeholder	A stakeholder is an individual or group with a vested interest in or expectation for organizational performance. Usually stakeholders can either have an effect on or are affected by an organization.
Resistance to change	Resistance to change refers to an attitude or behavior that shows unwillingness to make or support a change.
Short run	Short run refers to a period of time that permits an increase or decrease in current production volume with existing capacity, but one that is too short to permit enlargement of that capacity itself (eg, the building of new plants, training of additional workers, etc.).
Scope	Scope of a project is the sum total of all projects products and their requirements or features.
Yield	The interest rate that equates a future value or an annuity to a given present value is a yield.
Production	The creation of finished goods and services using the factors of production: land, labor, capital, entrepreneurship, and knowledge.
Inputs	The inputs used by a firm or an economy are the labor, raw materials, electricity and other resources it uses to produce its outputs.
Financial statement	Financial statement refers to a summary of all the transactions that have occurred over a particular period.
Intangible assets	Assets that have special rights but not physical substance are referred to as intangible assets.
Intangible asset	An intangible assets is defined as an asset that is not physical in nature. The most common types are trade secrets (e.g., customer lists and know-how), copyrights, patents, trademarks, and goodwill.
Economic growth	Economic growth refers to the increase over time in the capacity of an economy to produce goods and services and to improve the well-being of its citizens.
Tangible asset	Assets that have physical substance that cannot easily be converted into cash are referd to as a tangible asset.
Contribution	In business organization law, the cash or property contributed to a business by its owners is referred to as contribution.

Foundation	A Foundation is a type of philanthropic organization set up by either individuals or institutions as a legal entity (either as a corporation or trust) with the purpose of distributing grants to support causes in line with the goals of the foundation.
Users	Users refer to people in the organization who actually use the product or service purchased by the buying center.
Advertising	Advertising refers to paid, nonpersonal communication through various media by organizations and individuals who are in some way identified in the advertising message.
Innovation	Innovation refers to the first commercially successful introduction of a new product, the use of a new method of production, or the creation of a new form of business organization.
Knowledge base	Knowledge base refers to a database that includes decision rules for use of the data, which may be qualitative as well as quantitative.
Human capital	Human capital refers to the stock of knowledge and skill, embodied in an individual as a result of education, training, and experience that makes them more productive. The stock of knowledge and skill embodied in the population of an economy.
Ancillary	An ancillary receiver is a receiver who has been appointed in aid of, and in subordination to, the primary receiver.
Crown jewel	Crown jewel refers to a valuable asset of the target corporation's that the tender offeror particularly wants to acquire in the tender offer.
Financial capital	Common stock, preferred stock, bonds, and retained earnings are financial capital. Financial capital appears on the corporate balance sheet under long-term liabilities and equity.
Microsoft	Microsoft is a multinational computer technology corporation with 2004 global annual sales of US$39.79 billion and 71,553 employees in 102 countries and regions as of July 2006. It develops, manufactures, licenses, and supports a wide range of software products for computing devices.
Inventory	Tangible property held for sale in the normal course of business or used in producing goods or services for sale is an inventory.
Promotion	Promotion refers to all the techniques sellers use to motivate people to buy products or services. An attempt by marketers to inform people about products and to persuade them to participate in an exchange.
Corporation	A legal entity chartered by a state or the Federal government that is distinct and separate from the individuals who own it is a corporation. This separation gives the corporation unique powers which other legal entities lack.
Starbucks	Although it has endured much criticism for its purported monopoly on the global coffee-bean market, Starbucks purchases only 3% of the coffee beans grown worldwide. In 2000 the company introduced a line of fair trade products and now offers three options for socially conscious coffee drinkers. According to Starbucks, they purchased 4.8 million pounds of Certified Fair Trade coffee in fiscal year 2004 and 11.5 million pounds in 2005.
Contract	A contract is a "promise" or an "agreement" that is enforced or recognized by the law. In the civil law, a contract is considered to be part of the general law of obligations.
Supply chain	Supply chain refers to the flow of goods, services, and information from the initial sources of materials and services to the delivery of products to consumers.
Supply	Supply is the aggregate amount of any material good that can be called into being at a certain price point; it comprises one half of the equation of supply and demand. In classical economic theory, a curve representing supply is one of the factors that produce price.

Go to **Cram101.com** for the Practice Tests for this Chapter.

Venue	A requirement distinct from jurisdiction that the court be geographically situated so that it is the most appropriate and convenient court to try the case is the venue.
Sustainable competitive advantage	A strength, relative to competitors, in the markets served and the products offered is referred to as the sustainable competitive advantage.
Safeway	On April 18, 2005, Safeway began a 100 million dollar brand re-positioning campaign labeled "Ingredients for life". This was done in an attempt to differentiate itself from its competitors, and to increase brand involvement. Steve Burd described it as "branding the shopping experience".
Organizational culture	The mindset of employees, including their shared beliefs, values, and goals is called the organizational culture.
Prototype	A prototype is built to test the function of a new design before starting production of a product.
Commodity	Could refer to any good, but in trade a commodity is usually a raw material or primary product that enters into international trade, such as metals or basic agricultural products.
Variable	A variable is something measured by a number; it is used to analyze what happens to other things when the size of that number changes.
Discount	The difference between the face value of a bond and its selling price, when a bond is sold for less than its face value it's referred to as a discount.
American Airlines	American Airlines developed from a conglomeration of about 82 small airlines through a series of corporate acquisitions and reorganizations: initially, the name American Airways was used as a common brand by a number of independent air carriers. American Airlines is the largest airline in the world in terms of total passengers transported and fleet size, and the second-largest airline in the world.
Peak	Peak refers to the point in the business cycle when an economic expansion reaches its highest point before turning down. Contrasts with trough.
Customer service	The ability of logistics management to satisfy users in terms of time, dependability, communication, and convenience is called the customer service.
Comprehensive	A comprehensive refers to a layout accurate in size, color, scheme, and other necessary details to show how a final ad will look. For presentation only, never for reproduction.
Agent	A person who makes economic decisions for another economic actor. A hired manager operates as an agent for a firm's owner.
Deliverable	A deliverable refers to a product created as a result of project work.
PepsiCo	In many ways, PepsiCo differs from its main competitor, having three times as many employees, larger revenues, but a smaller net profit.
Buyer	A buyer refers to a role in the buying center with formal authority and responsibility to select the supplier and negotiate the terms of the contract.
Value chain	The sequence of business functions in which usefulness is added to the products or services of a company is a value chain.
Logistics	Those activities that focus on getting the right amount of the right products to the right place at the right time at the lowest possible cost is referred to as logistics.
Outbound	Communications originating inside an organization and destined for customers, prospects, or other people outside the organization are called outbound.

Human resource management	The process of evaluating human resource needs, finding people to fill those needs, and getting the best work from each employee by providing the right incentives and job environment, all with the goal of meeting the needs of the firm are called human resource management.
Resource management	Resource management is the efficient and effective deployment of an organization's resources when they are needed. Such resources may include financial resources, inventory, human skills, production resources, or information technology.
Federal Express	The company officially began operations on April 17, 1973, utilizing a network of 14 Dassault Falcon 20s which connected 25 U.S. cities. FedEx, the first cargo airline to use jet aircraft for its services, expanded greatly after the deregulation of the cargo airlines sector. Federal Express use of the hub-spoke distribution paradigm in air freight enabled it to become a world leader in its field.
Management	Management characterizes the process of leading and directing all or part of an organization, often a business, through the deployment and manipulation of resources. Early twentieth-century management writer Mary Parker Follett defined management as "the art of getting things done through people."
Procurement	Procurement is the acquisition of goods or services at the best possible total cost of ownership, in the right quantity, at the right time, in the right place for the direct benefit or use of the governments, corporations, or individuals generally via, but not limited to a contract.
Basic research	Involves discovering new knowledge rather than solving specific problems is called basic research.
Product design	Product Design is defined as the idea generation, concept development, testing and manufacturing or implementation of a physical object or service. It is possibly the evolution of former discipline name - Industrial Design.
Personnel	A collective term for all of the employees of an organization. Personnel is also commonly used to refer to the personnel management function or the organizational unit responsible for administering personnel programs.
Accounting	A system that collects and processes financial information about an organization and reports that information to decision makers is referred to as accounting.
Accord	An agreement whereby the parties agree to accept something different in satisfaction of the original contract is an accord.
Finished goods	Completed products awaiting sale are called finished goods. An item considered a finished good in a supplying plant might be considered a component or raw material in a receiving plant.
Trend	Trend refers to the long-term movement of an economic variable, such as its average rate of increase or decrease over enough years to encompass several business cycles.
Strategic management	A philosophy of management that links strategic planning with dayto-day decision making. Strategic management seeks a fit between an organization's external and internal environments.
Research and development	The use of resources for the deliberate discovery of new information and ways of doing things, together with the application of that information in inventing new products or processes is referred to as research and development.
Information technology	Information technology refers to technology that helps companies change business by allowing them to use new methods.

Go to **Cram101.com** for the Practice Tests for this Chapter.

Offshore outsourcing	Offshore outsourcing is the practice of hiring an external organization to perform some or all business functions in a country other than the one where the product or service will be sold or consumed.
Vendor	A person who sells property to a vendee is a vendor. The words vendor and vendee are more commonly applied to the seller and purchaser of real estate, and the words seller and buyer are more commonly applied to the seller and purchaser of personal property.
General Motors	General Motors is the world's largest automaker. Founded in 1908, today it employs about 327,000 people around the world. With global headquarters in Detroit, it manufactures its cars and trucks in 33 countries.
Motorola	The Six Sigma quality system was developed at Motorola even though it became most well known because of its use by General Electric. It was created by engineer Bill Smith, under the direction of Bob Galvin (son of founder Paul Galvin) when he was running the company.
Siemens	Siemens is the world's largest conglomerate company. Worldwide, Siemens and its subsidiaries employs 461,000 people (2005) in 190 countries and reported global sales of €75.4 billion in fiscal year 2005.
Nokia	Nokia Corporation is the world's largest manufacturer of mobile telephones (as of June 2006), with a global market share of approximately 34% in Q2 of 2006. It produces mobile phones for every major market and protocol, including GSM, CDMA, and W-CDMA (UMTS).
Wage	The payment for the service of a unit of labor, per unit time. In trade theory, it is the only payment to labor, usually unskilled labor. In empirical work, wage data may exclude other compenzation, which must be added to get the total cost of employment.
Labor	People's physical and mental talents and efforts that are used to help produce goods and services are called labor.
Domestic	From or in one's own country. A domestic producer is one that produces inside the home country. A domestic price is the price inside the home country. Opposite of 'foreign' or 'world.'.
Boeing	Boeing is the world's largest aircraft manufacturer by revenue. Headquartered in Chicago, Illinois, Boeing is the second-largest defense contractor in the world. In 2005, the company was the world's largest civil aircraft manufacturer in terms of value.
Union	A worker association that bargains with employers over wages and working conditions is called a union.
Change management	Change management is the process of developing a planned approach to change in an organization. Typically the objective is to maximize the collective benefits for all people involved in the change and minimize the risk of failure of implementing the change.
Gain	In finance, gain is a profit or an increase in value of an investment such as a stock or bond. Gain is calculated by fair market value or the proceeds from the sale of the investment minus the sum of the purchase price and all costs associated with it.
Consideration	Consideration in contract law, a basic requirement for an enforceable agreement under traditional contract principles, defined in this text as legal value, bargained for and given in exchange for an act or promise. In corporation law, cash or property contributed to a corporation in exchange for shares, or a promise to contribute such cash or property.
Southwest airlines	Southwest Airlines is a low-fare airline in the United States. It is the third-largest airline in the world, by number of passengers carried, and the largest in the United States by number of passengers carried domestically.
Journal	Book of original entry, in which transactions are recorded in a general ledger system, is

Go to **Cram101.com** for the Practice Tests for this Chapter.

referred to as a journal.

Drucker

Drucker as a business thinker took off in the 1940s, when his initial writings on politics and society won him access to the internal workings of General Motors, which was one of the largest companies in the world at that time. His experiences in Europe had left him fascinated with the problem of authority.

Harvard Business Review

Harvard Business Review is a research-based magazine written for business practitioners, it claims a high ranking business readership and enjoys the reverence of academics, executives, and management consultants. It has been the frequent publishing home for well known scholars and management thinkers.

Strategic alliance

Strategic alliance refers to a long-term partnership between two or more companies established to help each company build competitive market advantages.

Integration

Economic integration refers to reducing barriers among countries to transactions and to movements of goods, capital, and labor, including harmonization of laws, regulations, and standards. Integrated markets theoretically function as a unified market.

Organizational performance

Organizational performance comprises the actual output or results of an organization as measured against its intended outputs (or goals and objectives).

Diversification strategy

Diversification strategy is a corporate strategy that takes the organization away from both its current markets and products, as opposed to either market or product development.

Diversification

Investing in a collection of assets whose returns do not always move together, with the result that overall risk is lower than for individual assets is referred to as diversification.

Corporate level

Corporate level refers to level at which top management directs overall strategy for the entire organization.

Engineering Management

Engineering Management involves the overall management of organizations with an orientation to manufacturing, engineering, technology or production.

Business strategy

Business strategy, which refers to the aggregated operational strategies of single business firm or that of an SBU in a diversified corporation refers to the way in which a firm competes in its chosen arenas.

Case study

A case study is a particular method of qualitative research. Rather than using large samples and following a rigid protocol to examine a limited number of variables, case study methods involve an in-depth, longitudinal examination of a single instance or event: a case. They provide a systematic way of looking at events, collecting data, analyzing information, and reporting the results.

Premium	Premium refers to the fee charged by an insurance company for an insurance policy. The rate of losses must be relatively predictable: In order to set the premium (prices) insurers must be able to estimate them accurately.
Firm	An organization that employs resources to produce a good or service for profit and owns and operates one or more plants is referred to as a firm.
Market	A market is, as defined in economics, a social arrangement that allows buyers and sellers to discover information and carry out a voluntary exchange of goods or services.
Joint venture	Joint venture refers to an undertaking by two parties for a specific purpose and duration, taking any of several legal forms.
Forming	The first stage of team development, where the team is formed and the objectives for the team are set is referred to as forming.
Competitor	Other organizations in the same industry or type of business that provide a good or service to the same set of customers is referred to as a competitor.
Analyst	Analyst refers to a person or tool with a primary function of information analysis, generally with a more limited, practical and short term set of goals than a researcher.
Competitive advantage	A business is said to have a competitive advantage when its unique strengths, often based on cost, quality, time, and innovation, offer consumers a greater percieved value and there by differtiating it from its competitors.
Marketing	Promoting and selling products or services to customers, or prospective customers, is referred to as marketing.
Consumption	In Keynesian economics consumption refers to personal consumption expenditure, i.e., the purchase of currently produced goods and services out of income, out of savings (net worth), or from borrowed funds. It refers to that part of disposable income that does not go to saving.
Purchasing	Purchasing refers to the function in a firm that searches for quality material resources, finds the best suppliers, and negotiates the best price for goods and services.
Manufacturing	Production of goods primarily by the application of labor and capital to raw materials and other intermediate inputs, in contrast to agriculture, mining, forestry, fishing, and services a manufacturing.
Proprietary	Proprietary indicates that a party, or proprietor, exercises private ownership, control or use over an item of property, usually to the exclusion of other parties. Where a party, holds or claims proprietary interests in relation to certain types of property (eg. a creative literary work, or software), that property may also be the subject of intellectual property law (eg. copyright or patents).
Technology	The body of knowledge and techniques that can be used to combine economic resources to produce goods and services is called technology.
Industry	A group of firms that produce identical or similar products is an industry. It is also used specifically to refer to an area of economic production focused on manufacturing which involves large amounts of capital investment before any profit can be realized, also called "heavy industry".
Information technology	Information technology refers to technology that helps companies change business by allowing them to use new methods.
Brief	Brief refers to a statement of a party's case or legal arguments, usually prepared by an attorney. Also used to make legal arguments before appellate courts.

Go to **Cram101.com** for the Practice Tests for this Chapter.

Complexity	The technical sophistication of the product and hence the amount of understanding required to use it is referred to as complexity. It is the opposite of simplicity.
Economy	The income, expenditures, and resources that affect the cost of running a business and household are called an economy.
Core competency	A company's core competency are things that a firm can (alsosns) do well and that meet the following three conditions. 1. It provides customer benefits, 2. It is hard for competitors to imitate, and 3. it can be leveraged widely to many products and market. A core competency can take various forms, including technical/subject matter knowhow, a reliable process, and/or close relationships with customers and suppliers. It may also include product development or culture such as employee dedication. Modern business theories suggest that most activities that are not part of a company's core competency should be outsourced.
Core	A core is the set of feasible allocations in an economy that cannot be improved upon by subset of the set of the economy's consumers (a coalition). In construction, when the force in an element is within a certain center section, the core, the element will only be under compression.
Gain	In finance, gain is a profit or an increase in value of an investment such as a stock or bond. Gain is calculated by fair market value or the proceeds from the sale of the investment minus the sum of the purchase price and all costs associated with it.
Service	Service refers to a "non tangible product" that is not embodied in a physical good and that typically effects some change in another product, person, or institution. Contrasts with good.
Strategic intent	Strategic intent is when a firm relentlessly pursues a difficult strategic goa and concentrates its competitive actions and energies on achieving that goal.
Allocate	Allocate refers to the assignment of income for various tax purposes. A multistate corporation's nonbusiness income usually is distributed to the state where the nonbusiness assets are located; it is not apportioned with the rest of the entity's income.
Global competition	Global competition exists when competitive conditions across national markets are linked strongly enough to form a true international market and when leading competitors compete head to head in many different countries.
Option	A contract that gives the purchaser the option to buy or sell the underlying financial instrument at a specified price, called the exercise price or strike price, within a specific period of time.
Distribution	Distribution in economics, the manner in which total output and income is distributed among individuals or factors.
Corporation	A legal entity chartered by a state or the Federal government that is distinct and separate from the individuals who own it is a corporation. This separation gives the corporation unique powers which other legal entities lack.
Loyalty	Marketers tend to define customer loyalty as making repeat purchases. Some argue that it should be defined attitudinally as a strongly positive feeling about the brand.
Ford Motor Company	Ford Motor Company introduced methods for large-scale manufacturing of cars, and large-scale management of an industrial workforce, especially elaborately engineered manufacturing sequences typified by the moving assembly lines. Henry Ford's combination of highly efficient factories, highly paid workers, and low prices revolutionized manufacturing and came to be known around the world as Fordism by 1914.
Customer loyalty	Marketers tend to define customer loyalty as making repeat purchases. Some argue that it should be defined attitudinally as a strongly positive feeling about the brand.

Go to **Cram101.com** for the Practice Tests for this Chapter.

Profit	Profit refers to the return to the resource entrepreneurial ability; total revenue minus total cost.
Ford	Ford is an American company that manufactures and sells automobiles worldwide. Ford introduced methods for large-scale manufacturing of cars, and large-scale management of an industrial workforce, especially elaborately engineered manufacturing sequences typified by the moving assembly lines.
Customer defection	Customer defection refers to customers who do not continue to purchase from the enterprise. The words attrition and churn are often used to describe the same phenomenon.
Credit	Credit refers to a recording as positive in the balance of payments, any transaction that gives rise to a payment into the country, such as an export, the sale of an asset, or borrowing from abroad.
Issuer	The company that borrows money from investors by issuing bonds is referred to as issuer. They are legally responsible for the obligations of the issue and for reporting financial conditions, material developments and any other operational activities as required by the regulations of their jurisdictions.
Cemex	Although it is not a monopoly, Cemex, along with Holcim-Apasco, controls the Mexican cement market. This has given rise to allegations that because of the oligopolistic structure in the Mexican cement market (as in many other markets in Mexico) consumers pay a higher price for cement than in other countries. However given the peculiarities of the Mexican cement market, the fact that it is sold mostly in bags, and the fact that cement is not an easily transported commodity make this accuzation difficult, if not impossible to prove.
Cost Leadership Strategy	Using a serious commitment to reducing expenses that, in turn, lowers the price of the items sold in a relatively broad array of market segments is called cost leadership strategy.
Cost leadership	Organization's ability to achieve lower costs relative to competitors through productivity and efficiency improvements, elimination of waste, and tight cost control is cost leadership.
Integration	Economic integration refers to reducing barriers among countries to transactions and to movements of goods, capital, and labor, including harmonization of laws, regulations, and standards. Integrated markets theoretically function as a unified market.
Leadership	Management merely consists of leadership applied to business situations; or in other words: management forms a sub-set of the broader process of leadership.
Affiliation	A relationship with other websites in which a company can cross-promote and is credited for sales that accrue through their site is an affiliation.
Merrill Lynch	Merrill Lynch through its subsidiaries and affiliates, provides capital markets services, investment banking and advisory services, wealth management, asset management, insurance, banking and related products and services on a global basis. It is best known for its Global Private Client services and its strong sales force.
Exchange	The trade of things of value between buyer and seller so that each is better off after the trade is called the exchange.
Broker	In commerce, a broker is a party that mediates between a buyer and a seller. A broker who also acts as a seller or as a buyer becomes a principal party to the deal.
Microsoft	Microsoft is a multinational computer technology corporation with 2004 global annual sales of US$39.79 billion and 71,553 employees in 102 countries and regions as of July 2006. It develops, manufactures, licenses, and supports a wide range of software products for computing devices.
Supply	Supply is the aggregate amount of any material good that can be called into being at a

Go to **Cram101.com** for the Practice Tests for this Chapter.

certain price point; it comprises one half of the equation of supply and demand. In classical economic theory, a curve representing supply is one of the factors that produce price.

Dealer	People who link buyers with sellers by buying and selling securities at stated prices are referred to as a dealer.
Buyer	A buyer refers to a role in the buying center with formal authority and responsibility to select the supplier and negotiate the terms of the contract.
Interest	In finance and economics, interest is the price paid by a borrower for the use of a lender's money. In other words, interest is the amount of paid to "rent" money for a period of time.
Market segmentation	The process of dividing the total market into several groups whose members have similar characteristics is market segmentation.
Advertisement	Advertisement is the promotion of goods, services, companies and ideas, usually by an identified sponsor. Marketers see advertising as part of an overall promotional strategy.
End user	End user refers to the ultimate user of a product or service.
Revenue	Revenue is a U.S. business term for the amount of money that a company receives from its activities, mostly from sales of products and/or services to customers.
Marketing strategy	Marketing strategy refers to the means by which a marketing goal is to be achieved, usually characterized by a specified target market and a marketing program to reach it.
Effective communication	When the intended meaning equals the perceived meaning it is called effective communication.
Benefit segmentation	Dividing the market by determining which benefits of the product to talk about is benefit segmentation.
Perceptual mapping	Perceptual mapping is a graphics technique used by marketers that attempts to visually display the perceptions of customers or potential customers. Typically the position of a product, product line, brand, or company is displayed relative to their competition.
Family life cycle	Family life cycle refers to concept that demonstrates changing purchasing behavior as a person or a family matures.
Social class	Social class refers to the hierarchical distinctions between individuals or groups in societies or cultures. While anthropologists, historians and sociologists identify class as a social structure emerging from pre-history, the idea of social class entered the English lexicon about the 1770s.
Production	The creation of finished goods and services using the factors of production: land, labor, capital, entrepreneurship, and knowledge.
Economics	The social science dealing with the use of scarce resources to obtain the maximum satisfaction of society's virtually unlimited economic wants is an economics.
Users	Users refer to people in the organization who actually use the product or service purchased by the buying center.
Generation x	Generation x refers to the 15 percent of the U.S. population born between 1965 and 1976 a period also known as the baby bust.
Shareholder	A shareholder is an individual or company (including a corporation) that legally owns one or more shares of stock in a joined stock company.
Holding	The holding is a court's determination of a matter of law based on the issue presented in the particular case. In other words: under this law, with these facts, this result.
Stock	In financial terminology, stock is the capital raized by a corporation, through the issuance

and sale of shares.

Fund	Independent accounting entity with a self-balancing set of accounts segregated for the purposes of carrying on specific activities is referred to as a fund.
Distribution channel	A distribution channel is a chain of intermediaries, each passing a product down the chain to the next organization, before it finally reaches the consumer or end-user.
Channel	Channel, in communications (sometimes called communications channel), refers to the medium used to convey information from a sender (or transmitter) to a receiver.
Niche	In industry, a niche is a situation or an activity perfectly suited to a person. A niche can imply a working position or an area suited to a person who occupies it. Basically, a job where a person is able to succeed and thrive.
Generation y	Generation y refers to Americans born after 1976, the year that many baby boomers began having children.
PepsiCo	In many ways, PepsiCo differs from its main competitor, having three times as many employees, larger revenues, but a smaller net profit.
Productivity	Productivity refers to the total output of goods and services in a given period of time divided by work hours.
Business intelligence	Business intelligence refers to data about the past history, present status, or future projections for a business organization.
Data mining	The extraction of hidden predictive information from large databases is referred to as data mining.
Research and development	The use of resources for the deliberate discovery of new information and ways of doing things, together with the application of that information in inventing new products or processes is referred to as research and development.
Consumer good	Products and services that are ultimately consumed rather than used in the production of another good are a consumer good.
Innovation	Innovation refers to the first commercially successful introduction of a new product, the use of a new method of production, or the creation of a new form of business organization.
Marketing mix	The marketing mix approach to marketing is a model of crafting and implementing marketing strategies. It stresses the "mixing" or blending of various factors in such a way that both organizational and consumer (target markets) objectives are attained.
Mass media	Mass media refers to non-personal channels of communication that allow a message to be sent to many individuals at one time.
Investment	Investment refers to spending for the production and accumulation of capital and additions to inventories. In a financial sense, buying an asset with the expectation of making a return.
Michael Porter	Michael Porter is a leading contributor to strategic management theory, Porter's main academic objectives focus on how a firm or a region, can build a competitive advantage and develop competitive strategy. Porter's strategic system consists primarily of 5 forces analysis, strategic groups, the value chain, and market positioning stratagies.
Strategic fit	In business planning, the strategic fit is an indication of how well a company's mission and strategies fit its internal capabilities and its external environment.
Southwest airlines	Southwest Airlines is a low-fare airline in the United States. It is the third-largest airline in the world, by number of passengers carried, and the largest in the United States by number of passengers carried domestically.

Go to **Cram101.com** for the Practice Tests for this Chapter.

Positioning	The art and science of fitting the product or service to one or more segments of the market in such a way as to set it meaningfully apart from competition is called positioning.
Customer service	The ability of logistics management to satisfy users in terms of time, dependability, communication, and convenience is called the customer service.
Organizational culture	The mindset of employees, including their shared beliefs, values, and goals is called the organizational culture.
Continental Airlines	Continental Airlines is an airline of the United States. Based in Houston, Texas, it is the 6th largest airline in the U.S. and the 8th largest in the world. Continental's tagline, since 1998, has been Work Hard, Fly Right.
Subsidiary	A company that is controlled by another company or corporation is a subsidiary.
US airways	US Airways is an airline based in Tempe, Arizona, owned by US Airways Group, Inc.. As of May 2006, the combined airline is the fifth largest airline in the United States and has a fleet of 358 mainline jet aircraft and 295 express aircraft connecting 237 destinations in North America, Central America, the Caribbean, Hawaii, and Europe.
Sears	Before the Sears catalog, farmers typically bought supplies (often at very high prices) from local general stores. Sears took advantage of this by publishing his catalog with clearly stated prices, so that consumers could know what he was selling and at what price, and order and obtain them conveniently. The catalog business soon grew quickly.
Scope	Scope of a project is the sum total of all projects products and their requirements or features.
Differentiation Strategy	Differentiation strategy requires innovation and significant points of difference in product offerings, brand image, higher quality, advanced technology, or superior service in a relatively broad array of market segments.
Assignment	A transfer of property or some right or interest is referred to as assignment.
Internal environment	Variables that are under some degree of control by organizational members is the internal enviroment. Internal environment scans are conducted to identify an organization's internal capabilities, performance levels, strengths, and weaknesses.
Inventory control	Inventory control, in the field of loss prevention, are systems designed to introduce technical barriers to shoplifting.
Total cost	The sum of fixed cost and variable cost is referred to as total cost.
Inventory	Tangible property held for sale in the normal course of business or used in producing goods or services for sale is an inventory.
Logistics	Those activities that focus on getting the right amount of the right products to the right place at the right time at the lowest possible cost is referred to as logistics.
Outbound	Communications originating inside an organization and destined for customers, prospects, or other people outside the organization are called outbound.
Raw material	Raw material refers to a good that has not been transformed by production; a primary product.
Procurement	Procurement is the acquisition of goods or services at the best possible total cost of ownership, in the right quantity, at the right time, in the right place for the direct benefit or use of the governments, corporations, or individuals generally via, but not limited to a contract.
Discount	The difference between the face value of a bond and its selling price, when a bond is sold for less than its face value it's referred to as a discount.

Go to **Cram101.com** for the Practice Tests for this Chapter.

79

Inventory management	The planning, coordinating, and controlling activities related to the flow of inventory into, through, and out of an organization is referred to as inventory management.
Management system	A management system is the framework of processes and procedures used to ensure that an organization can fulfill all tasks required to achieve its objectives.
Management	Management characterizes the process of leading and directing all or part of an organization, often a business, through the deployment and manipulation of resources. Early twentieth-century management writer Mary Parker Follett defined management as "the art of getting things done through people."
Wholesale	According to the United Nations Statistics Division Wholesale is the resale of new and used goods to retailers, to industrial, commercial, institutional or professional users, or to other wholesalers, or involves acting as an agent or broker in buying merchandise for, or selling merchandise, to such persons or companies.
Retailing	All activities involved in selling, renting, and providing goods and services to ultimate consumers for personal, family, or household use is referred to as retailing.
Brand	A name, symbol, or design that identifies the goods or services of one seller or group of sellers and distinguishes them from the goods and services of competitors is a brand.
Strategy formulation	The process of deciding on a strategic direction by defining a company's mission and goals, its external opportunities and threats, and its internal strengths and weaknesses is referred to as a strategy formulation.
Turnover	Turnover in a financial context refers to the rate at which a provider of goods cycles through its average inventory. Turnover in a human resources context refers to the characteristic of a given company or industry, relative to rate at which an employer gains and loses staff.
Price competition	Price competition is where a company tries to distinguish its product or service from competing products on the basis of low price.
Margin	A deposit by a buyer in stocks with a seller or a stockbroker, as security to cover fluctuations in the market in reference to stocks that the buyer has purchased but for which he has not paid is a margin. Commodities are also traded on margin.
Profit margin	Profit margin is a measure of profitability. It is calculated using a formula and written as a percentage or a number. Profit margin = Net income before tax and interest / Revenue.
Entry barrier	An entry barrier or barrier to entry is an obstacle in the path of a potential firm which wants to enter a given market.
Differentiated product	A firm's product that is not identical to products of other firms in the same industry is a differentiated product.
Expense	In accounting, an expense represents an event in which an asset is used up or a liability is incurred. In terms of the accounting equation, expenses reduce owners' equity.
Caterpillar	Caterpillar is a United States based corporation headquartered in Peoria, Illinois. Caterpillar is "the world's largest manufacturer of construction and mining equipment, diesel and natural gas engines, and industrial gas turbines."
Toyota	Toyota is a Japanese multinational corporation that manufactures automobiles, trucks and buses. Toyota is the world's second largest automaker by sales. Toyota also provides financial services through its subsidiary, Toyota Financial Services, and participates in other lines of business.
Product innovations	Innovations that introduce new goods or services to better meet customer needs are product innovations.

Go to **Cram101.com** for the Practice Tests for this Chapter.

Product innovation	The development and sale of a new or improved product is a product innovation. Production of a new product on a commercial basis.
Brand loyalty	The degree to which customers are satisfied, like the brand, and are committed to further purchase is referred to as brand loyalty.
United Nations	An international organization created by multilateral treaty in 1945 to promote social and economic cooperation among nations and to protect human rights is the United Nations.
Brand image	The advertising metric that measures the type and favorability of consumer perceptions of the brand is referred to as the brand image.
Portfolio	In finance, a portfolio is a collection of investments held by an institution or a private individual. Holding but not always a portfolio is part of an investment and risk-limiting strategy called diversification. By owning several assets, certain types of risk (in particular specific risk) can be reduced.
Bargaining power	Bargaining power refers to the ability to influence the setting of prices or wages, usually arising from some sort of monopoly or monopsony position
Philip Morris	Philip Morris, is the world's largest commercial tobacco company by sales. Philip Morris was begun by a London tobacconist of the same name. He was one of the first people to sell hand-rolled cigarettes in the 1860s, selling them under the brand names Oxford and Cambridge Blues, following the adoption of cigarette smoking by British soldiers returning from the Crimean War.
Domestic	From or in one's own country. A domestic producer is one that produces inside the home country. A domestic price is the price inside the home country. Opposite of 'foreign' or 'world.'.
Customs	Customs is an authority or agency in a country responsible for collecting customs duties and for controlling the flow of people, animals and goods (including personal effects and hazardous items) in and out of the country.
Altria	Altria Group, Inc. based in New York City, is one of the world's largest food, beverage, and tobacco corporations and a component of the Dow Jones Industrial Average and S&P 500. It owns the brands Marlboro under its Philip Morris USA arm and retains a majority stake in Kraft Foods and a 36% interest in SABMiller.
Agent	A person who makes economic decisions for another economic actor. A hired manager operates as an agent for a firm's owner.
Market segments	Market segments refer to the groups that result from the process of market segmentation; these groups ideally have common needs and will respond similarly to a marketing action.
Balance	In banking and accountancy, the outstanding balance is the amount of money owned, (or due), that remains in a deposit account (or a loan account) at a given date, after all past remittances, payments and withdrawal have been accounted for. It can be positive (then, in the balance sheet of a firm, it is an asset) or negative (a liability).
Outsourcing	Outsourcing refers to a production activity that was previously done inside a firm or plant that is now conducted outside that firm or plant.
Acquisition	A company's purchase of the property and obligations of another company is an acquisition.
Liability	A liability is a present obligation of the enterprise arizing from past events, the settlement of which is expected to result in an outflow from the enterprise of resources embodying economic benefits.
Merger	Merger refers to the combination of two firms into a single firm.

Go to **Cram101.com** for the Practice Tests for this Chapter.

Appeal	Appeal refers to the act of asking an appellate court to overturn a decision after the trial court's final judgment has been entered.
Personnel	A collective term for all of the employees of an organization. Personnel is also commonly used to refer to the personnel management function or the organizational unit responsible for administering personnel programs.
Product development	In business and engineering, new product development is the complete process of bringing a new product to market. There are two parallel aspects to this process : one involves product engineering ; the other marketing analysis. Marketers see new product development as the first stage in product life cycle management, engineers as part of Product Lifecycle Management.
Preference	The act of a debtor in paying or securing one or more of his creditors in a manner more favorable to them than to other creditors or to the exclusion of such other creditors is a preference. In the absence of statute, a preference is perfectly good, but to be legal it must be bona fide, and not a mere subterfuge of the debtor to secure a future benefit to himself or to prevent the application of his property to his debts.
BMW	BMW is an independent German company and manufacturer of automobiles and motorcycles. BMW is the world's largest premium carmaker and is the parent company of the BMW MINI and Rolls-Royce car brands, and, formerly, Rover.
Forbes	David Churbuck founded online Forbes in 1996. The site drew attention when it uncovered Stephen Glass' journalistic fraud in The New Republic in 1998, a scoop that gave credibility to internet journalism.
Cabinet	The heads of the executive departments of a jurisdiction who report to and advise its chief executive; examples would include the president's cabinet, the governor's cabinet, and the mayor's cabinet.
Five competitive forces	There are five competitive forces which can be used to estimate the attractiveness and profitability of entering a business market. They consist of the threat of new entrants, competitive rivalry, the threat of substitute products, the power of buyers, and the power of suppliers
Home Depot	Home Depot has recently added self checkout registers at most of its stores in North America. These automated kiosks allow the customer to scan the barcode of the item they wish to purchase, then insert money to pay for the items, and receive any change automatically. The customer no longer needs to interact with a store employee during checkout.
Targeting	In advertizing, targeting is to select a demographic or other group of people to advertise to, and create advertisements appropriately.
Trend	Trend refers to the long-term movement of an economic variable, such as its average rate of increase or decrease over enough years to encompass several business cycles.
Standardization	Standardization, in the context related to technologies and industries, is the process of establishing a technical standard among competing entities in a market, where this will bring benefits without hurting competition.
Commodity	Could refer to any good, but in trade a commodity is usually a raw material or primary product that enters into international trade, such as metals or basic agricultural products.
Production line	A production line is a set of sequential operations established in a factory whereby materials are put through a refining process to produce an end-product that is suitable for onward consumption; or components are assembled to make a finished article.
Flexible manufacturing	A series of manufacturing machines, controlled and integrated by a computer, which is designed to perform a series of manufacturing operations automatically are referred to as a

Go to **Cram101.com** for the Practice Tests for this Chapter.

system	flexible manufacturing system.
Total quality management	The broad set of management and control processes designed to focus an entire organization and all of its employees on providing products or services that do the best possible job of satisfying the customer is called total quality management.
Quality management	Quality management is a method for ensuring that all the activities necessary to design, develop and implement a product or service are effective and efficient with respect to the system and its performance.
Flexible manufacturing	Flexible manufacturing refers to designing machines to do multiple tasks so that they can produce a variety of products.
Intervention	Intervention refers to an activity in which a government buys or sells its currency in the foreign exchange market in order to affect its currency's exchange rate.
Fiscal year	A fiscal year is a 12-month period used for calculating annual ("yearly") financial reports in businesses and other organizations. In many jurisdictions, regulatory laws regarding accounting require such reports once per twelve months, but do not require that the twelve months constitute a calendar year (i.e. January to December).
Allegation	An allegation is a statement of a fact by a party in a pleading, which the party claims it will prove. Allegations remain assertions without proof, only claims until they are proved.
Value pricing	When marketers provide consumers with brand-name goods and services at fair prices, we have value pricing.
Preparation	Preparation refers to usually the first stage in the creative process. It includes education and formal training.
Advertising Age	Advertising Age is the world's leading source of news, analysis, information and data on advertising, marketing and media. The magazine was started as a broadsheet newspaper in Chicago in 1930.
Advertising	Advertising refers to paid, nonpersonal communication through various media by organizations and individuals who are in some way identified in the advertising message.
Competitive Strategy	An outline of how a business intends to compete with other firms in the same industry is called competitive strategy.
Intangible assets	Assets that have special rights but not physical substance are referred to as intangible assets.
Intangible asset	An intangible assets is defined as an asset that is not physical in nature. The most common types are trade secrets (e.g., customer lists and know-how), copyrights, patents, trademarks, and goodwill.
Tangible asset	Assets that have physical substance that cannot easily be converted into cash are referd to as a tangible asset.
Tangible	Having a physical existence is referred to as the tangible. Personal property other than real estate, such as cars, boats, stocks, or other assets.
Asset	An item of property, such as land, capital, money, a share in ownership, or a claim on others for future payment, such as a bond or a bank deposit is an asset.
Customer relationship management	Learning as much as possible about customers and doing everything you can to satisfy them or even delight them with goods and services over time is customer relationship management.
Relationship management	A method for developing long-term associations with customers is referred to as relationship management.

Go to **Cram101.com** for the Practice Tests for this Chapter.

Points	Loan origination fees that may be deductible as interest by a buyer of property. A seller of property who pays points reduces the selling price by the amount of the points paid for the buyer.
Enterprise resource planning	Computer-based production and operations system that links multiple firms into one integrated production unit is enterprise resource planning.
Enterprise	Enterprise refers to another name for a business organization. Other similar terms are business firm, sometimes simply business, sometimes simply firm, as well as company, and entity.
Information system	An information system is a system whether automated or manual, that comprises people, machines, and/or methods organized to collect, process, transmit, and disseminate data that represent user information.
Installations	Support goods, consisting of buildings and fixed equipment are called installations.
Customer satisfaction	Customer satisfaction is a business term which is used to capture the idea of measuring how satisfied an enterprise's customers are with the organization's efforts in a marketplace.
Continuous improvement	The constant effort to eliminate waste, reduce response time, simplify the design of both products and processes, and improve quality and customer service is referred to as continuous improvement.
General Motors	General Motors is the world's largest automaker. Founded in 1908, today it employs about 327,000 people around the world. With global headquarters in Detroit, it manufactures its cars and trucks in 33 countries.
Empowerment	Giving employees the authority and responsibility to respond quickly to customer requests is called empowerment.
Gap	In December of 1995, Gap became the first major North American retailer to accept independent monitoring of the working conditions in a contract factory producing its garments. Gap is the largest specialty retailer in the United States.
Quality measures	Ratios that are used to measure a firm's performance in the area of quality management are referred to as quality measures.
Strategic choice	Strategic choice refers to an organization's strategy; the ways an organization will attempt to fulfill its mission and achieve its long-term goals.
Foundation	A Foundation is a type of philanthropic organization set up by either individuals or institutions as a legal entity (either as a corporation or trust) with the purpose of distributing grants to support causes in line with the goals of the foundation.
Standardized product	Standardized product refers to a product whose buyers are indifferent to the seller from whom they purchase it, as long as the price charged by all sellers is the same; a product all units of which are identical and thus are perfect substitutes.
Warehouse clubs	Large retail stores that require a yearly fee to shop at the store are called warehouse clubs.
Warehouse	Warehouse refers to a location, often decentralized, that a firm uses to store, consolidate, age, or mix stock; house product-recall programs; or ease tax burdens.
Costco	Costco focuses on selling products at low prices, often at very high volume. These goods are usually bulk-packaged and marketed primarily to large families and small businesses. As a warehouse club, Costco is only open to members and their guests, except for purchases of liquor, gasoline and prescription drugs in some U.S. states due to state law and liquor license restrictions.

Go to **Cram101.com** for the Practice Tests for this Chapter.

Earnings per share	Earnings per share refers to annual profit of the corporation divided by the number of shares outstanding.
Gross margin	Gross margin is an ambiguous phrase that expresses the relationship between gross profit and sales revenue as Gross Margin = Revenue - costs of good sold.
Cash flow	In finance, cash flow refers to the amounts of cash being received and spent by a business during a defined period of time, sometimes tied to a specific project. Most of the time they are being used to determine gaps in the liquid position of a company.
Shares	Shares refer to an equity security, representing a shareholder's ownership of a corporation. Shares are one of a finite number of equal portions in the capital of a company, entitling the owner to a proportion of distributed, non-reinvested profits known as dividends and to a portion of the value of the company in case of liquidation.
Regulation	Regulation refers to restrictions state and federal laws place on business with regard to the conduct of its activities.
Labor	People's physical and mental talents and efforts that are used to help produce goods and services are called labor.
International diversification	Achieving diversification through many different foreign investments that are influenced by a variety of factors is referred to as international diversification. By diversifying across nations whose economic cycles are not perfectly correlated, investors can typically reduce the variability of their returns.
Strategic management	A philosophy of management that links strategic planning with dayto-day decision making. Strategic management seeks a fit between an organization's external and internal environments.
Entrepreneurship	The assembling of resources to produce new or improved products and technologies is referred to as entrepreneurship.
Management team	A management team is directly responsible for managing the day-to-day operations (and profitability) of a company.
Diversification	Investing in a collection of assets whose returns do not always move together, with the result that overall risk is lower than for individual assets is referred to as diversification.
Composition	An out-of-court settlement in which creditors agree to accept a fractional settlement on their original claim is referred to as composition.
Status quo	Status quo is a Latin term meaning the present, current, existing state of affairs.
Journal	Book of original entry, in which transactions are recorded in a general ledger system, is referred to as a journal.
Context	The effect of the background under which a message often takes on more and richer meaning is a context. Context is especially important in cross-cultural interactions because some cultures are said to be high context or low context.
New product development	New product development is the complete process of bringing a new product to market. There are two parallel aspects to this process : one involves product engineering ; the other marketing analysis.
Small business	Small business refers to a business that is independently owned and operated, is not dominant in its field of operation, and meets certain standards of size in terms of employees or annual receipts.
Assessment	Collecting information and providing feedback to employees about their behavior,

	communication style, or skills is an assessment.
Export	In economics, an export is any good or commodity, shipped or otherwise transported out of a country, province, town to another part of the world in a legitimate fashion, typically for use in trade or sale.
Harvard Business Review	Harvard Business Review is a research-based magazine written for business practitioners, it claims a high ranking business readership and enjoys the reverence of academics, executives, and management consultants. It has been the frequent publishing home for well known scholars and management thinkers.

92

Go to **Cram101.com** for the Practice Tests for this Chapter.

Strategic management	A philosophy of management that links strategic planning with dayto-day decision making. Strategic management seeks a fit between an organization's external and internal environments.
Competitor	Other organizations in the same industry or type of business that provide a good or service to the same set of customers is referred to as a competitor.
Management	Management characterizes the process of leading and directing all or part of an organization, often a business, through the deployment and manipulation of resources. Early twentieth-century management writer Mary Parker Follett defined management as "the art of getting things done through people."
Competitor analysis	Competitor analysis in marketing and strategic management is an assessment of the strengths and weaknesses of current and potential competitors.
Market	A market is, as defined in economics, a social arrangement that allows buyers and sellers to discover information and carry out a voluntary exchange of goods or services.
Airbus	In 2003, for the first time in its 33-year history, Airbus delivered more jet-powered airliners than Boeing. Boeing states that the Boeing 777 has outsold its Airbus counterparts, which include the A340 family as well as the A330-300. The smaller A330-200 competes with the 767, outselling its Boeing counterpart.
Service	Service refers to a "non tangible product" that is not embodied in a physical good and that typically effects some change in another product, person, or institution. Contrasts with good.
Delta Air Lines	Delta Air Lines currently has the largest route network "footprint" of any airline. The airline also serves Puerto Rico, and the U.S. Virgin Islands, in addition to 95 countries.
Subsidiary	A company that is controlled by another company or corporation is a subsidiary.
Boeing	Boeing is the world's largest aircraft manufacturer by revenue. Headquartered in Chicago, Illinois, Boeing is the second-largest defense contractor in the world. In 2005, the company was the world's largest civil aircraft manufacturer in terms of value.
Southwest airlines	Southwest Airlines is a low-fare airline in the United States. It is the third-largest airline in the world, by number of passengers carried, and the largest in the United States by number of passengers carried domestically.
Discount	The difference between the face value of a bond and its selling price, when a bond is sold for less than its face value it's referred to as a discount.
Profit	Profit refers to the return to the resource entrepreneurial ability; total revenue minus total cost.
Industry	A group of firms that produce identical or similar products is an industry. It is also used specifically to refer to an area of economic production focused on manufacturing which involves large amounts of capital investment before any profit can be realized, also called "heavy industry".
Revenue	Revenue is a U.S. business term for the amount of money that a company receives from its activities, mostly from sales of products and/or services to customers.
Analyst	Analyst refers to a person or tool with a primary function of information analysis, generally with a more limited, practical and short term set of goals than a researcher.
DIRECTV	DirecTV was launched in 1994 by General Motors subsidiary Hughes Electronics. It was the first high-powered direct broadcast satellite service in the world. Digital Equipment Corporation provided the customer-care out of their existing technical support center in Colorado Springs, Colorado.

Go to **Cram101.com** for the Practice Tests for this Chapter.

Channel	Channel, in communications (sometimes called communications channel), refers to the medium used to convey information from a sender (or transmitter) to a receiver.
Credit	Credit refers to a recording as positive in the balance of payments, any transaction that gives rise to a payment into the country, such as an export, the sale of an asset, or borrowing from abroad.
Firm	An organization that employs resources to produce a good or service for profit and owns and operates one or more plants is referred to as a firm.
PepsiCo	In many ways, PepsiCo differs from its main competitor, having three times as many employees, larger revenues, but a smaller net profit.
Targeting	In advertizing, targeting is to select a demographic or other group of people to advertise to, and create advertisements appropriately.
Context	The effect of the background under which a message often takes on more and richer meaning is a context. Context is especially important in cross-cultural interactions because some cultures are said to be high context or low context.
Market position	Market position is a measure of the position of a company or product on a market.
Competitive advantage	A business is said to have a competitive advantage when its unique strengths, often based on cost, quality, time, and innovation, offer consumers a greater percieved value and there by differtiating it from its competitors.
Gain	In finance, gain is a profit or an increase in value of an investment such as a stock or bond. Gain is calculated by fair market value or the proceeds from the sale of the investment minus the sum of the purchase price and all costs associated with it.
Acquisition	A company's purchase of the property and obligations of another company is an acquisition.
Economy	The income, expenditures, and resources that affect the cost of running a business and household are called an economy.
Scope	Scope of a project is the sum total of all projects products and their requirements or features.
Integration	Economic integration refers to reducing barriers among countries to transactions and to movements of goods, capital, and labor, including harmonization of laws, regulations, and standards. Integrated markets theoretically function as a unified market.
Union	A worker association that bargains with employers over wages and working conditions is called a union.
Market share	That fraction of an industry's output accounted for by an individual firm or group of firms is called market share.
Points	Loan origination fees that may be deductible as interest by a buyer of property. A seller of property who pays points reduces the selling price by the amount of the points paid for the buyer.
Insurance	Insurance refers to a system by which individuals can reduce their exposure to risk of large losses by spreading the risks among a large number of persons.
Interest	In finance and economics, interest is the price paid by a borrower for the use of a lender's money. In other words, interest is the amount of paid to "rent" money for a period of time.
Health insurance	Health insurance is a type of insurance whereby the insurer pays the medical costs of the insured if the insured becomes sick due to covered causes, or due to accidents. The insurer may be a private organization or a government agency.

Go to **Cram101.com** for the Practice Tests for this Chapter.

Core competency	A company's core competency are things that a firm can (alsosns) do well and that meet the following three conditions. 1. It provides customer benefits, 2. It is hard for competitors to imitate, and 3. it can be leveraged widely to many products and market. A core competency can take various forms, including technical/subject matter knowhow, a reliable process, and/or close relationships with customers and suppliers. It may also include product development or culture such as employee dedication. Modern business theories suggest that most activities that are not part of a company's core competency should be outsourced.
Technology	The body of knowledge and techniques that can be used to combine economic resources to produce goods and services is called technology.
Core	A core is the set of feasible allocations in an economy that cannot be improved upon by subset of the set of the economy's consumers (a coalition). In construction, when the force in an element is within a certain center section, the core, the element will only be under compression.
Market segments	Market segments refer to the groups that result from the process of market segmentation; these groups ideally have common needs and will respond similarly to a marketing action.
Tangible	Having a physical existence is referred to as the tangible. Personal property other than real estate, such as cars, boats, stocks, or other assets.
Walgreens	Walgreens is a convenience store and pharmacy chain in the United States that operates more than 5,000 stores in 46 states and Puerto Rico. It became responsible for many firsts in its field, including: the first pharmacy chain to use child-resistant prescription caps, the first chain to have a drive-thru pharmacy ,and the first pharmacy to have all their stores linked via satellite with the introduction of Intercom Plus in 1981.
Net income	Net income is equal to the income that a firm has after subtracting costs and expenses from the total revenue. Expenses will typically include tax expense.
Trust	An arrangement in which shareholders of independent firms agree to give up their stock in exchange for trust certificates that entitle them to a share of the trust's common profits.
Toyota	Toyota is a Japanese multinational corporation that manufactures automobiles, trucks and buses. Toyota is the world's second largest automaker by sales. Toyota also provides financial services through its subsidiary, Toyota Financial Services, and participates in other lines of business.
Volkswagen	Volkswagen or VW is an automobile manufacturer based in Wolfsburg, Germany in the state of Lower Saxony. It forms the core of this Group, one of the world's four largest car producers. Its German tagline is "Aus Liebe zum Automobil", which is translated as "For the love of the car" - or, For Love of the People's Cars,".
Manufacturing	Production of goods primarily by the application of labor and capital to raw materials and other intermediate inputs, in contrast to agriculture, mining, forestry, fishing, and services a manufacturing.
Endowment	Endowment refers to the amount of something that a person or country simply has, rather than their having somehow to acquire it.
Incentive	An incentive is any factor (financial or non-financial) that provides a motive for a particular course of action, or counts as a reason for preferring one choice to the alternatives.
General Motors	General Motors is the world's largest automaker. Founded in 1908, today it employs about 327,000 people around the world. With global headquarters in Detroit, it manufactures its cars and trucks in 33 countries.
Corporation	A legal entity chartered by a state or the Federal government that is distinct and separate

Go to **Cram101.com** for the Practice Tests for this Chapter.

	from the individuals who own it is a corporation. This separation gives the corporation unique powers which other legal entities lack.
Brand	A name, symbol, or design that identifies the goods or services of one seller or group of sellers and distinguishes them from the goods and services of competitors is a brand.
Ford	Ford is an American company that manufactures and sells automobiles worldwide. Ford introduced methods for large-scale manufacturing of cars, and large-scale management of an industrial workforce, especially elaborately engineered manufacturing sequences typified by the moving assembly lines.
Profit margin	Profit margin is a measure of profitability. It is calculated using a formula and written as a percentage or a number. Profit margin = Net income before tax and interest / Revenue.
Margin	A deposit by a buyer in stocks with a seller or a stockbroker, as security to cover fluctuations in the market in reference to stocks that the buyer has purchased but for which he has not paid is a margin. Commodities are also traded on margin.
Configuration	An organization's shape, which reflects the division of labor and the means of coordinating the divided tasks is configuration.
Operation	A standardized method or technique that is performed repetitively, often on different materials resulting in different finished goods is called an operation.
Wall Street Journal	Dow Jones & Company was founded in 1882 by reporters Charles Dow, Edward Jones and Charles Bergstresser. Jones converted the small Customers' Afternoon Letter into The Wall Street Journal, first published in 1889, and began delivery of the Dow Jones News Service via telegraph. The Journal featured the Jones 'Average', the first of several indexes of stock and bond prices on the New York Stock Exchange.
Business Week	Business Week is a business magazine published by McGraw-Hill. It was first published in 1929 under the direction of Malcolm Muir, who was serving as president of the McGraw-Hill Publishing company at the time. It is considered to be the standard both in industry and among students.
Journal	Book of original entry, in which transactions are recorded in a general ledger system, is referred to as a journal.
Shares	Shares refer to an equity security, representing a shareholder's ownership of a corporation. Shares are one of a finite number of equal portions in the capital of a company, entitling the owner to a proportion of distributed, non-reinvested profits known as dividends and to a portion of the value of the company in case of liquidation.
Financial capital	Common stock, preferred stock, bonds, and retained earnings are financial capital. Financial capital appears on the corporate balance sheet under long-term liabilities and equity.
Capital	Capital generally refers to financial wealth, especially that used to start or maintain a business. In classical economics, capital is one of four factors of production, the others being land and labor and entrepreneurship.
Forming	The first stage of team development, where the team is formed and the objectives for the team are set is referred to as forming.
Research and development	The use of resources for the deliberate discovery of new information and ways of doing things, together with the application of that information in inventing new products or processes is referred to as research and development.
Price war	Price war refers to successive and continued decreases in the prices charged by firms in an oligopolistic industry. Each firm lowers its price below rivals' prices, hoping to increase its sales and revenues at its rivals' expense.

Nestle	Nestle is the world's biggest food and beverage company. In the 1860s, a pharmacist, developed a food for babies who were unable to be breastfed. His first success was a premature infant who could not tolerate his own mother's milk nor any of the usual substitutes. The value of the new product was quickly recognized when his new formula saved the child's life.
Domestic	From or in one's own country. A domestic producer is one that produces inside the home country. A domestic price is the price inside the home country. Opposite of 'foreign' or 'world.'.
Joint venture	Joint venture refers to an undertaking by two parties for a specific purpose and duration, taking any of several legal forms.
Distribution channel	A distribution channel is a chain of intermediaries, each passing a product down the chain to the next organization, before it finally reaches the consumer or end-user.
Distribution	Distribution in economics, the manner in which total output and income is distributed among individuals or factors.
Loyalty	Marketers tend to define customer loyalty as making repeat purchases. Some argue that it should be defined attitudinally as a strongly positive feeling about the brand.
Product life cycle	Product life cycle refers to a series of phases in a product's sales and cash flows over time; these phases, in order of occurrence, are introductory, growth, maturity, and decline.
Cisco Systems	While Cisco Systems was not the first company to develop and sell a router (a device that forwards computer traffic from one network to another), it did create the first commercially successful multi-protocol router to allow previously incompatible computers to communicate using different network protocols.
Investment	Investment refers to spending for the production and accumulation of capital and additions to inventories. In a financial sense, buying an asset with the expectation of making a return.
Marketing	Promoting and selling products or services to customers, or prospective customers, is referred to as marketing.
Product innovations	Innovations that introduce new goods or services to better meet customer needs are product innovations.
Product innovation	The development and sale of a new or improved product is a product innovation. Production of a new product on a commercial basis.
Innovation	Innovation refers to the first commercially successful introduction of a new product, the use of a new method of production, or the creation of a new form of business organization.
Mistake	In contract law a mistake is incorrect understanding by one or more parties to a contract and may be used as grounds to invalidate the agreement. Common law has identified three different types of mistake in contract: unilateral mistake, mutual mistake, and common mistake.
Late Movers	Late movers often imitate the technological advances of other businesses or reduce risks by waiting until a new market is established. The competitive advantage held by businesses that are late in entering a market.
Mortgage	Mortgage refers to a note payable issued for property, such as a house, usually repaid in equal installments consisting of part principle and part interest, over a specified period.
Customer value	Customer value refers to the unique combination of benefits received by targeted buyers that includes quality, price, convenience, on-time delivery, and both before-sale and after-sale service.
Complexity	The technical sophistication of the product and hence the amount of understanding required to

Go to **Cram101.com** for the Practice Tests for this Chapter.

use it is referred to as complexity. It is the opposite of simplicity.

ExxonMobil	ExxonMobil is the largest publicly traded integrated oil and gas company in the world, formed on November 30, 1999, by the merger of Exxon and Mobil. It is the sixth-largest company in the world as ranked by the Forbes Global 2000 and the largest company in the world (by revenue) as ranked by the Fortune Global 500.
Market capitalization	Market capitalization is a business term that refers to the aggregate value of a firm's outstanding common shares. In essence, market capitalization reflects the total value of a firm's equity currently available on the market. This measure differs from equity value to the extent that a firm has outstanding stock options or other securities convertible to common shares. The size and growth of a firm's market capitalization is often one of the critical measurements of a public company's success or failure.
Cost leadership	Organization's ability to achieve lower costs relative to competitors through productivity and efficiency improvements, elimination of waste, and tight cost control is cost leadership.
Leadership	Management merely consists of leadership applied to business situations; or in other words: management forms a sub-set of the broader process of leadership.
Authority	Authority in agency law, refers to an agent's ability to affect his principal's legal relations with third parties. Also used to refer to an actor's legal power or ability to do something. In addition, sometimes used to refer to a statute, case, or other legal source that justifies a particular result.
Perceived quality	A dimension of quality identified by David Garvin that refers to a subjective assessment of a product's quality based on criteria defined by the observer is a perceived quality.
Quality dimension	A quality dimension refers to aspects of quality that help to better define what quality is. These include perceived quality, conformance, reliability, durability, and so on.
Serviceability	A dimension of quality that refers to a product's ease of repair is referred to as serviceability.
Conformance	A dimension of quality that refers to the extent to which a product lies within an allowable range of deviation from its specification is called the conformance.
Assessment	Collecting information and providing feedback to employees about their behavior, communication style, or skills is an assessment.
Credibility	The extent to which a source is perceived as having knowledge, skill, or experience relevant to a communication topic and can be trusted to give an unbiased opinion or present objective information on the issue is called credibility.
Quality improvement	Quality is inversely proportional to variability thus quality Improvement is the reduction of variability in products and processes.
Consumer Reports	Consumer Reports is known for publishing reviews and comparisons of consumer products and services based on reporting and results from its in-house testing laboratory. Consumer Reports does not accept advertizing nor permit the commercial use of its reviews for selling products.
Warranty	An obligation of a company to replace defective goods or correct any deficiencies in performance or quality of a product is called a warranty.
Honda	With more than 14 million internal combustion engines built each year, Honda is the largest engine-maker in the world. In 2004, the company began to produce diesel motors, which were both very quiet whilst not requiring particulate filters to pass pollution standards. It is arguable, however, that the foundation of their success is the motorcycle division.
Option	A contract that gives the purchaser the option to buy or sell the underlying financial

	instrument at a specified price, called the exercise price or strike price, within a specific period of time.
Home Depot	Home Depot has recently added self checkout registers at most of its stores in North America. These automated kiosks allow the customer to scan the barcode of the item they wish to purchase, then insert money to pay for the items, and receive any change automatically. The customer no longer needs to interact with a store employee during checkout.
Retailing	All activities involved in selling, renting, and providing goods and services to ultimate consumers for personal, family, or household use is referred to as retailing.
Warehouse	Warehouse refers to a location, often decentralized, that a firm uses to store, consolidate, age, or mix stock; house product-recall programs; or ease tax burdens.
Damages	The sum of money recoverable by a plaintiff who has received a judgment in a civil case is called damages.
Market leader	The market leader is dominant in its industry. It has substantial market share and often extensive distribution arrangements with retailers. It typically is the industry leader in developing innovative new business models and new products (although not always).
Compaq	Compaq was founded in February 1982 by Rod Canion, Jim Harris and Bill Murto, three senior managers from semiconductor manufacturer Texas Instruments. Each invested $1,000 to form the company. Their first venture capital came from Ben Rosen and Sevin-Rosen partners. It is often told that the architecture of the original PC was first sketched out on a placemat by the founders while dining in the Houston restaurant, House of Pies.
Diversification	Investing in a collection of assets whose returns do not always move together, with the result that overall risk is lower than for individual assets is referred to as diversification.
Accounting	A system that collects and processes financial information about an organization and reports that information to decision makers is referred to as accounting.
Proprietary	Proprietary indicates that a party, or proprietor, exercises private ownership, control or use over an item of property, usually to the exclusion of other parties. Where a party, holds or claims proprietary interests in relation to certain types of property (eg. a creative literary work, or software), that property may also be the subject of intellectual property law (eg. copyright or patents).
Walt Disney	As the co-founder of Walt Disney Productions, Walt became one of the most well-known motion picture producers in the world. The corporation he co-founded, now known as The Walt Disney Company, today has annual revenues of approximately US $30 billion.
Disney	Disney is one of the largest media and entertainment corporations in the world. Founded on October 16, 1923 by brothers Walt and Roy Disney as a small animation studio, today it is one of the largest Hollywood studios and also owns nine theme parks and several television networks, including the American Broadcasting Company (ABC).
Patent	The legal right to the proceeds from and control over the use of an invented product or process, granted for a fixed period of time, usually 20 years. Patent is one form of intellectual property that is subject of the TRIPS agreement.
Food and Drug Administration	The Food and Drug Administration is an agency of the United States Department of Health and Human Services and is responsible for regulating food (human and animal), dietary supplements, drugs (human and animal), cosmetics, medical devices (human and animal) and radiation emitting devices (including non-medical devices), biologics, and blood products in the United States.
Administration	Administration refers to the management and direction of the affairs of governments and

institutions; a collective term for all policymaking officials of a government; the execution and implementation of public policy.

Pfizer	Pfizer is the world's largest pharmaceutical company based in New York City. It produces the number-one selling drug Lipitor (atorvastatin, used to lower blood cholesterol).
Reverse engineering	Reverse engineering refers to the process of learning how a product is made by taking it apart and examining it.
Controlling	A management function that involves determining whether or not an organization is progressing toward its goals and objectives, and taking corrective action if it is not is called controlling.
Allocate	Allocate refers to the assignment of income for various tax purposes. A multistate corporation's nonbusiness income usually is distributed to the state where the nonbusiness assets are located; it is not apportioned with the rest of the entity's income.
Sustainable competitive advantage	A strength, relative to competitors, in the markets served and the products offered is referred to as the sustainable competitive advantage.
Shareholder	A shareholder is an individual or company (including a corporation) that legally owns one or more shares of stock in a joined stock company.
Consumer demand	Consumer demand or consumption is also known as personal consumption expenditure. It is the largest part of aggregate demand or effective demand at the macroeconomic level. There are two variants of consumption in the aggregate demand model, including induced consumption and autonomous consumption.
Business unit	The lowest level of the company which contains the set of functions that carry a product through its life span from concept through manufacture, distribution, sales and service is a business unit.
Strategic business unit	Strategic business unit is understood as a business unit within the overall corporate identity which is distinguishable from other business because it serves a defined external market where management can conduct strategic planning in relation to products and markets. When companies become really large, they are best thought of as being composed of a number of businesses
Customer service	The ability of logistics management to satisfy users in terms of time, dependability, communication, and convenience is called the customer service.
Total quality management	The broad set of management and control processes designed to focus an entire organization and all of its employees on providing products or services that do the best possible job of satisfying the customer is called total quality management.
Quality management	Quality management is a method for ensuring that all the activities necessary to design, develop and implement a product or service are effective and efficient with respect to the system and its performance.
Smart card	A stored-value card that contains a computer chip that allows it to be loaded with digital cash from the owner's bank account whenever needed is called a smart card.
Users	Users refer to people in the organization who actually use the product or service purchased by the buying center.
Competitive market	A market in which no buyer or seller has market power is called a competitive market.
Annual report	An annual report is prepared by corporate management that presents financial information including financial statements, footnotes, and the management discussion and analysis.

Economies of scale	In economics, returns to scale and economies of scale are related terms that describe what happens as the scale of production increases. They are different terms and not to be used interchangeably.
Product line	A group of products that are physically similar or are intended for a similar market are called the product line.
Extension	Extension refers to an out-of-court settlement in which creditors agree to allow the firm more time to meet its financial obligations. A new repayment schedule will be developed, subject to the acceptance of creditors.
Interdependence	The extent to which departments depend on each other for resources or materials to accomplish their tasks is referred to as interdependence.
Mutual interdependence	Mutual interdependence refers to a situation in which a change in price strategy by one firm will affect the sales and profits of another firm. Any firm that makes such a change can expect the other rivals to react to the change. Occurs in oligopolies.
Specific factor	Specific factor refers to a factor of production that is unable to move into or out of an industry. The term is used to describe both factors that would not be of any use in other industries and -- more loosely -- factors that could be used elsewhere but are not.
Adoption	In corporation law, a corporation's acceptance of a pre-incorporation contract by action of its board of directors, by which the corporation becomes liable on the contract, is referred to as adoption.
Deming	Deming is widely credited with improving production in the United States during World War II, although he is perhaps best known for his work in Japan. There, from 1950 onward he taught top management how to improve design (and thus service), product quality, testing and sales (the latter through global markets).

Firm	An organization that employs resources to produce a good or service for profit and owns and operates one or more plants is referred to as a firm.
Unrelated diversification	A business strategy in which an organization operates several businesses that are not associated with one another is unrelated diversification.
Diversification strategy	Diversification strategy is a corporate strategy that takes the organization away from both its current markets and products, as opposed to either market or product development.
Diversification	Investing in a collection of assets whose returns do not always move together, with the result that overall risk is lower than for individual assets is referred to as diversification.
Incentive	An incentive is any factor (financial or non-financial) that provides a motive for a particular course of action, or counts as a reason for preferring one choice to the alternatives.
Technology	The body of knowledge and techniques that can be used to combine economic resources to produce goods and services is called technology.
Industry	A group of firms that produce identical or similar products is an industry. It is also used specifically to refer to an area of economic production focused on manufacturing which involves large amounts of capital investment before any profit can be realized, also called "heavy industry".
Sony	Sony is a multinational corporation and one of the world's largest media conglomerates founded in Tokyo, Japan. One of its divisions Sony Electronics is one of the leading manufacturers of electronics, video, communications, and information technology products for the consumer and professional markets.
Distribution	Distribution in economics, the manner in which total output and income is distributed among individuals or factors.
Business unit	The lowest level of the company which contains the set of functions that carry a product through its life span from concept through manufacture, distribution, sales and service is a business unit.
Time Warner	Time Warner is the world's largest media company with major Internet, publishing, film, telecommunications and television divisions.
Bertelsmann	Bertelsmann is a transnational media corporation founded in 1835, based in Gütersloh, Germany. Bertelsmann made headlines on May 17, 2002, when it announced it would acquire the assets of Napster for $8 million.
Convergence	The blending of various facets of marketing functions and communication technology to create more efficient and expanded synergies is a convergence.
Security	Security refers to a claim on the borrower future income that is sold by the borrower to the lender. A security is a type of transferable interest representing financial value.
Analyst	Analyst refers to a person or tool with a primary function of information analysis, generally with a more limited, practical and short term set of goals than a researcher.
Acquisition	A company's purchase of the property and obligations of another company is an acquisition.
Users	Users refer to people in the organization who actually use the product or service purchased by the buying center.
Swap	In finance a swap is a derivative, where two counterparties exchange one stream of cash flows against another stream. These streams are called the legs of the swap. The cash flows are calculated over a notional principal amount. Swaps are often used to hedge certain risks, for

113

instance interest rate risk. Another use is speculation.

Business model	A business model is the instrument by which a business intends to generate revenue and profits. It is a summary of how a company means to serve its employees and customers, and involves both strategy (what an business intends to do) as well as an implementation.
Market	A market is, as defined in economics, a social arrangement that allows buyers and sellers to discover information and carry out a voluntary exchange of goods or services.
Levy	Levy refers to imposing and collecting a tax or tariff.
Core competency	A company's core competency are things that a firm can (alsosns) do well and that meet the following three conditions. 1. It provides customer benefits, 2. It is hard for competitors to imitate, and 3. it can be leveraged widely to many products and market. A core competency can take various forms, including technical/subject matter knowhow, a reliable process, and/or close relationships with customers and suppliers. It may also include product development or culture such as employee dedication. Modern business theories suggest that most activities that are not part of a company's core competency should be outsourced.
Core	A core is the set of feasible allocations in an economy that cannot be improved upon by subset of the set of the economy's consumers (a coalition). In construction, when the force in an element is within a certain center section, the core, the element will only be under compression.
Competitive advantage	A business is said to have a competitive advantage when its unique strengths, often based on cost, quality, time, and innovation, offer consumers a greater percieved value and there by differtiating it from its competitors.
Gain	In finance, gain is a profit or an increase in value of an investment such as a stock or bond. Gain is calculated by fair market value or the proceeds from the sale of the investment minus the sum of the purchase price and all costs associated with it.
Portfolio	In finance, a portfolio is a collection of investments held by an institution or a private individual. Holding but not always a portfolio is part of an investment and risk-limiting strategy called diversification. By owning several assets, certain types of risk (in particular specific risk) can be reduced.
Management	Management characterizes the process of leading and directing all or part of an organization, often a business, through the deployment and manipulation of resources. Early twentieth-century management writer Mary Parker Follett defined management as "the art of getting things done through people."
Competitiveness	Competitiveness usually refers to characteristics that permit a firm to compete effectively with other firms due to low cost or superior technology, perhaps internationally.
Balance	In banking and accountancy, the outstanding balance is the amount of money owned, (or due), that remains in a deposit account (or a loan account) at a given date, after all past remittances, payments and withdrawal have been accounted for. It can be positive (then, in the balance sheet of a firm, it is an asset) or negative (a liability).
Economy	The income, expenditures, and resources that affect the cost of running a business and household are called an economy.
Multipoint competition	Multipoint competition arises when two or more enterprises encounter each other in different regional markets, national markets, or industries.
Vertical integration	Vertical integration refers to production of different stages of processing of a product within the same firm.
Integration	Economic integration refers to reducing barriers among countries to transactions and to

Go to **Cram101.com** for the Practice Tests for this Chapter.

	movements of goods, capital, and labor, including harmonization of laws, regulations, and standards. Integrated markets theoretically function as a unified market.
Competitor	Other organizations in the same industry or type of business that provide a good or service to the same set of customers is referred to as a competitor.
Distribution channel	A distribution channel is a chain of intermediaries, each passing a product down the chain to the next organization, before it finally reaches the consumer or end-user.
Service	Service refers to a "non tangible product" that is not embodied in a physical good and that typically effects some change in another product, person, or institution. Contrasts with good.
Channel	Channel, in communications (sometimes called communications channel), refers to the medium used to convey information from a sender (or transmitter) to a receiver.
Revenue	Revenue is a U.S. business term for the amount of money that a company receives from its activities, mostly from sales of products and/or services to customers.
Trademark	A distinctive word, name, symbol, device, or combination thereof, which enables consumers to identify favored products or services and which may find protection under state or federal law is a trademark.
Brand	A name, symbol, or design that identifies the goods or services of one seller or group of sellers and distinguishes them from the goods and services of competitors is a brand.
Business strategy	Business strategy, which refers to the aggregated operational strategies of single business firm or that of an SBU in a diversified corporation refers to the way in which a firm competes in its chosen arenas.
Collaboration	Collaboration occurs when the interaction between groups is very important to goal attainment and the goals are compatible. Wherein people work together —applying both to the work of individuals as well as larger collectives and societies.
Total revenue	Total revenue refers to the total number of dollars received by a firm from the sale of a product; equal to the total expenditures for the product produced by the firm; equal to the quantity sold multiplied by the price at which it is sold.
Business operations	Business operations are those activities involved in the running of a business for the purpose of producing value for the stakeholders. The outcome of business operations is the harvesting of value from assets owned by a business.
Cooperative	A business owned and controlled by the people who use it, producers, consumers, or workers with similar needs who pool their resources for mutual gain is called cooperative.
Bankruptcy	Bankruptcy is a legally declared inability or impairment of ability of an individual or organization to pay their creditors.
Operation	A standardized method or technique that is performed repetitively, often on different materials resulting in different finished goods is called an operation.
Bid	A bid price is a price offered by a buyer when he/she buys a good. In the context of stock trading on a stock exchange, the bid price is the highest price a buyer of a stock is willing to pay for a share of that given stock.
Shares	Shares refer to an equity security, representing a shareholder's ownership of a corporation. Shares are one of a finite number of equal portions in the capital of a company, entitling the owner to a proportion of distributed, non-reinvested profits known as dividends and to a portion of the value of the company in case of liquidation.
General Electric	In 1876, Thomas Alva Edison opened a new laboratory in Menlo Park, New Jersey. Out of the

Go to **Cram101.com** for the Practice Tests for this Chapter.

laboratory was to come perhaps the most famous invention of all—a successful development of the incandescent electric lamp. By 1890, Edison had organized his various businesses into the Edison General Electric Company.

Asset	An item of property, such as land, capital, money, a share in ownership, or a claim on others for future payment, such as a bond or a bank deposit is an asset.
Private sector	The households and business firms of the economy are referred to as private sector.
Conglomerate	A conglomerate is a large company that consists of divisions of often seemingly unrelated businesses.
Market power	The ability of a single economic actor to have a substantial influence on market prices is market power.
Scope	Scope of a project is the sum total of all projects products and their requirements or features.
Economies of scope	The ability to use one resource to provide many different products and services is referred to as economies of scope.
Manufacturing	Production of goods primarily by the application of labor and capital to raw materials and other intermediate inputs, in contrast to agriculture, mining, forestry, fishing, and services a manufacturing.
Tangible	Having a physical existence is referred to as the tangible. Personal property other than real estate, such as cars, boats, stocks, or other assets.
Production	The creation of finished goods and services using the factors of production: land, labor, capital, entrepreneurship, and knowledge.
Inputs	The inputs used by a firm or an economy are the labor, raw materials, electricity and other resources it uses to produce its outputs.
Cost structure	The relative proportion of an organization's fixed, variable, and mixed costs is referred to as cost structure.
Compaq	Compaq was founded in February 1982 by Rod Canion, Jim Harris and Bill Murto, three senior managers from semiconductor manufacturer Texas Instruments. Each invested $1,000 to form the company. Their first venture capital came from Ben Rosen and Sevin-Rosen partners. It is often told that the architecture of the original PC was first sketched out on a placemat by the founders while dining in the Houston restaurant, House of Pies.
Facilitation	Facilitation refers to helping a team or individual achieve a goal. Often used in meetings or with teams to help the teams achieve their objectives.
Expense	In accounting, an expense represents an event in which an asset is used up or a liability is incurred. In terms of the accounting equation, expenses reduce owners' equity.
Allocate	Allocate refers to the assignment of income for various tax purposes. A multistate corporation's nonbusiness income usually is distributed to the state where the nonbusiness assets are located; it is not apportioned with the rest of the entity's income.
Value creation	Value creation refers to performing activities that increase the value of goods or services to consumers.
Intangibility	A unique element of services-services cannot be held, touched, or seen before the purchase decision which is referred to as intangibility.
Corporation	A legal entity chartered by a state or the Federal government that is distinct and separate from the individuals who own it is a corporation. This separation gives the corporation unique powers which other legal entities lack.

Go to **Cram101.com** for the Practice Tests for this Chapter.

Merger	Merger refers to the combination of two firms into a single firm.
Franchising	Franchising is a method of doing business wherein a franchisor licenses trademarks and tried and proven methods of doing business to a franchisee in exchange for a recurring payment, and usually a percentage piece of gross sales or gross profits as well as the annual fees. The term " franchising " is used to describe a wide variety of business systems which may or may not fall into the legal definition provided above.
Marketing	Promoting and selling products or services to customers, or prospective customers, is referred to as marketing.
Estate	An estate is the totality of the legal rights, interests, entitlements and obligations attaching to property. In the context of wills and probate, it refers to the totality of the property which the deceased owned or in which some interest was held.
Market value	Market value refers to the price of an asset agreed on between a willing buyer and a willing seller; the price an asset could demand if it is sold on the open market.
Accounting	A system that collects and processes financial information about an organization and reports that information to decision makers is referred to as accounting.
Preparation	Preparation refers to usually the first stage in the creative process. It includes education and formal training.
Exchange	The trade of things of value between buyer and seller so that each is better off after the trade is called the exchange.
Mortgage	Mortgage refers to a note payable issued for property, such as a house, usually repaid in equal installments consisting of part principle and part interest, over a specified period.
Product line	A group of products that are physically similar or are intended for a similar market are called the product line.
Joint venture	Joint venture refers to an undertaking by two parties for a specific purpose and duration, taking any of several legal forms.
Capital requirement	The capital requirement is a bank regulation, which sets a framework on how banks and depository institutions must handle their capital. The categorization of assets and capital is highly standardized so that it can be risk weighted.
Cash flow	In finance, cash flow refers to the amounts of cash being received and spent by a business during a defined period of time, sometimes tied to a specific project. Most of the time they are being used to determine gaps in the liquid position of a company.
Capital	Capital generally refers to financial wealth, especially that used to start or maintain a business. In classical economics, capital is one of four factors of production, the others being land and labor and entrepreneurship.
Margin	A deposit by a buyer in stocks with a seller or a stockbroker, as security to cover fluctuations in the market in reference to stocks that the buyer has purchased but for which he has not paid is a margin. Commodities are also traded on margin.
Franchise	A contractual right to sell certain products or services, use certain trademarks, or perform activities in a geographical region is called a franchise.
Budget	Budget refers to an account, usually for a year, of the planned expenditures and the expected receipts of an entity. For a government, the receipts are tax revenues.
Strike	The withholding of labor services by an organized group of workers is referred to as a strike.
Interest	In finance and economics, interest is the price paid by a borrower for the use of a lender's

money. In other words, interest is the amount of paid to "rent" money for a period of time.

Complement	A good that is used in conjunction with another good is a complement. For example, cameras and film would complement eachother.
Travelocity	According to Sabre Holdings, Travelocity is the sixth-largest travel agency in the United States. In addition to its primary US consumer site, Travelocity operates a full-service business agency, Travelocity Business, and comparable websites in Canada, Germany, France, the Scandinavian countries, and the United Kingdom, and is a partner in Asian travel hubs Tabini and Zuji.
Loyalty	Marketers tend to define customer loyalty as making repeat purchases. Some argue that it should be defined attitudinally as a strongly positive feeling about the brand.
Consultant	A professional that provides expert advice in a particular field or area in which customers occassionaly require this type of knowledge is a consultant.
Insurance	Insurance refers to a system by which individuals can reduce their exposure to risk of large losses by spreading the risks among a large number of persons.
Holding	The holding is a court's determination of a matter of law based on the issue presented in the particular case. In other words: under this law, with these facts, this result.
Property	Assets defined in the broadest legal sense. Property includes the unrealized receivables of a cash basis taxpayer, but not services rendered.
Synergy	Corporate synergy occurs when corporations interact congruently. A corporate synergy refers to a financial benefit that a corporation expects to realize when it merges with or acquires another corporation.
Stakeholder	A stakeholder is an individual or group with a vested interest in or expectation for organizational performance. Usually stakeholders can either have an effect on or are affected by an organization.
Ford	Ford is an American company that manufactures and sells automobiles worldwide. Ford introduced methods for large-scale manufacturing of cars, and large-scale management of an industrial workforce, especially elaborately engineered manufacturing sequences typified by the moving assembly lines.
Honda	With more than 14 million internal combustion engines built each year, Honda is the largest engine-maker in the world. In 2004, the company began to produce diesel motors, which were both very quiet whilst not requiring particulate filters to pass pollution standards. It is arguable, however, that the foundation of their success is the motorcycle division.
Forward integration	Practice in corporate vertical marketing system in which a producer also owns retail shops is a forward integration.
Petition	A petition is a request to an authority, most commonly a government official or public entity. In the colloquial sense, a petition is a document addressed to some official and signed by numerous individuals.
Market share	That fraction of an industry's output accounted for by an individual firm or group of firms is called market share.
United parcel service	United Parcel Service is the world's largest package delivery company, delivering more than 14 million packages a day to more than 200 countries around the world. It has recently expanded its operations to include logistics and other transportation-related areas.
Core business	The core business of an organization is an idealized construct intended to express that organization's "main" or "essential" activity.

Go to **Cram101.com** for the Practice Tests for this Chapter.

Market price	Market price is an economic concept with commonplace familiarity; it is the price that a good or service is offered at, or will fetch, in the marketplace; it is of interest mainly in the study of microeconomics.
Transaction cost	A transaction cost is a cost incurred in making an economic exchange. For example, most people, when buying or selling a stock, must pay a commission to their broker; that commission is a transaction cost of doing the stock deal.
Economies of scale	In economics, returns to scale and economies of scale are related terms that describe what happens as the scale of production increases. They are different terms and not to be used interchangeably.
Buyer	A buyer refers to a role in the buying center with formal authority and responsibility to select the supplier and negotiate the terms of the contract.
Profit margin	Profit margin is a measure of profitability. It is calculated using a formula and written as a percentage or a number. Profit margin = Net income before tax and interest / Revenue.
Profit	Profit refers to the return to the resource entrepreneurial ability; total revenue minus total cost.
General Motors	General Motors is the world's largest automaker. Founded in 1908, today it employs about 327,000 people around the world. With global headquarters in Detroit, it manufactures its cars and trucks in 33 countries.
Contract	A contract is a "promise" or an "agreement" that is enforced or recognized by the law. In the civil law, a contract is considered to be part of the general law of obligations.
Supply	Supply is the aggregate amount of any material good that can be called into being at a certain price point; it comprises one half of the equation of supply and demand. In classical economic theory, a curve representing supply is one of the factors that produce price.
Intel	Intel Corporation, founded in 1968 and based in Santa Clara, California, USA, is the world's largest semiconductor company. Intel is best known for its PC microprocessors, where it maintains roughly 80% market share.
Inventory management	The planning, coordinating, and controlling activities related to the flow of inventory into, through, and out of an organization is referred to as inventory management.
Inventory	Tangible property held for sale in the normal course of business or used in producing goods or services for sale is an inventory.
Enterprise	Enterprise refers to another name for a business organization. Other similar terms are business firm, sometimes simply business, sometimes simply firm, as well as company, and entity.
Strategic group	A strategic group is a concept used in strategic management that groups companies within an industry that have similar business models or similar combinations of strategies.
Operating profit	Operating profit is a measure of a company's earning power from ongoing operations, equal to earnings before the deduction of interest payments and income taxes.
Research and development	The use of resources for the deliberate discovery of new information and ways of doing things, together with the application of that information in inventing new products or processes is referred to as research and development.
Contribution	In business organization law, the cash or property contributed to a business by its owners is referred to as contribution.
Disney	Disney is one of the largest media and entertainment corporations in the world. Founded on October 16, 1923 by brothers Walt and Roy Disney as a small animation studio, today it is one

Go to **Cram101.com** for the Practice Tests for this Chapter.

of the largest Hollywood studios and also owns nine theme parks and several television networks, including the American Broadcasting Company (ABC).

Investment	Investment refers to spending for the production and accumulation of capital and additions to inventories. In a financial sense, buying an asset with the expectation of making a return.
Business risk	The risk related to the inability of the firm to hold its competitive position and maintain stability and growth in earnings is business risk.
Purchasing	Purchasing refers to the function in a firm that searches for quality material resources, finds the best suppliers, and negotiates the best price for goods and services.
Equity	Equity is the name given to the set of legal principles, in countries following the English common law tradition, which supplement strict rules of law where their application would operate harshly, so as to achieve what is sometimes referred to as "natural justice."
Shareholder	A shareholder is an individual or company (including a corporation) that legally owns one or more shares of stock in a joined stock company.
Stock	In financial terminology, stock is the capital raized by a corporation, through the issuance and sale of shares.
Personnel	A collective term for all of the employees of an organization. Personnel is also commonly used to refer to the personnel management function or the organizational unit responsible for administering personnel programs.
DIRECTV	DirecTV was launched in 1994 by General Motors subsidiary Hughes Electronics. It was the first high-powered direct broadcast satellite service in the world. Digital Equipment Corporation provided the customer-care out of their existing technical support center in Colorado Springs, Colorado.
Capital market	A financial market in which long-term debt and equity instruments are traded is referred to as a capital market. The capital market includes the stock market and the bond market.
Disclosure	Disclosure means the giving out of information, either voluntarily or to be in compliance with legal regulations or workplace rules.
Management team	A management team is directly responsible for managing the day-to-day operations (and profitability) of a company.
Intervention	Intervention refers to an activity in which a government buys or sells its currency in the foreign exchange market in order to affect its currency's exchange rate.
Resource allocation	Resource allocation refers to the manner in which an economy distributes its resources among the potential uses so as to produce a particular set of final goods.
Stock market	An organized marketplace in which common stocks are traded. In the United States, the largest stock market is the New York Stock Exchange, on which are traded the stocks of the largest U.S. companies.
Discount	The difference between the face value of a bond and its selling price, when a bond is sold for less than its face value it's referred to as a discount.
Siemens	Siemens is the world's largest conglomerate company. Worldwide, Siemens and its subsidiaries employs 461,000 people (2005) in 190 countries and reported global sales of €75.4 billion in fiscal year 2005.
Trust	An arrangement in which shareholders of independent firms agree to give up their stock in exchange for trust certificates that entitle them to a share of the trust's common profits.
Restructuring	Restructuring is the corporate management term for the act of partially dismantling and reorganizing a company for the purpose of making it more efficient and therefore more

profitable.

Household	An economic unit that provides the economy with resources and uses the income received to purchase goods and services that satisfy economic wants is called household.
Option	A contract that gives the purchaser the option to buy or sell the underlying financial instrument at a specified price, called the exercise price or strike price, within a specific period of time.
Transparency	Transparency refers to a concept that describes a company being so open to other companies working with it that the once-solid barriers between them become see-through and electronic information is shared as if the companies were one.
Sales orientation	The sales orientation era ran from the mid-1950s to the early 1970s, and is therefore after the production orientation era but before the marketing orientation era. During WWII world industry geared up for accelerated wartime production. When the war was over this stimulated industrial machine turned to producing consumer products.
Advertising agency	A firm that specializes in the creation, production, and placement of advertising messages and may provide other services that facilitate the marketing communications process is an advertising agency.
Advertising	Advertising refers to paid, nonpersonal communication through various media by organizations and individuals who are in some way identified in the advertising message.
Service business	A business firm that provides services to consumers, such as accounting and legal services, is referred to as a service business.
Internal environment	Variables that are under some degree of control by organizational members is the internal enviroment. Internal environment scans are conducted to identify an organization's internal capabilities, performance levels, strengths, and weaknesses.
Regulation	Regulation refers to restrictions state and federal laws place on business with regard to the conduct of its activities.
Antitrust	Government intervention to alter market structure or prevent abuse of market power is called antitrust.
Antitrust policy	The use of the antitrust laws to promote competition and economic efficiency is referred to as antitrust policy.
Antitrust laws	Legislation that prohibits anticompetitive business activities such as price fixing, bid rigging, monopolization, and tying contracts is referred to as antitrust laws.
Policy	Similar to a script in that a policy can be a less than completely rational decision-making method. Involves the use of a pre-existing set of decision steps for any problem that presents itself.
Horizontal integration	Horizontal integration refers to production of different varieties of the same product, or different products at the same level of processing, within a single firm. This may, but need not, take place in subsidiaries in different countries.
Conglomerate diversification	Conglomerate diversification happens where there is neither technological nor marketing synergy and required reaching new customer groups and individuals.
Partnership	In the common law, a partnership is a type of business entity in which partners share with each other the profits or losses of the business undertaking in which they have all invested.
Forming	The first stage of team development, where the team is formed and the objectives for the team are set is referred to as forming.
Premium	Premium refers to the fee charged by an insurance company for an insurance policy. The rate

Go to **Cram101.com** for the Practice Tests for this Chapter.

of losses must be relatively predictable: In order to set the premium (prices) insurers must be able to estimate them accurately.

Banner ad	A banner ad is a form of advertising on the World Wide Web. This form of online advertising entails embedding an advertisement into a web page.
Google	As it has grown, Google has found itself the focus of various controversies related to its business practices and services. For example, Google Print's effort to digitize millions of books and make the full text searchable has led to copyright disputes with the Authors Guild, cooperation with the governments of China, France and Germany to filter search results in accordance to regional laws and regulations has led to claims of censorship.
Mergers and acquisitions	The phrase mergers and acquisitions refers to the aspect of corporate finance strategy and management dealing with the merging and acquiring of different companies as well as other assets. Usually mergers occur in a friendly setting where executives from the respective companies participate in a due diligence process to ensure a successful combination of all parts.
Investment banker	Investment banker refers to a financial organization that specializes in selling primary offerings of securities. Investment bankers can also perform other financial functions, such as advising clients, negotiating mergers and takeovers, and selling secondary offerings.
Horizontal merger	Horizontal merger refers to the merger into a single firm of two firms producing the same product and selling it in the same geographic market.
Corporate tax	Corporate tax refers to a direct tax levied by various jurisdictions on the profits made by companies or associations. As a general principle, this varies substantially between jurisdictions.
Business Week	Business Week is a business magazine published by McGraw-Hill. It was first published in 1929 under the direction of Malcolm Muir, who was serving as president of the McGraw-Hill Publishing company at the time. It is considered to be the standard both in industry and among students.
Target firm	The firm that is being studied or benchmarked against is referred to as target firm.
Takeover	A takeover in business refers to one company (the acquirer) purchasing another (the target). Such events resemble mergers, but without the formation of a new company.
Yahoo	Yahoo is an American computer services company. It operates an Internet portal, the Yahoo Directory and a host of other services including the popular Yahoo Mail. Yahoo is the most visited website on the Internet today with more than 400 million unique users. The global network of Yahoo! websites received 3.4 billion page views per day on average as of October 2005.
Financial assets	Financial assets refer to monetary claims or obligations by one party against another party. Examples are bonds, mortgages, bank loans, and equities.
Free cash flow	Cash provided by operating activities adjusted for capital expenditures and dividends paid is referred to as free cash flow.
Dividend	Amount of corporate profits paid out for each share of stock is referred to as dividend.
Capital gain	Capital gain refers to the gain in value that the owner of an asset experiences when the price of the asset rises, including when the currency in which the asset is denominated appreciates.
Fund	Independent accounting entity with a self-balancing set of accounts segregated for the purposes of carrying on specific activities is referred to as a fund.
Tax reform	Tax reform is the process of changing the way taxes are collected or managed by the

government. Some seek to reduce the level of taxation of all people by the government. Some seek to make the tax system more/less progressive in its effect. Some may be trying to make the tax system more understandable, or more accountable.

Retained earnings	Cumulative earnings of a company that are not distributed to the owners and are reinvested in the business are called retained earnings.
Interest expense	The cost a business incurs to borrow money. With respect to bonds payable, the interest expense is calculated by multiplying the market rate of interest by the carrying value of the bonds on the date of the payment.
Deductible	The dollar sum of costs that an insured individual must pay before the insurer begins to pay is called deductible.
Leverage	Leverage is using given resources in such a way that the potential positive or negative outcome is magnified. In finance, this generally refers to borrowing.
Allowance	Reduction in the selling price of goods extended to the buyer because the goods are defective or of lower quality than the buyer ordered and to encourage a buyer to keep merchandise that would otherwise be returned is the allowance.
Depreciation	Depreciation is an accounting and finance term for the method of attributing the cost of an asset across the useful life of the asset. Depreciation is a reduction in the value of a currency in floating exchange rate.
Financial accounting standards board	Financial accounting standards board refers to the private sector body given the primary responsibility to work out the detailed rules that become generally accepted accounting principles.
Financial accounting Standards	Financial Accounting Standards refers to a set of standards that dictate accounting rules concerning financial reporting; establish generally accepted accounting principles.
Accounting Standards Board	The role of the Accounting Standards Board is to issue accounting standards in the United Kingdom. It is recognized for that purpose under the Companies Act 1985. It took over the task of setting accounting standards from the Accounting Standards Committee (ASC) in 1990.
Financial accounting	Financial accounting is the branch of accountancy concerned with the preparation of financial statements for external decision makers, such as stockholders, suppliers, banks and government agencies. The fundamental need for financial accounting is to reduce principal-agent problem by measuring and monitoring agents' performance.
Pooling of interests	Pooling of interests refers to a method of financial recording for mergers, in which the financial statements of the firms are combined, subject to minor adjustments, and goodwill is not created.
Sears	Before the Sears catalog, farmers typically bought supplies (often at very high prices) from local general stores. Sears took advantage of this by publishing his catalog with clearly stated prices, so that consumers could know what he was selling and at what price, and order and obtain them conveniently. The catalog business soon grew quickly.
Federal Communications Commission	Federal Communications Commission refers to the federal authority empowered to license radio and TV stations and to assign wavelengths to stations 'in the public interest'.
Free enterprise	Free enterprise refers to a system in which economic agents are free to own property and engage in commercial transactions.
Frequency	Frequency refers to the speed of the up and down movements of a fluctuating economic variable; that is, the number of times per unit of time that the variable completes a cycle

Go to **Cram101.com** for the Practice Tests for this Chapter.

133

of up and down movement.

Market leader	The market leader is dominant in its industry. It has substantial market share and often extensive distribution arrangements with retailers. It typically is the industry leader in developing innovative new business models and new products (although not always).
Home Depot	Home Depot has recently added self checkout registers at most of its stores in North America. These automated kiosks allow the customer to scan the barcode of the item they wish to purchase, then insert money to pay for the items, and receive any change automatically. The customer no longer needs to interact with a store employee during checkout.
Divestiture	In finance and economics, divestiture is the reduction of some kind of asset, for either financial or social goals. A divestment is the opposite of an investment.
Retail sale	The sale of goods and services to consumers for their own use is a retail sale.
Return on investment	Return on investment refers to the return a businessperson gets on the money he and other owners invest in the firm; for example, a business that earned $100 on a $1,000 investment would have a ROI of 10 percent: 100 divided by 1000.
Leadership	Management merely consists of leadership applied to business situations; or in other words: management forms a sub-set of the broader process of leadership.
Commodity	Could refer to any good, but in trade a commodity is usually a raw material or primary product that enters into international trade, such as metals or basic agricultural products.
Volkswagen	Volkswagen or VW is an automobile manufacturer based in Wolfsburg, Germany in the state of Lower Saxony. It forms the core of this Group, one of the world's four largest car producers. Its German tagline is "Aus Liebe zum Automobil", which is translated as "For the love of the car" - or, For Love of the People's Cars,".
Net profit	Net profit is an accounting term which is commonly used in business. It is equal to the gross revenue for a given time period minus associated expenses.
Brand image	The advertising metric that measures the type and favorability of consumer perceptions of the brand is referred to as the brand image.
Chrysler	The Chrysler Corporation was an American automobile manufacturer that existed independently from 1925–1998. The company was formed by Walter Percy Chrysler on June 6, 1925, with the remaining assets of Maxwell Motor Company.
Compromise	Compromise occurs when the interaction is moderately important to meeting goals and the goals are neither completely compatible nor completely incompatible.
Utility	Utility refers to the want-satisfying power of a good or service; the satisfaction or pleasure a consumer obtains from the consumption of a good or service.
Microsoft	Microsoft is a multinational computer technology corporation with 2004 global annual sales of US$39.79 billion and 71,553 employees in 102 countries and regions as of July 2006. It develops, manufactures, licenses, and supports a wide range of software products for computing devices.
Excess capacity	Excess capacity refers to plant resources that are underused when imperfectly competitive firms produce less output than that associated with purely competitive firms, who by definiation, are achieving minimum average total cost.
Physical asset	A physical asset is an item of economic value that has a tangible or material existence. A physical asset usually refers to cash, equipment, inventory and properties owned by a business.
Tacit knowledge	Knowledge that has not been articulated. Tacit knowledge is often subconscious and relatively

Go to **Cram101.com** for the Practice Tests for this Chapter.

difficult to communicate to other people. Tacit knowledge consists often of habits and culture that we do not recognize in ourselves.

Liability	A liability is a present obligation of the enterprise arizing from past events, the settlement of which is expected to result in an outflow from the enterprise of resources embodying economic benefits.
Board of directors	The group of individuals elected by the stockholders of a corporation to oversee its operations is a board of directors.
Golden Parachute	Highly attractive termination payments made to current management in the event of a takeover of the company is called a golden parachute.
Poison pill	Poison pill refers to a strategy that makes a firm unattractive as a potential takeover candidate. These are attempts by a potential acquirer to obtain a control block of shares in a target company, and thereby gain control of the board and, through it, the company's management.
Tactic	A short-term immediate decision that, in its totality, leads to the achievement of strategic goals is called a tactic.
Optimum	Optimum refers to the best. Usually refers to a most preferred choice by consumers subject to a budget constraint or a profit maximizing choice by firms or industry subject to a technological constraint.
Strategic management	A philosophy of management that links strategic planning with dayto-day decision making. Strategic management seeks a fit between an organization's external and internal environments.
Citibank	In April of 2006, Citibank struck a deal with 7-Eleven to put its ATMs in over 5,500 convenience stores in the U.S. In the same month, it also announced it would sell all of its Buffalo and Rochester New York branches and accounts to M&T Bank.
Competitive Strategy	An outline of how a business intends to compete with other firms in the same industry is called competitive strategy.
Variance	Variance refers to a measure of how much an economic or statistical variable varies across values or observations. Its calculation is the same as that of the covariance, being the covariance of the variable with itself.
Harvard Business Review	Harvard Business Review is a research-based magazine written for business practitioners, it claims a high ranking business readership and enjoys the reverence of academics, executives, and management consultants. It has been the frequent publishing home for well known scholars and management thinkers.
Financial management	The job of managing a firm's resources so it can meet its goals and objectives is called financial management.
Market development	Selling existing products to new markets is called market development.
Legal system	Legal system refers to system of rules that regulate behavior and the processes by which the laws of a country are enforced and through which redress of grievances is obtained.
Complexity	The technical sophistication of the product and hence the amount of understanding required to use it is referred to as complexity. It is the opposite of simplicity.
Keiretsu	Keiretsu is a set of companies with interlocking business relationships and shareholdings. It is a type of business group.
Journal	Book of original entry, in which transactions are recorded in a general ledger system, is

referred to as a journal.

Foreign direct investment	Foreign direct investment refers to the buying of permanent property and businesses in foreign nations.
Management science	Management science is the discipline of using mathematics, and other analytical methods, to help make better business decisions.
Direct investment	Direct investment refers to a domestic firm actually investing in and owning a foreign subsidiary or division.
Entrepreneurship	The assembling of resources to produce new or improved products and technologies is referred to as entrepreneurship.
International Business	International business refers to any firm that engages in international trade or investment.
Hierarchy	A system of grouping people in an organization according to rank from the top down in which all subordinate managers must report to one person is called a hierarchy.
Market structure	Market structure refers to the way that suppliers and demanders in an industry interact to determine price and quantity. Market structures range from perfect competition to monopoly.
Federal Reserve	The Federal Reserve System was created via the Federal Reserve Act of December 23rd, 1913. All national banks were required to join the system and other banks could join. The Reserve Banks opened for business on November 16th, 1914. Federal Reserve Notes were created as part of the legislation, to provide an elastic supply of currency.
Corporate Strategy	Corporate strategy is concerned with the firm's choice of business, markets and activities and thus it defines the overall scope and direction of the business.
Capital structure	Capital Structure refers to the way a corporation finances itself through some combination of equity sales, equity options, bonds, and loans. Optimal capital structure refers to the particular combination that minimizes the cost of capital while maximizing the stock price.
Forbes	David Churbuck founded online Forbes in 1996. The site drew attention when it uncovered Stephen Glass' journalistic fraud in The New Republic in 1998, a scoop that gave credibility to internet journalism.
Marketing management	Marketing management refers to the process of planning and executing the conception, pricing, promotion, and distribution of ideas, goods, and services to create mutually beneficial exchanges.
Intangible assets	Assets that have special rights but not physical substance are referred to as intangible assets.
Intangible asset	An intangible assets is defined as an asset that is not physical in nature. The most common types are trade secrets (e.g., customer lists and know-how), copyrights, patents, trademarks, and goodwill.
Personal finance	Personal finance is the application of the principles of financial economics to an individual's (or a family's) financial decisions.
Human capital	Human capital refers to the stock of knowledge and skill, embodied in an individual as a result of education, training, and experience that makes them more productive. The stock of knowledge and skill embodied in the population of an economy.
Accumulation	The acquisition of an increasing quantity of something. The accumulation of factors, especially capital, is a primary mechanism for economic growth.
Contingency perspective	Contingency perspective suggests that, in most organizations, situations and outcomes are contingent on, or influenced by, other variables.

Emerging markets	The term emerging markets is commonly used to describe business and market activity in industrializing or emerging regions of the world. It is sometimes loosely used as a replacement for emerging economies, but really signifies a business phenomenon that is not fully described by or constrained to geography or economic strength; such countries are considered to be in a transitional phase between developing and developed status.
Emerging market	The term emerging market is commonly used to describe business and market activity in industrializing or emerging regions of the world.
Case study	A case study is a particular method of qualitative research. Rather than using large samples and following a rigid protocol to examine a limited number of variables, case study methods involve an in-depth, longitudinal examination of a single instance or event: a case. They provide a systematic way of looking at events, collecting data, analyzing information, and reporting the results.
Economics	The social science dealing with the use of scarce resources to obtain the maximum satisfaction of society's virtually unlimited economic wants is an economics.

Competitiveness	Competitiveness usually refers to characteristics that permit a firm to compete effectively with other firms due to low cost or superior technology, perhaps internationally.
Acquisition	A company's purchase of the property and obligations of another company is an acquisition.
Firm	An organization that employs resources to produce a good or service for profit and owns and operates one or more plants is referred to as a firm.
Competitive advantage	A business is said to have a competitive advantage when its unique strengths, often based on cost, quality, time, and innovation, offer consumers a greater percieved value and there by differtiating it from its competitors.
Restructuring	Restructuring is the corporate management term for the act of partially dismantling and reorganizing a company for the purpose of making it more efficient and therefore more profitable.
Corporation	A legal entity chartered by a state or the Federal government that is distinct and separate from the individuals who own it is a corporation. This separation gives the corporation unique powers which other legal entities lack.
DIRECTV	DirecTV was launched in 1994 by General Motors subsidiary Hughes Electronics. It was the first high-powered direct broadcast satellite service in the world. Digital Equipment Corporation provided the customer-care out of their existing technical support center in Colorado Springs, Colorado.
Management	Management characterizes the process of leading and directing all or part of an organization, often a business, through the deployment and manipulation of resources. Early twentieth-century management writer Mary Parker Follett defined management as "the art of getting things done through people."
Television network	Television network refers to the provider of news and programming to a series of affiliated local television stations.
Committee	A long-lasting, sometimes permanent team in the organization structure created to deal with tasks that recur regularly is the committee.
Hearing	A hearing is a proceeding before a court or other decision-making body or officer. A hearing is generally distinguished from a trial in that it is usually shorter and often less formal.
Controlling interest	A firm has a controlling interest in another business entity when it owns more than 50 percent of that entity's voting stock.
General Motors	General Motors is the world's largest automaker. Founded in 1908, today it employs about 327,000 people around the world. With global headquarters in Detroit, it manufactures its cars and trucks in 33 countries.
Controlling	A management function that involves determining whether or not an organization is progressing toward its goals and objectives, and taking corrective action if it is not is called controlling.
Interest	In finance and economics, interest is the price paid by a borrower for the use of a lender's money. In other words, interest is the amount of paid to "rent" money for a period of time.
Industry	A group of firms that produce identical or similar products is an industry. It is also used specifically to refer to an area of economic production focused on manufacturing which involves large amounts of capital investment before any profit can be realized, also called "heavy industry".
Time Warner	Time Warner is the world's largest media company with major Internet, publishing, film, telecommunications and television divisions.

Go to **Cram101.com** for the Practice Tests for this Chapter.

Merger	Merger refers to the combination of two firms into a single firm.
Distribution	Distribution in economics, the manner in which total output and income is distributed among individuals or factors.
Foundation	A Foundation is a type of philanthropic organization set up by either individuals or institutions as a legal entity (either as a corporation or trust) with the purpose of distributing grants to support causes in line with the goals of the foundation.
Market capitalization	Market capitalization is a business term that refers to the aggregate value of a firm's outstanding common shares. In essence, market capitalization reflects the total value of a firm's equity currently available on the market. This measure differs from equity value to the extent that a firm has outstanding stock options or other securities convertible to common shares. The size and growth of a firm's market capitalization is often one of the critical measurements of a public company's success or failure.
Market	A market is, as defined in economics, a social arrangement that allows buyers and sellers to discover information and carry out a voluntary exchange of goods or services.
Viacom	Viacom is an American-based media conglomerate with various worldwide interests in cable and satellite television networks (MTV Networks and BET), video gaming (part of Sega of America), and movie production and distribution (the Paramount Pictures movie studio and DreamWorks).
Mergers and acquisitions	The phrase mergers and acquisitions refers to the aspect of corporate finance strategy and management dealing with the merging and acquiring of different companies as well as other assets. Usually mergers occur in a friendly setting where executives from the respective companies participate in a due diligence process to ensure a successful combination of all parts.
Takeover	A takeover in business refers to one company (the acquirer) purchasing another (the target). Such events resemble mergers, but without the formation of a new company.
Primary market	The market for the raising of new funds as opposed to the trading of securities already in existence is called primary market.
Core business	The core business of an organization is an idealized construct intended to express that organization's "main" or "essential" activity.
Market power	The ability of a single economic actor to have a substantial influence on market prices is market power.
Volatility	Volatility refers to the extent to which an economic variable, such as a price or an exchange rate, moves up and down over time.
Option	A contract that gives the purchaser the option to buy or sell the underlying financial instrument at a specified price, called the exercise price or strike price, within a specific period of time.
Core	A core is the set of feasible allocations in an economy that cannot be improved upon by subset of the set of the economy's consumers (a coalition). In construction, when the force in an element is within a certain center section, the core, the element will only be under compression.
Operation	A standardized method or technique that is performed repetitively, often on different materials resulting in different finished goods is called an operation.
DaimlerChrysler	In 2002, the merged company, DaimlerChrysler, appeared to run two independent product lines, with few signs of corporate integration. In 2003, however, it was alleged by the Detroit News that the "merger of equals" was, in fact, a takeover.
Chrysler	The Chrysler Corporation was an American automobile manufacturer that existed independently

from 1925–1998. The company was formed by Walter Percy Chrysler on June 6, 1925, with the remaining assets of Maxwell Motor Company.

Portfolio	In finance, a portfolio is a collection of investments held by an institution or a private individual. Holding but not always a portfolio is part of an investment and risk-limiting strategy called diversification. By owning several assets, certain types of risk (in particular specific risk) can be reduced.
Target firm	The firm that is being studied or benchmarked against is referred to as target firm.
Subsidiary	A company that is controlled by another company or corporation is a subsidiary.
Bid	A bid price is a price offered by a buyer when he/she buys a good. In the context of stock trading on a stock exchange, the bid price is the highest price a buyer of a stock is willing to pay for a share of that given stock.
Safeway	On April 18, 2005, Safeway began a 100 million dollar brand re-positioning campaign labeled "Ingredients for life". This was done in an attempt to differentiate itself from its competitors, and to increase brand involvement. Steve Burd described it as "branding the shopping experience".
Asset	An item of property, such as land, capital, money, a share in ownership, or a claim on others for future payment, such as a bond or a bank deposit is an asset.
Investment	Investment refers to spending for the production and accumulation of capital and additions to inventories. In a financial sense, buying an asset with the expectation of making a return.
Competitor	Other organizations in the same industry or type of business that provide a good or service to the same set of customers is referred to as a competitor.
Service	Service refers to a "non tangible product" that is not embodied in a physical good and that typically effects some change in another product, person, or institution. Contrasts with good.
ExxonMobil	ExxonMobil is the largest publicly traded integrated oil and gas company in the world, formed on November 30, 1999, by the merger of Exxon and Mobil. It is the sixth-largest company in the world as ranked by the Forbes Global 2000 and the largest company in the world (by revenue) as ranked by the Fortune Global 500.
Inventory management	The planning, coordinating, and controlling activities related to the flow of inventory into, through, and out of an organization is referred to as inventory management.
Human resources	Human resources refers to the individuals within the firm, and to the portion of the firm's organization that deals with hiring, firing, training, and other personnel issues.
PeopleSoft	PeopleSoft, Inc. was a software company that provided HRMS (human resource management), CRM), Manufacturing, Financials, EPM and Student Administration software solutions to large corporations, governments, and organizations. PeopleSoft was acquired in a hostile takeover by the Oracle Corporation.
Inventory	Tangible property held for sale in the normal course of business or used in producing goods or services for sale is an inventory.
Oracle	In 2004, sales at Oracle grew at a rate of 14.5% to $6.2 billion, giving it 41.3% and the top share of the relational-database market. Their main competitors in the database arena are IBM DB2 and Microsoft SQL Server, and to a lesser extent Sybase, Teradata, Informix, and MySQL. In the applications arena, their main competitor is SAP.
Shell	One of the original Seven Sisters, Royal Dutch/Shell is the world's third-largest oil company by revenue, and a major player in the petrochemical industry and the solar energy business. Shell has six core businesses: Exploration and Production, Gas and Power, Downstream,

Go to **Cram101.com** for the Practice Tests for this Chapter.

Chemicals, Renewables, and Trading/Shipping, and operates in more than 140 countries.

Microsoft	Microsoft is a multinational computer technology corporation with 2004 global annual sales of US$39.79 billion and 71,553 employees in 102 countries and regions as of July 2006. It develops, manufactures, licenses, and supports a wide range of software products for computing devices.
Department of Justice	The United States Department of Justice is a Cabinet department in the United States government designed to enforce the law and defend the interests of the United States according to the law and to ensure fair and impartial administration of justice for all Americans. This department is administered by the United States Attorney General, one of the original members of the cabinet.
Antitrust	Government intervention to alter market structure or prevent abuse of market power is called antitrust.
Shareholder	A shareholder is an individual or company (including a corporation) that legally owns one or more shares of stock in a joined stock company.
Appeal	Appeal refers to the act of asking an appellate court to overturn a decision after the trial court's final judgment has been entered.
Poison pill	Poison pill refers to a strategy that makes a firm unattractive as a potential takeover candidate. These are attempts by a potential acquirer to obtain a control block of shares in a target company, and thereby gain control of the board and, through it, the company's management.
Consolidation	The combination of two or more firms, generally of equal size and market power, to form an entirely new entity is a consolidation.
Economy	The income, expenditures, and resources that affect the cost of running a business and household are called an economy.
Analyst	Analyst refers to a person or tool with a primary function of information analysis, generally with a more limited, practical and short term set of goals than a researcher.
Enterprise	Enterprise refers to another name for a business organization. Other similar terms are business firm, sometimes simply business, sometimes simply firm, as well as company, and entity.
Holding	The holding is a court's determination of a matter of law based on the issue presented in the particular case. In other words: under this law, with these facts, this result.
Incentive	An incentive is any factor (financial or non-financial) that provides a motive for a particular course of action, or counts as a reason for preferring one choice to the alternatives.
Gain	In finance, gain is a profit or an increase in value of an investment such as a stock or bond. Gain is calculated by fair market value or the proceeds from the sale of the investment minus the sum of the purchase price and all costs associated with it.
Objection	In the trial of a case the formal remonstrance made by counsel to something that has been said or done, in order to obtain the court's ruling thereon is an objection.
Market share	That fraction of an industry's output accounted for by an individual firm or group of firms is called market share.
Revenue	Revenue is a U.S. business term for the amount of money that a company receives from its activities, mostly from sales of products and/or services to customers.
Synergy	Corporate synergy occurs when corporations interact congruently. A corporate synergy refers

Go to **Cram101.com** for the Practice Tests for this Chapter.

	to a financial benefit that a corporation expects to realize when it merges with or acquires another corporation.
Excess capacity	Excess capacity refers to plant resources that are underused when imperfectly competitive firms produce less output than that associated with purely competitive firms, who by definiation, are achieving minimum average total cost.
Core competency	A company's core competency are things that a firm can (alsosns) do well and that meet the following three conditions. 1. It provides customer benefits, 2. It is hard for competitors to imitate, and 3. it can be leveraged widely to many products and market. A core competency can take various forms, including technical/subject matter knowhow, a reliable process, and/or close relationships with customers and suppliers. It may also include product development or culture such as employee dedication. Modern business theories suggest that most activities that are not part of a company's core competency should be outsourced.
Integration	Economic integration refers to reducing barriers among countries to transactions and to movements of goods, capital, and labor, including harmonization of laws, regulations, and standards. Integrated markets theoretically function as a unified market.
Complement	A good that is used in conjunction with another good is a complement. For example, cameras and film would complement eachother.
Technology	The body of knowledge and techniques that can be used to combine economic resources to produce goods and services is called technology.
Sony	Sony is a multinational corporation and one of the world's largest media conglomerates founded in Tokyo, Japan. One of its divisions Sony Electronics is one of the leading manufacturers of electronics, video, communications, and information technology products for the consumer and professional markets.
Honeywell	Honeywell is a major American multinational corporation that produces electronic control systems and automation equipment. It is a major supplier of engineering services and avionics for NASA, Boeing and the United States Department of Defense.
Barriers to entry	In economics and especially in the theory of competition, barriers to entry are obstacles in the path of a firm which wants to enter a given market.
Entry barrier	An entry barrier or barrier to entry is an obstacle in the path of a potential firm which wants to enter a given market.
Expense	In accounting, an expense represents an event in which an asset is used up or a liability is incurred. In terms of the accounting equation, expenses reduce owners' equity.
Differentiated product	A firm's product that is not identical to products of other firms in the same industry is a differentiated product.
Economies of scale	In economics, returns to scale and economies of scale are related terms that describe what happens as the scale of production increases. They are different terms and not to be used interchangeably.
Buyer	A buyer refers to a role in the buying center with formal authority and responsibility to select the supplier and negotiate the terms of the contract.
Market access	The ability of firms from one country to sell in another is market access.
Emerging markets	The term emerging markets is commonly used to describe business and market activity in industrializing or emerging regions of the world. It is sometimes loosely used as a replacement for emerging economies, but really signifies a business phenomenon that is not fully described by or constrained to geography or economic strength; such countries are considered to be in a transitional phase between developing and developed status.

Go to **Cram101.com** for the Practice Tests for this Chapter.

Purchasing power	The amount of goods that money will buy, usually measured by the CPI is referred to as purchasing power.
Emerging market	The term emerging market is commonly used to describe business and market activity in industrializing or emerging regions of the world.
Purchasing	Purchasing refers to the function in a firm that searches for quality material resources, finds the best suppliers, and negotiates the best price for goods and services.
Frequency	Frequency refers to the speed of the up and down movements of a fluctuating economic variable; that is, the number of times per unit of time that the variable completes a cycle of up and down movement.
Acquirer	An acquirer is a company offering debit and credit card acceptance services for merchants. Often the company is partially or wholly owned by a bank, sometimes a bank itself offers acquiring services.
Domestic	From or in one's own country. A domestic producer is one that produces inside the home country. A domestic price is the price inside the home country. Opposite of 'foreign' or 'world.'.
Regulation	Regulation refers to restrictions state and federal laws place on business with regard to the conduct of its activities.
Accounting	A system that collects and processes financial information about an organization and reports that information to decision makers is referred to as accounting.
Financial crisis	A loss of confidence in a country's currency or other financial assets causing international investors to withdraw their funds from the country is referred to as a financial crisis.
Devaluation	Lowering the value of a nation's currency relative to other currencies is called devaluation.
Innovation	Innovation refers to the first commercially successful introduction of a new product, the use of a new method of production, or the creation of a new form of business organization.
Patent	The legal right to the proceeds from and control over the use of an invented product or process, granted for a fixed period of time, usually 20 years. Patent is one form of intellectual property that is subject of the TRIPS agreement.
Manufacturing	Production of goods primarily by the application of labor and capital to raw materials and other intermediate inputs, in contrast to agriculture, mining, forestry, fishing, and services a manufacturing.
Marketing	Promoting and selling products or services to customers, or prospective customers, is referred to as marketing.
Novartis	Novartis was created in 1996 from the merger of Ciba-Geigy and Sandoz Laboratories, both Swiss companies with long individual histories. At the time of the merger, it was the largest corporate merger in history.
Diversification	Investing in a collection of assets whose returns do not always move together, with the result that overall risk is lower than for individual assets is referred to as diversification.
Product line	A group of products that are physically similar or are intended for a similar market are called the product line.
Unrelated diversification	A business strategy in which an organization operates several businesses that are not associated with one another is unrelated diversification.
Diversification strategy	Diversification strategy is a corporate strategy that takes the organization away from both its current markets and products, as opposed to either market or product development.

Go to **Cram101.com** for the Practice Tests for this Chapter.

Conglomerate	A conglomerate is a large company that consists of divisions of often seemingly unrelated businesses.
Scope	Scope of a project is the sum total of all projects products and their requirements or features.
Argument	The discussion by counsel for the respective parties of their contentions on the law and the facts of the case being tried in order to aid the jury in arriving at a correct and just conclusion is called argument.
Human resource management	The process of evaluating human resource needs, finding people to fill those needs, and getting the best work from each employee by providing the right incentives and job environment, all with the goal of meeting the needs of the firm are called human resource management.
Resource management	Resource management is the efficient and effective deployment of an organization's resources when they are needed. Such resources may include financial resources, inventory, human skills, production resources, or information technology.
Knowledge base	Knowledge base refers to a database that includes decision rules for use of the data, which may be qualitative as well as quantitative.
Property	Assets defined in the broadest legal sense. Property includes the unrealized receivables of a cash basis taxpayer, but not services rendered.
Corporate culture	The whole collection of beliefs, values, and behaviors of a firm that send messages to those within and outside the company about how business is done is the corporate culture.
Control system	A control system is a device or set of devices that manage the behavior of other devices. Some devices or systems are not controllable.A control system is an interconnection of components connected or related in such a manner as to command, direct, or regulate itself or another system.
Budget	Budget refers to an account, usually for a year, of the planned expenditures and the expected receipts of an entity. For a government, the receipts are tax revenues.
Human capital	Human capital refers to the stock of knowledge and skill, embodied in an individual as a result of education, training, and experience that makes them more productive. The stock of knowledge and skill embodied in the population of an economy.
Capital	Capital generally refers to financial wealth, especially that used to start or maintain a business. In classical economics, capital is one of four factors of production, the others being land and labor and entrepreneurship.
Personnel	A collective term for all of the employees of an organization. Personnel is also commonly used to refer to the personnel management function or the organizational unit responsible for administering personnel programs.
Turnover	Turnover in a financial context refers to the rate at which a provider of goods cycles through its average inventory. Turnover in a human resources context refers to the characteristic of a given company or industry, relative to rate at which an employer gains and loses staff.
Integration process	The way information such as product knowledge, meanings, and beliefs is combined to evaluate two or more alternatives is referred to as an integration process.
Due diligence	Due diligence is the effort made by an ordinarily prudent or reasonable party to avoid harm to another party or himself. Failure to make this effort is considered negligence. Failure to make this effort is considered negligence.
Evaluation	The consumer's appraisal of the product or brand on important attributes is called

Go to **Cram101.com** for the Practice Tests for this Chapter.

	evaluation.
Investment banker	Investment banker refers to a financial organization that specializes in selling primary offerings of securities. Investment bankers can also perform other financial functions, such as advising clients, negotiating mergers and takeovers, and selling secondary offerings.
Consultant	A professional that provides expert advice in a particular field or area in which customers occassionaly require this type of knowledge is a consultant.
Premium	Premium refers to the fee charged by an insurance company for an insurance policy. The rate of losses must be relatively predictable: In order to set the premium (prices) insurers must be able to estimate them accurately.
Investment banks	Investment banks, assist public and private corporations in raising funds in the capital markets (both equity and debt), as well as in providing strategic advisory services for mergers, acquisitions and other types of financial transactions. They also act as intermediaries in trading for clients. Investment banks differ from commercial banks, which take deposits and make commercial and retail loans.
Credit Suisse First Boston	Credit Suisse First Boston is a leading global investment bank serving institutional, corporate, government and high net worth clients. The Firm operates under a "One-Bank" policy as part of the Zurich-based Credit Suisse Group, a leading global financial services company.
Citibank	In April of 2006, Citibank struck a deal with 7-Eleven to put its ATMs in over 5,500 convenience stores in the U.S. In the same month, it also announced it would sell all of its Buffalo and Rochester New York branches and accounts to M&T Bank.
Credit	Credit refers to a recording as positive in the balance of payments, any transaction that gives rise to a payment into the country, such as an export, the sale of an asset, or borrowing from abroad.
Financial innovation	The development of new financial products-new ways of borrowing and lending is referred to as financial innovation.
Junk bond	In finance, a junk bond is a bond that is rated below investment grade. These bonds have a higher risk of defaulting, but typically pay high yields in order to make them attractive to investors.
Bond	Bond refers to a debt instrument, issued by a borrower and promising a specified stream of payments to the purchaser, usually regular interest payments plus a final repayment of principal.
Interest rate	The rate of return on bonds, loans, or deposits. When one speaks of 'the' interest rate, it is usually in a model where there is only one.
Bondholder	The individual or entity that purchases a bond, thus loaning money to the company that issued the bond is the bondholder.
Collateral	Property that is pledged to the lender to guarantee payment in the event that the borrower is unable to make debt payments is called collateral.
Lender	Suppliers and financial institutions that lend money to companies is referred to as a lender.
Coors	Coors became the first American brewer to package beer in an all-aluminum two-piece beverage can in 1959.
Shareholder value	For a publicly traded company, shareholder value is the part of its capitalization that is equity as opposed to long-term debt. In the case of only one type of stock, this would roughly be the number of outstanding shares times current shareprice.
Economic profit	In Economics, a firm is said to be making an economic profit when its revenue exceeds the

total opportunity cost of its inputs. It is said to be making an accounting profit if its revenues exceed the total price the firm pays for those inputs. This is sometimes referred to as producer's surplus.

Profit	Profit refers to the return to the resource entrepreneurial ability; total revenue minus total cost.
Shares	Shares refer to an equity security, representing a shareholder's ownership of a corporation. Shares are one of a finite number of equal portions in the capital of a company, entitling the owner to a proportion of distributed, non-reinvested profits known as dividends and to a portion of the value of the company in case of liquidation.
Euro	The common currency of a subset of the countries of the EU, adopted January 1, 1999 is called euro.
Stock	In financial terminology, stock is the capital raized by a corporation, through the issuance and sale of shares.
Long run	In economic models, the long run time frame assumes no fixed factors of production. Firms can enter or leave the marketplace, and the cost (and availability) of land, labor, raw materials, and capital goods can be assumed to vary.
Short run	Short run refers to a period of time that permits an increase or decrease in current production volume with existing capacity, but one that is too short to permit enlargement of that capacity itself (eg, the building of new plants, training of additional workers, etc.).
Economies of scope	The ability to use one resource to provide many different products and services is referred to as economies of scope.
Yield	The interest rate that equates a future value or an annuity to a given present value is a yield.
Direct cost	A direct cost is a cost that can be identified specifically with a particular sponsored project, an instructional activity, or any other institutional activity, or that can be directly assigned to such activities relatively easily with a high degree of accuracy.
Indirect cost	Indirect cost refers to a cost that cannot be traced to a particular department.
Negotiation	Negotiation is the process whereby interested parties resolve disputes, agree upon courses of action, bargain for individual or collective advantage, and/or attempt to craft outcomes which serve their mutual interests.
Holding company	A corporation whose purpose or function is to own or otherwise hold the shares of other corporations either for investment or control is called holding company.
Advertising	Advertising refers to paid, nonpersonal communication through various media by organizations and individuals who are in some way identified in the advertising message.
Downturn	A decline in a stock market or economic cycle is a downturn.
Hedge	Hedge refers to a process of offsetting risk. In the foreign exchange market, hedgers use the forward market to cover a transaction or open position and thereby reduce exchange risk. The term applies most commonly to trade.
Promotion	Promotion refers to all the techniques sellers use to motivate people to buy products or services. An attempt by marketers to inform people about products and to persuade them to participate in an exchange.
Business unit	The lowest level of the company which contains the set of functions that carry a product through its life span from concept through manufacture, distribution, sales and service is a business unit.

Go to **Cram101.com** for the Practice Tests for this Chapter.

Divestment	In finance and economics, divestment or divestiture is the reduction of some kind of asset, for either financial or social goals. A divestment is the opposite of an investment.
Return on investment	Return on investment refers to the return a businessperson gets on the money he and other owners invest in the firm; for example, a business that earned $100 on a $1,000 investment would have a ROI of 10 percent: 100 divided by 1000.
Financial control	A process in which a firm periodically compares its actual revenues, costs, and expenses with its projected ones is called financial control.
Stakeholder	A stakeholder is an individual or group with a vested interest in or expectation for organizational performance. Usually stakeholders can either have an effect on or are affected by an organization.
Mistake	In contract law a mistake is incorrect understanding by one or more parties to a contract and may be used as grounds to invalidate the agreement. Common law has identified three different types of mistake in contract: unilateral mistake, mutual mistake, and common mistake.
Slowdown	A slowdown is an industrial action in which employees perform their duties but seek to reduce productivity or efficiency in their performance of these duties. A slowdown may be used as either a prelude or an alternative to a strike, as it is seen as less disruptive as well as less risky and costly for workers and their union.
Bankruptcy	Bankruptcy is a legally declared inability or impairment of ability of an individual or organization to pay their creditors.
Bureaucratic control	The use of rules, policies, hierarchy of authority, reward systems, and other formal devices to influence employee behavior and assess performance is referred to as bureaucratic control.
Complexity	The technical sophistication of the product and hence the amount of understanding required to use it is referred to as complexity. It is the opposite of simplicity.
Policy	Similar to a script in that a policy can be a less than completely rational decision-making method. Involves the use of a pre-existing set of decision steps for any problem that presents itself.
Warren Buffett	Warren Buffett is an American stock investor, businessman and philanthropist. Nicknamed the "Oracle of Omaha" or the "Sage of Omaha", he has amassed an enormous fortune from astute investments, particularly through his company Berkshire Hathaway, in which he holds a greater than 38% stake.
Contract	A contract is a "promise" or an "agreement" that is enforced or recognized by the law. In the civil law, a contract is considered to be part of the general law of obligations.
Leverage	Leverage is using given resources in such a way that the potential positive or negative outcome is magnified. In finance, this generally refers to borrowing.
Production	The creation of finished goods and services using the factors of production: land, labor, capital, entrepreneurship, and knowledge.
Equity	Equity is the name given to the set of legal principles, in countries following the English common law tradition, which supplement strict rules of law where their application would operate harshly, so as to achieve what is sometimes referred to as "natural justice."
Organizational culture	The mindset of employees, including their shared beliefs, values, and goals is called the organizational culture.
Insurance	Insurance refers to a system by which individuals can reduce their exposure to risk of large losses by spreading the risks among a large number of persons.
American Express	From the early 1980s until the late 1990s, American Express was known for cutting its

Go to **Cram101.com** for the Practice Tests for this Chapter.

Go to **Cram101.com** for the Practice Tests for this Chapter.
And, **NEVER** highlight a book again!

merchant fees (also known as a "discount rate") to fine merchants and restaurants if they only accepted American Express and no other credit or charge cards. This prompted competitors such as Visa and MasterCard to cry foul for a while, as the tactics "locked" restaurants into American Express.

Wells Fargo	Following completion of the First Security acquisition, Wells Fargo had total assets of $263 billion. Its strategy echoed that of the old Norwest: making selective acquisitions and pursuing cross-selling of an ever-wider array of credit and investment products to its vast customer base.
Gillette	On October 1, 2005, Gillette finalized its purchase by Procter & Gamble. As a result of this merger, the Gillette Company no longer exists. Its last day of market trading - symbol G on the New York Stock Exchange - was September 30, 2005. The merger created the world's largest personal care and household products company.
Downsizing	The process of eliminating managerial and non-managerial positions are called downsizing.
Composition	An out-of-court settlement in which creditors agree to accept a fractional settlement on their original claim is referred to as composition.
Trend	Trend refers to the long-term movement of an economic variable, such as its average rate of increase or decrease over enough years to encompass several business cycles.
Continental Airlines	Continental Airlines is an airline of the United States. Based in Houston, Texas, it is the 6th largest airline in the U.S. and the 8th largest in the world. Continental's tagline, since 1998, has been Work Hard, Fly Right.
Layoff	A layoff is the termination of an employee or (more commonly) a group of employees for business reasons, such as the decision that certain positions are no longer necessary.
Divestiture	In finance and economics, divestiture is the reduction of some kind of asset, for either financial or social goals. A divestment is the opposite of an investment.
Management team	A management team is directly responsible for managing the day-to-day operations (and profitability) of a company.
Corporate Strategy	Corporate strategy is concerned with the firm's choice of business, markets and activities and thus it defines the overall scope and direction of the business.
Samsung	On November 30, 2005 Samsung pleaded guilty to a charge it participated in a worldwide DRAM price fixing conspiracy during 1999-2002 that damaged competition and raized PC prices.
Leveraged buyout	An attempt by employees, management, or a group of investors to purchase an organization primarily through borrowing is a leveraged buyout.
Buyout	A buyout is an investment transaction by which the entire or a controlling part of the stock of a company is sold. A firm buysout the stake of the company to strengthen its influence on the company's decision making body. A buyout can take the forms of a leveraged buyout or a management buyout.
Financial distress	Financial distress is a term in Corporate Finance used to indicate a condition when promises to creditors of a company are broken or honored with difficulty. Sometimes financial distress can lead to bankruptcy. Financial distress is usually associated with some costs to the company and these are known as Costs of Financial Distress. A common example of a cost of financial distress is bankrupty costs.
Enron	Enron Corportaion's global reputation was undermined by persistent rumours of bribery and political pressure to secure contracts in Central America, South America, Africa, and the Philippines. Especially controversial was its $3 billion contract with the Maharashtra State Electricity Board in India, where it is alleged that Enron officials used political

Go to **Cram101.com** for the Practice Tests for this Chapter.

connections within the Clinton and Bush administrations to exert pressure on the board.

Wall Street Journal	Dow Jones & Company was founded in 1882 by reporters Charles Dow, Edward Jones and Charles Bergstresser. Jones converted the small Customers' Afternoon Letter into The Wall Street Journal, first published in 1889, and began delivery of the Dow Jones News Service via telegraph. The Journal featured the Jones 'Average', the first of several indexes of stock and bond prices on the New York Stock Exchange.
Journal	Book of original entry, in which transactions are recorded in a general ledger system, is referred to as a journal.
Fund	Independent accounting entity with a self-balancing set of accounts segregated for the purposes of carrying on specific activities is referred to as a fund.
Commercial bank	A firm that engages in the business of banking is a commercial bank.
Going private	The process by which all publicly owned shares of common stock are repurchased or retired, thereby eliminating listing fees, annual reports, and other expenses involved with publicly owned companies is going private.
Malfeasance	Malfeasance refers to the doing of an act that a person ought not to do at all. It is to be distinguished from misfeasance; the improper doing of an act that a person might lawfully do.
Stock exchange	A stock exchange is a corporation or mutual organization which provides facilities for stock brokers and traders, to trade company stocks and other securities.
Exchange	The trade of things of value between buyer and seller so that each is better off after the trade is called the exchange.
NASDAQ	NASDAQ is an American electronic stock exchange. It was founded in 1971 by the National Association of Securities Dealers who divested it in a series of sales in 2000 and 2001.
Public company	A public company is a company owned by the public rather than by a relatively few individuals. There are two different meanings for this term: (1) A company that is owned by stockholders who are members of the general public and trade shares publicly, often through a listing on a stock exchange. Ownership is open to anyone that has the money and inclination to buy shares in the company. It is differentiated from privately held companies where the shares are held by a small group of individuals, who are often members of one or a small group of families or otherwise related individuals, or other companies. The variant of this type of company in the United Kingdom and Ireland is known as a public limited compan, and (2) A government-owned corporation. This meaning of a "public company" comes from the fact that government debt is sometimes referred to as "public debt" although there are no "public bonds", government finance is sometimes called "public finance", among similar uses. This is the less-common meaning.
Bethlehem Steel	During its life, Bethlehem Steel was one of the largest shipbuilding companies in the world and was one of the most powerful symbols of American manufacturing leadership. It was the second largest steel producer in the United States, but following its 2001 bankruptcy, the company was dissolved and the remaining assets sold to International Steel Group in 2003.
Security	Security refers to a claim on the borrower future income that is sold by the borrower to the lender. A security is a type of transferable interest representing financial value.
Administration	Administration refers to the management and direction of the affairs of governments and institutions; a collective term for all policymaking officials of a government; the execution and implementation of public policy.
Tariff	A tax imposed by a nation on an imported good is called a tariff.
World Trade	The World Trade Organization is an international, multilateral organization, which sets the

Organization	rules for the global trading system and resolves disputes between its member states, all of whom are signatories to its approximately 30 agreements.
Union	A worker association that bargains with employers over wages and working conditions is called a union.
Management buyout	A management buyout is a form of acquisition where a company's existing managers buy or acquire a large part of the company.
Partnership	In the common law, a partnership is a type of business entity in which partners share with each other the profits or losses of the business undertaking in which they have all invested.
Financial market	In economics, a financial market is a mechanism which allows people to trade money for securities or commodities such as gold or other precious metals. In general, any commodity market might be considered to be a financial market, if the usual purpose of traders is not the immediate consumption of the commodity, but rather as a means of delaying or accelerating consumption over time.
Stock market	An organized marketplace in which common stocks are traded. In the United States, the largest stock market is the New York Stock Exchange, on which are traded the stocks of the largest U.S. companies.
Strategic control	Strategic control processes allow managers to evaluate a company's marketing program from a critical long-term perspective. This involves a detailed and objective analysis of a company's organization and its ability to maximize its strengths and market opportunities.
Globalization	The increasing world-wide integration of markets for goods, services and capital that attracted special attention in the late 1990s is called globalization.
Deregulation	The lessening or complete removal of government regulations on an industry, especially concerning the price that firms are allowed to charge and leaving price to be determined by market forces a deregulation.
Internal environment	Variables that are under some degree of control by organizational members is the internal enviroment. Internal environment scans are conducted to identify an organization's internal capabilities, performance levels, strengths, and weaknesses.
Information technology	Information technology refers to technology that helps companies change business by allowing them to use new methods.
Management science	Management science is the discipline of using mathematics, and other analytical methods, to help make better business decisions.
Recovery	Characterized by rizing output, falling unemployment, rizing profits, and increasing economic activity following a decline is a recovery.
Strategic cost analysis	A broad-based managerial-accounting analysis that compares a firms' costs to the unit costs of key competitors process by process is referred to as strategic cost analysis. This shows which internal activities are a source of cost advantage or disadvantage.
Harvard Business Review	Harvard Business Review is a research-based magazine written for business practitioners, it claims a high ranking business readership and enjoys the reverence of academics, executives, and management consultants. It has been the frequent publishing home for well known scholars and management thinkers.
Strategic management	A philosophy of management that links strategic planning with dayto-day decision making. Strategic management seeks a fit between an organization's external and internal environments.
Business Week	Business Week is a business magazine published by McGraw-Hill. It was first published in 1929 under the direction of Malcolm Muir, who was serving as president of the McGraw-Hill

	Publishing company at the time. It is considered to be the standard both in industry and among students.
Inputs	The inputs used by a firm or an economy are the labor, raw materials, electricity and other resources it uses to produce its outputs.
Weber	Weber was a German political economist and sociologist who is considered one of the founders of the modern study of sociology and public administration. His major works deal with rationalization in sociology of religion and government, but he also wrote much in the field of economics. His most popular work is his essay The Protestant Ethic and the Spirit of Capitalism.
Economics	The social science dealing with the use of scarce resources to obtain the maximum satisfaction of society's virtually unlimited economic wants is an economics.
Change management	Change management is the process of developing a planned approach to change in an organization. Typically the objective is to maximize the collective benefits for all people involved in the change and minimize the risk of failure of implementing the change.
Strategic alliance	Strategic alliance refers to a long-term partnership between two or more companies established to help each company build competitive market advantages.
Joint venture	Joint venture refers to an undertaking by two parties for a specific purpose and duration, taking any of several legal forms.
Wealth effect	The tendency for people to increase their consumption spending when the value of their financial and real assets rises and to decrease their consumption spending when the value of those assets falls is a wealth effect.
Preparation	Preparation refers to usually the first stage in the creative process. It includes education and formal training.
Preference	The act of a debtor in paying or securing one or more of his creditors in a manner more favorable to them than to other creditors or to the exclusion of such other creditors is a preference. In the absence of statute, a preference is perfectly good, but to be legal it must be bona fide, and not a mere subterfuge of the debtor to secure a future benefit to himself or to prevent the application of his property to his debts.
Hierarchy	A system of grouping people in an organization according to rank from the top down in which all subordinate managers must report to one person is called a hierarchy.
Entrepreneurship	The assembling of resources to produce new or improved products and technologies is referred to as entrepreneurship.
Privatization	A process in which investment bankers take companies that were previously owned by the government to the public markets is referred to as privatization.
Facilitator	A facilitator is someone who skilfully helps a group of people understand their common objectives and plan to achieve them without personally taking any side of the argument.
Leadership	Management merely consists of leadership applied to business situations; or in other words: management forms a sub-set of the broader process of leadership.

Go to **Cram101.com** for the Practice Tests for this Chapter.

International diversification	Achieving diversification through many different foreign investments that are influenced by a variety of factors is referred to as international diversification. By diversifying across nations whose economic cycles are not perfectly correlated, investors can typically reduce the variability of their returns.
Strategic management	A philosophy of management that links strategic planning with dayto-day decision making. Strategic management seeks a fit between an organization's external and internal environments.
Diversification	Investing in a collection of assets whose returns do not always move together, with the result that overall risk is lower than for individual assets is referred to as diversification.
Management	Management characterizes the process of leading and directing all or part of an organization, often a business, through the deployment and manipulation of resources. Early twentieth-century management writer Mary Parker Follett defined management as "the art of getting things done through people."
Firm	An organization that employs resources to produce a good or service for profit and owns and operates one or more plants is referred to as a firm.
International Business	International business refers to any firm that engages in international trade or investment.
Transnational	Transnational focuses on the heightened interconnectivity between people all around the world and the loosening of boundaries between countries.
Liability	A liability is a present obligation of the enterprise arizing from past events, the settlement of which is expected to result in an outflow from the enterprise of resources embodying economic benefits.
Trend	Trend refers to the long-term movement of an economic variable, such as its average rate of increase or decrease over enough years to encompass several business cycles.
International strategy	Trying to create value by transferring core competencies to foreign markets where indigenous competitors lack those competencies is called international strategy.
Market	A market is, as defined in economics, a social arrangement that allows buyers and sellers to discover information and carry out a voluntary exchange of goods or services.
Innovation	Innovation refers to the first commercially successful introduction of a new product, the use of a new method of production, or the creation of a new form of business organization.
Foreign direct investment	Foreign direct investment refers to the buying of permanent property and businesses in foreign nations.
World Trade Organization	The World Trade Organization is an international, multilateral organization, which sets the rules for the global trading system and resolves disputes between its member states, all of whom are signatories to its approximately 30 agreements.
Direct investment	Direct investment refers to a domestic firm actually investing in and owning a foreign subsidiary or division.
Manufacturing	Production of goods primarily by the application of labor and capital to raw materials and other intermediate inputs, in contrast to agriculture, mining, forestry, fishing, and services a manufacturing.
Investment	Investment refers to spending for the production and accumulation of capital and additions to inventories. In a financial sense, buying an asset with the expectation of making a return.
Industry	A group of firms that produce identical or similar products is an industry. It is also used

specifically to refer to an area of economic production focused on manufacturing which involves large amounts of capital investment before any profit can be realized, also called "heavy industry".

Labor	People's physical and mental talents and efforts that are used to help produce goods and services are called labor.
Wage	The payment for the service of a unit of labor, per unit time. In trade theory, it is the only payment to labor, usually unskilled labor. In empirical work, wage data may exclude other compenzation, which must be added to get the total cost of employment.
Analyst	Analyst refers to a person or tool with a primary function of information analysis, generally with a more limited, practical and short term set of goals than a researcher.
Economy	The income, expenditures, and resources that affect the cost of running a business and household are called an economy.
Expense	In accounting, an expense represents an event in which an asset is used up or a liability is incurred. In terms of the accounting equation, expenses reduce owners' equity.
Deflation	Deflation is an increase in the market value of money which is equivalent to a decrease in the general price level, over a period of time. The term is also used to refer to a decrease in the size of the money supply
Export	In economics, an export is any good or commodity, shipped or otherwise transported out of a country, province, town to another part of the world in a legitimate fashion, typically for use in trade or sale.
Asset	An item of property, such as land, capital, money, a share in ownership, or a claim on others for future payment, such as a bond or a bank deposit is an asset.
General Motors	General Motors is the world's largest automaker. Founded in 1908, today it employs about 327,000 people around the world. With global headquarters in Detroit, it manufactures its cars and trucks in 33 countries.
Volkswagen	Volkswagen or VW is an automobile manufacturer based in Wolfsburg, Germany in the state of Lower Saxony. It forms the core of this Group, one of the world's four largest car producers. Its German tagline is "Aus Liebe zum Automobil", which is translated as "For the love of the car" - or, For Love of the People's Cars,".
Operation	A standardized method or technique that is performed repetitively, often on different materials resulting in different finished goods is called an operation.
Barriers to entry	In economics and especially in the theory of competition, barriers to entry are obstacles in the path of a firm which wants to enter a given market.
Complexity	The technical sophistication of the product and hence the amount of understanding required to use it is referred to as complexity. It is the opposite of simplicity.
Human resources	Human resources refers to the individuals within the firm, and to the portion of the firm's organization that deals with hiring, firing, training, and other personnel issues.
Joint venture	Joint venture refers to an undertaking by two parties for a specific purpose and duration, taking any of several legal forms.
Subsidiary	A company that is controlled by another company or corporation is a subsidiary.
Licensing	Licensing is a form of strategic alliance which involves the sale of a right to use certain proprietary knowledge (so called intellectual property) in a defined way.
Exporting	Selling products to another country is called exporting.

Go to **Cram101.com** for the Practice Tests for this Chapter.

Domestic	From or in one's own country. A domestic producer is one that produces inside the home country. A domestic price is the price inside the home country. Opposite of 'foreign' or 'world.'.
Service	Service refers to a "non tangible product" that is not embodied in a physical good and that typically effects some change in another product, person, or institution. Contrasts with good.
Forming	The first stage of team development, where the team is formed and the objectives for the team are set is referred to as forming.
Incentive	An incentive is any factor (financial or non-financial) that provides a motive for a particular course of action, or counts as a reason for preferring one choice to the alternatives.
Yield	The interest rate that equates a future value or an annuity to a given present value is a yield.
Competitor	Other organizations in the same industry or type of business that provide a good or service to the same set of customers is referred to as a competitor.
Production	The creation of finished goods and services using the factors of production: land, labor, capital, entrepreneurship, and knowledge.
Manufacturing costs	Costs incurred in a manufacturing process, which consist of direct material, direct labor, and manufacturing overhead are referred to as manufacturing costs.
Raw material	Raw material refers to a good that has not been transformed by production; a primary product.
Supply	Supply is the aggregate amount of any material good that can be called into being at a certain price point; it comprises one half of the equation of supply and demand. In classical economic theory, a curve representing supply is one of the factors that produce price.
Integration	Economic integration refers to reducing barriers among countries to transactions and to movements of goods, capital, and labor, including harmonization of laws, regulations, and standards. Integrated markets theoretically function as a unified market.
Commodity	Could refer to any good, but in trade a commodity is usually a raw material or primary product that enters into international trade, such as metals or basic agricultural products.
Technology	The body of knowledge and techniques that can be used to combine economic resources to produce goods and services is called technology.
Benetton	Benetton has been known in the United States for producing a long-running series of controversial, sometimes offensive, advertisements that have caused a number of media critics to accuse the company of deliberately creating controversy in order to sell its products. This publicity campaign originated when photographer Oliviero Toscani was given carte blanche by the Benetton management.
Downturn	A decline in a stock market or economic cycle is a downturn.
Brand	A name, symbol, or design that identifies the goods or services of one seller or group of sellers and distinguishes them from the goods and services of competitors is a brand.
Globalization	The increasing world-wide integration of markets for goods, services and capital that attracted special attention in the late 1990s is called globalization.
Purchasing	Purchasing refers to the function in a firm that searches for quality material resources, finds the best suppliers, and negotiates the best price for goods and services.
Internationa-ization	Internationalization refers to another term for fragmentation. Used by Grossman and Helpman.

174

Emerging markets	The term emerging markets is commonly used to describe business and market activity in industrializing or emerging regions of the world. It is sometimes loosely used as a replacement for emerging economies, but really signifies a business phenomenon that is not fully described by or constrained to geography or economic strength; such countries are considered to be in a transitional phase between developing and developed status.
Economic system	Economic system refers to a particular set of institutional arrangements and a coordinating mechanism for solving the economizing problem; a method of organizing an economy, of which the market system and the command system are the two general types.
Emerging market	The term emerging market is commonly used to describe business and market activity in industrializing or emerging regions of the world.
Devaluation	Lowering the value of a nation's currency relative to other currencies is called devaluation.
International firm	International firm refers to those firms who have responded to stiff competition domestically by expanding their sales abroad. They may start a production facility overseas and send some of their managers, who report to a global division, to that country.
Economies of scale	In economics, returns to scale and economies of scale are related terms that describe what happens as the scale of production increases. They are different terms and not to be used interchangeably.
Localization	As an element of wireless marketing strategy, transmitting messages that are relevant to the user's current geographical location are referred to as localization.
Labor force	In economics the labor force is the group of people who have a potential for being employed.
Contract	A contract is a "promise" or an "agreement" that is enforced or recognized by the law. In the civil law, a contract is considered to be part of the general law of obligations.
Tariff	A tax imposed by a nation on an imported good is called a tariff.
Scope	Scope of a project is the sum total of all projects products and their requirements or features.
Competitive advantage	A business is said to have a competitive advantage when its unique strengths, often based on cost, quality, time, and innovation, offer consumers a greater percieved value and there by diffentiating it from its competitors.
Host country	The country in which the parent-country organization seeks to locate or has already located a facility is a host country.
Capital	Capital generally refers to financial wealth, especially that used to start or maintain a business. In classical economics, capital is one of four factors of production, the others being land and labor and entrepreneurship.
Market share	That fraction of an industry's output accounted for by an individual firm or group of firms is called market share.
Market potential	Market potential refers to maximum total sales of a product by all firms to a segment during a specified time period under specified environmental conditions and marketing efforts of the firms.
Cultural values	The values that employees need to have and act on for the organization to act on the strategic values are called cultural values.
Option	A contract that gives the purchaser the option to buy or sell the underlying financial instrument at a specified price, called the exercise price or strike price, within a specific period of time.
Return on	Return on investment refers to the return a businessperson gets on the money he and other

Go to **Cram101.com** for the Practice Tests for this Chapter.

investment	owners invest in the firm; for example, a business that earned $100 on a $1,000 investment would have a ROI of 10 percent: 100 divided by 1000.
Siemens	Siemens is the world's largest conglomerate company. Worldwide, Siemens and its subsidiaries employs 461,000 people (2005) in 190 countries and reported global sales of €75.4 billion in fiscal year 2005.
Productivity	Productivity refers to the total output of goods and services in a given period of time divided by work hours.
Reverse engineering	Reverse engineering refers to the process of learning how a product is made by taking it apart and examining it.
Product development	In business and engineering, new product development is the complete process of bringing a new product to market. There are two parallel aspects to this process : one involves product engineering ; the other marketing analysis. Marketers see new product development as the first stage in product life cycle management, engineers as part of Product Lifecycle Management.
New product development	New product development is the complete process of bringing a new product to market. There are two parallel aspects to this process : one involves product engineering ; the other marketing analysis.
Honda	With more than 14 million internal combustion engines built each year, Honda is the largest engine-maker in the world. In 2004, the company began to produce diesel motors, which were both very quiet whilst not requiring particulate filters to pass pollution standards. It is arguable, however, that the foundation of their success is the motorcycle division.
Ford	Ford is an American company that manufactures and sells automobiles worldwide. Ford introduced methods for large-scale manufacturing of cars, and large-scale management of an industrial workforce, especially elaborately engineered manufacturing sequences typified by the moving assembly lines.
Core competency	A company's core competency are things that a firm can (alsosns) do well and that meet the following three conditions. 1. It provides customer benefits, 2. It is hard for competitors to imitate, and 3. it can be leveraged widely to many products and market. A core competency can take various forms, including technical/subject matter knowhow, a reliable process, and/or close relationships with customers and suppliers. It may also include product development or culture such as employee dedication. Modern business theories suggest that most activities that are not part of a company's core competency should be outsourced.
Synergy	Corporate synergy occurs when corporations interact congruently. A corporate synergy refers to a financial benefit that a corporation expects to realize when it merges with or acquires another corporation.
Core	A core is the set of feasible allocations in an economy that cannot be improved upon by subset of the set of the economy's consumers (a coalition). In construction, when the force in an element is within a certain center section, the core, the element will only be under compression.
Users	Users refer to people in the organization who actually use the product or service purchased by the buying center.
Cost leadership	Organization's ability to achieve lower costs relative to competitors through productivity and efficiency improvements, elimination of waste, and tight cost control is cost leadership.
Leadership	Management merely consists of leadership applied to business situations; or in other words: management forms a sub-set of the broader process of leadership.
Factors of	Economic resources: land, capital, labor, and entrepreneurial ability are called factors of

Go to **Cram101.com** for the Practice Tests for this Chapter.

production	production.
Michael Porter	Michael Porter is a leading contributor to strategic management theory, Porter's main academic objectives focus on how a firm or a region, can build a competitive advantage and develop competitive strategy. Porter's strategic system consists primarily of 5 forces analysis, strategic groups, the value chain, and market positioning stratagies.
Brand equity	The combination of factors such as awareness, loyalty, perceived quality, images, and emotions people associate with a given brand name is referred to as brand equity.
Equity	Equity is the name given to the set of legal principles, in countries following the English common law tradition, which supplement strict rules of law where their application would operate harshly, so as to achieve what is sometimes referred to as "natural justice."
Niche market	A niche market or market niche is a focused, targetable portion of a market. By definition, then, a business that focuses on a niche market is addressing a need for a product or service that is not being addressed by mainstream providers.
Niche	In industry, a niche is a situation or an activity perfectly suited to a person. A niche can imply a working position or an area suited to a person who occupies it. Basically, a job where a person is able to succeed and thrive.
Process improvement	Process improvement is the activity of elevating the performance of a process, especially that of a business process with regard to its goal.
Cooperative	A business owned and controlled by the people who use it, producers, consumers, or workers with similar needs who pool their resources for mutual gain is called cooperative.
Structural attributes	Attributes having to do with physical characteristics of a product such as power steering or red paint are called structural attributes.
Policy	Similar to a script in that a policy can be a less than completely rational decision-making method. Involves the use of a pre-existing set of decision steps for any problem that presents itself.
Acquisition	A company's purchase of the property and obligations of another company is an acquisition.
Margin	A deposit by a buyer in stocks with a seller or a stockbroker, as security to cover fluctuations in the market in reference to stocks that the buyer has purchased but for which he has not paid is a margin. Commodities are also traded on margin.
Discount	The difference between the face value of a bond and its selling price, when a bond is sold for less than its face value it's referred to as a discount.
Monopoly	A monopoly is defined as a persistent market situation where there is only one provider of a kind of product or service.
Gain	In finance, gain is a profit or an increase in value of an investment such as a stock or bond. Gain is calculated by fair market value or the proceeds from the sale of the investment minus the sum of the purchase price and all costs associated with it.
Strategic choice	Strategic choice refers to an organization's strategy; the ways an organization will attempt to fulfill its mission and achieve its long-term goals.
Corporate Strategy	Corporate strategy is concerned with the firm's choice of business, markets and activities and thus it defines the overall scope and direction of the business.
Authority	Authority in agency law, refers to an agent's ability to affect his principal's legal relations with third parties. Also used to refer to an actor's legal power or ability to do something. In addition, sometimes used to refer to a statute, case, or other legal source that justifies a particular result.

Go to **Cram101.com** for the Practice Tests for this Chapter.

Corporate level	Corporate level refers to level at which top management directs overall strategy for the entire organization.
Business unit	The lowest level of the company which contains the set of functions that carry a product through its life span from concept through manufacture, distribution, sales and service is a business unit.
Multidomestic strategy	Emphasizing the need to be responsive to the unique conditions prevailing in different national markets is referred to as a multidomestic strategy.
Preference	The act of a debtor in paying or securing one or more of his creditors in a manner more favorable to them than to other creditors or to the exclusion of such other creditors is a preference. In the absence of statute, a preference is perfectly good, but to be legal it must be bona fide, and not a mere subterfuge of the debtor to secure a future benefit to himself or to prevent the application of his property to his debts.
Interest	In finance and economics, interest is the price paid by a borrower for the use of a lender's money. In other words, interest is the amount of paid to "rent" money for a period of time.
Points	Loan origination fees that may be deductible as interest by a buyer of property. A seller of property who pays points reduces the selling price by the amount of the points paid for the buyer.
Standardized product	Standardized product refers to a product whose buyers are indifferent to the seller from whom they purchase it, as long as the price charged by all sellers is the same; a product all units of which are identical and thus are perfect substitutes.
Global strategy	Global strategy refers to strategy focusing on increasing profitability by reaping cost reductions from experience curve and location economies.
Strategic business unit	Strategic business unit is understood as a business unit within the overall corporate identity which is distinguishable from other business because it serves a defined external market where management can conduct strategic planning in relation to products and markets. When companies become really large, they are best thought of as being composed of a number of businesses
Transnational strategy	Plan to exploit experience-based cost and location economies, transfer core competencies with the firm, and pay attention to local responsiveness is called transnational strategy.
Stock exchange	A stock exchange is a corporation or mutual organization which provides facilities for stock brokers and traders, to trade company stocks and other securities.
Exchange	The trade of things of value between buyer and seller so that each is better off after the trade is called the exchange.
Stock	In financial terminology, stock is the capital raized by a corporation, through the issuance and sale of shares.
Cemex	Although it is not a monopoly, Cemex, along with Holcim-Apasco, controls the Mexican cement market. This has given rise to allegations that because of the oligopolistic structure in the Mexican cement market (as in many other markets in Mexico) consumers pay a higher price for cement than in other countries. However given the peculiarities of the Mexican cement market, the fact that it is sold mostly in bags, and the fact that cement is not an easily transported commodity make this accuzation difficult, if not impossible to prove.
Market position	Market position is a measure of the position of a company or product on a market.
Cost structure	The relative proportion of an organization's fixed, variable, and mixed costs is referred to as cost structure.
Revenue	Revenue is a U.S. business term for the amount of money that a company receives from its

Go to **Cram101.com** for the Practice Tests for this Chapter.

	activities, mostly from sales of products and/or services to customers.
Supply network	A supply network is a pattern of temporal and spatial processes carried out at facility nodes and over distribution links, which adds value for customers through the manufacture and delivery of products.
Logistics	Those activities that focus on getting the right amount of the right products to the right place at the right time at the lowest possible cost is referred to as logistics.
Receiver	A person that is appointed as a custodian of other people's property by a court of law or a creditor of the owner, pending a lawsuit or reorganization is called a receiver.
DaimlerChrysler	In 2002, the merged company, DaimlerChrysler, appeared to run two independent product lines, with few signs of corporate integration. In 2003, however, it was alleged by the Detroit News that the "merger of equals" was, in fact, a takeover.
Chrysler	The Chrysler Corporation was an American automobile manufacturer that existed independently from 1925–1998. The company was formed by Walter Percy Chrysler on June 6, 1925, with the remaining assets of Maxwell Motor Company.
Profit	Profit refers to the return to the resource entrepreneurial ability; total revenue minus total cost.
Toyota	Toyota is a Japanese multinational corporation that manufactures automobiles, trucks and buses. Toyota is the world's second largest automaker by sales. Toyota also provides financial services through its subsidiary, Toyota Financial Services, and participates in other lines of business.
Nissan	Nissan is Japan's second largest car company after Toyota. Nissan is among the top three Asian rivals of the "big three" in the US.
Price competition	Price competition is where a company tries to distinguish its product or service from competing products on the basis of low price.
Controlling interest	A firm has a controlling interest in another business entity when it owns more than 50 percent of that entity's voting stock.
Operating margin	In business, operating margin is the ratio of operating income divided by net sales.
Controlling	A management function that involves determining whether or not an organization is progressing toward its goals and objectives, and taking corrective action if it is not is called controlling.
Regulation	Regulation refers to restrictions state and federal laws place on business with regard to the conduct of its activities.
Sony	Sony is a multinational corporation and one of the world's largest media conglomerates founded in Tokyo, Japan. One of its divisions Sony Electronics is one of the leading manufacturers of electronics, video, communications, and information technology products for the consumer and professional markets.

Go to **Cram101.com** for the Practice Tests for this Chapter.

Innovation	Innovation refers to the first commercially successful introduction of a new product, the use of a new method of production, or the creation of a new form of business organization.
Entrepreneurship	The assembling of resources to produce new or improved products and technologies is referred to as entrepreneurship.
Strategic alliance	Strategic alliance refers to a long-term partnership between two or more companies established to help each company build competitive market advantages.
Cooperative	A business owned and controlled by the people who use it, producers, consumers, or workers with similar needs who pool their resources for mutual gain is called cooperative.
Venture capital	Venture capital is capital provided by outside investors for financing of new, growing or struggling businesses. Venture capital investments generally are high risk investments but offer the potential for above average returns.
Capital	Capital generally refers to financial wealth, especially that used to start or maintain a business. In classical economics, capital is one of four factors of production, the others being land and labor and entrepreneurship.
Initial public offering	Firms in the process of becoming publicly traded companies will issue shares of stock using an initial public offering, which is merely the process of selling stock for the first time to interested investors.
Agent	A person who makes economic decisions for another economic actor. A hired manager operates as an agent for a firm's owner.
Firm	An organization that employs resources to produce a good or service for profit and owns and operates one or more plants is referred to as a firm.
Balanced scorecard	A framework for implementing strategy by translating an organization's mission and strategy into a set of performance measures is called balanced scorecard.
Strategic management	A philosophy of management that links strategic planning with dayto-day decision making. Strategic management seeks a fit between an organization's external and internal environments.
Accounting	A system that collects and processes financial information about an organization and reports that information to decision makers is referred to as accounting.
Management	Management characterizes the process of leading and directing all or part of an organization, often a business, through the deployment and manipulation of resources. Early twentieth-century management writer Mary Parker Follett defined management as "the art of getting things done through people."
Leadership	Management merely consists of leadership applied to business situations; or in other words: management forms a sub-set of the broader process of leadership.
Performance measurement	The process by which someone evaluates an employee's work behaviors by measurement and comparison with previously established standards, documents the results, and communicates the results to the employee is called performance measurement.
Harvard Business Review	Harvard Business Review is a research-based magazine written for business practitioners, it claims a high ranking business readership and enjoys the reverence of academics, executives, and management consultants. It has been the frequent publishing home for well known scholars and management thinkers.
Journal	Book of original entry, in which transactions are recorded in a general ledger system, is referred to as a journal.
Foreign	A company owned in a foreign country by another company is referred to as foreign subsidiary.

Go to **Cram101.com** for the Practice Tests for this Chapter.

subsidiary	
Competitiveness	Competitiveness usually refers to characteristics that permit a firm to compete effectively with other firms due to low cost or superior technology, perhaps internationally.
Subsidiary	A company that is controlled by another company or corporation is a subsidiary.
Corporate culture	The whole collection of beliefs, values, and behaviors of a firm that send messages to those within and outside the company about how business is done is the corporate culture.
Context	The effect of the background under which a message often takes on more and richer meaning is a context. Context is especially important in cross-cultural interactions because some cultures are said to be high context or low context.
Brand	A name, symbol, or design that identifies the goods or services of one seller or group of sellers and distinguishes them from the goods and services of competitors is a brand.
Social capital	Capital that provides services to the public. Most social capital takes the form of public goods and public services.
International management	International management refers to the management of business operations conducted in more than one country.
Internationa-ization	Internationalization refers to another term for fragmentation. Used by Grossman and Helpman.
Transaction cost	A transaction cost is a cost incurred in making an economic exchange. For example, most people, when buying or selling a stock, must pay a commission to their broker; that commission is a transaction cost of doing the stock deal.
Business ethics	The study of what makes up good and bad conduct as related to business activities and values is business ethics.
Control system	A control system is a device or set of devices that manage the behavior of other devices. Some devices or systems are not controllable.A control system is an interconnection of components connected or related in such a manner as to command, direct, or regulate itself or another system.
Invisible hand	Invisible hand refers to a phrase coined by Adam Smith to describe the process that turns self-directed gain into social and economic benefits for all.
Controlling	A management function that involves determining whether or not an organization is progressing toward its goals and objectives, and taking corrective action if it is not is called controlling.
Compliance	A type of influence process where a receiver accepts the position advocated by a source to obtain favorable outcomes or to avoid punishment is the compliance.
Paradox	As used in economics, paradox means something unexpected, rather than the more extreme normal meaning of something seemingly impossible. Some paradoxes are just theoretical results that go against what one thinks of as normal.
Corporate governance	Corporate governance is the set of processes, customs, policies, laws and institutions affecting the way a corporation is directed, administered or controlled.
Globalization	The increasing world-wide integration of markets for goods, services and capital that attracted special attention in the late 1990s is called globalization.
Business Week	Business Week is a business magazine published by McGraw-Hill. It was first published in 1929 under the direction of Malcolm Muir, who was serving as president of the McGraw-Hill Publishing company at the time. It is considered to be the standard both in industry and among students.

Go to **Cram101.com** for the Practice Tests for this Chapter.

Jack Welch	In 1986, GE acquired NBC. During the 90s, Jack Welch helped to modernize GE by emphasizing a shift from manufacturing to services. He also made hundreds of acquisitions and made a push to dominate markets abroad. Welch adopted the Six Sigma quality program in late 1995.
American Management Association	American Management Association International is the world's largest membership-based management development and executive training organization. Their products include instructor led seminars, workshops, conferences, customized corporate programs, online learning, books, newsletters, research surveys and reports.
Management science	Management science is the discipline of using mathematics, and other analytical methods, to help make better business decisions.
Investment	Investment refers to spending for the production and accumulation of capital and additions to inventories. In a financial sense, buying an asset with the expectation of making a return.
Stakeholder	A stakeholder is an individual or group with a vested interest in or expectation for organizational performance. Usually stakeholders can either have an effect on or are affected by an organization.
Human resource management	The process of evaluating human resource needs, finding people to fill those needs, and getting the best work from each employee by providing the right incentives and job environment, all with the goal of meeting the needs of the firm are called human resource management.
Competitive advantage	A business is said to have a competitive advantage when its unique strengths, often based on cost, quality, time, and innovation, offer consumers a greater percieved value and there by differtiating it from its competitors.
Resource management	Resource management is the efficient and effective deployment of an organization's resources when they are needed. Such resources may include financial resources, inventory, human skills, production resources, or information technology.
Learning organization	A firm, which values continuous learning and is consistently looking to adapt and change with its environment is referred to as learning organization.
Management team	A management team is directly responsible for managing the day-to-day operations (and profitability) of a company.
Business unit	The lowest level of the company which contains the set of functions that carry a product through its life span from concept through manufacture, distribution, sales and service is a business unit.
Expatriate manager	A national of one country appointed to a management position in another country is an expatriate manager.
Expatriate	Employee sent by his or her company to live and manage operations in a different country is called an expatriate.
Downsizing	The process of eliminating managerial and non-managerial positions are called downsizing.
Hysteresis	Hysteresis refers to a departure from full employment levels as a result of past high unemployment.
Inventory	Tangible property held for sale in the normal course of business or used in producing goods or services for sale is an inventory.
Industry	A group of firms that produce identical or similar products is an industry. It is also used specifically to refer to an area of economic production focused on manufacturing which involves large amounts of capital investment before any profit can be realized, also called "heavy industry".

Go to **Cram101.com** for the Practice Tests for this Chapter.

Market	A market is, as defined in economics, a social arrangement that allows buyers and sellers to discover information and carry out a voluntary exchange of goods or services.
Organizational performance	Organizational performance comprises the actual output or results of an organization as measured against its intended outputs (or goals and objectives).
Extended enterprise	Extended Enterprise is a concept typically applied to a networked organization in which a dominant enterprise "extends" its boundaries to all or some of its suppliers. An extended enterprise can be seen as a particular case of a virtual enterprise and therefore a manifestation of a Collaborative Network.
Charismatic leader	A leader who has the ability to motivate subordinates to transcend their expected performance is a charismatic leader.
Management buyout	A management buyout is a form of acquisition where a company's existing managers buy or acquire a large part of the company.
Centralization	A structural policy in which decision-making authority is concentrated at the top of the organizational hierarchy is referred to as centralization.
Privatization	A process in which investment bankers take companies that were previously owned by the government to the public markets is referred to as privatization.
Composition	An out-of-court settlement in which creditors agree to accept a fractional settlement on their original claim is referred to as composition.
Enterprise	Enterprise refers to another name for a business organization. Other similar terms are business firm, sometimes simply business, sometimes simply firm, as well as company, and entity.
Buyout	A buyout is an investment transaction by which the entire or a controlling part of the stock of a company is sold. A firm buysout the stake of the company to strengthen its influence on the company's decision making body. A buyout can take the forms of a leveraged buyout or a management buyout.
Trust	An arrangement in which shareholders of independent firms agree to give up their stock in exchange for trust certificates that entitle them to a share of the trust's common profits.
Asset	An item of property, such as land, capital, money, a share in ownership, or a claim on others for future payment, such as a bond or a bank deposit is an asset.
Restructuring	Restructuring is the corporate management term for the act of partially dismantling and reorganizing a company for the purpose of making it more efficient and therefore more profitable.
Intellectual capital	Intellectual capital makes an organization worth more than its balance sheet value. For many years, intellectual capital and goodwill meant the same thing. Today, intellectual capital management is far broader. It seeks to explain how knowledge, collaboration, and process-engagement create decisions and actions that lead to cost allocations, productivity, and finally financial performance.
Policy	Similar to a script in that a policy can be a less than completely rational decision-making method. Involves the use of a pre-existing set of decision steps for any problem that presents itself.
Labor market	Any arrangement that brings buyers and sellers of labor services together to agree on conditions of work and pay is called a labor market.
Labor	People's physical and mental talents and efforts that are used to help produce goods and services are called labor.

Go to **Cram101.com** for the Practice Tests for this Chapter.

Level 5 leadership	Level 5 leadership is the Executive who "builds enduring greatness through a paradoxical blend of personal humility and professional will." Every one of the good-to-great companies has level 5 leaders in the critical transition phase.
Technology	The body of knowledge and techniques that can be used to combine economic resources to produce goods and services is called technology.
Leverage	Leverage is using given resources in such a way that the potential positive or negative outcome is magnified. In finance, this generally refers to borrowing.
Learning by doing	The improvement in technology that takes place in some industries, early in their history, as they learn by experience so that average cost falls as accumulated output rises is called learning by doing.
Business strategy	Business strategy, which refers to the aggregated operational strategies of single business firm or that of an SBU in a diversified corporation refers to the way in which a firm competes in its chosen arenas.
Strategy implementation	Strategy implementation refers to the process of devising structures and allocating resources to enact the strategy a company has chosen.
Manufacturing	Production of goods primarily by the application of labor and capital to raw materials and other intermediate inputs, in contrast to agriculture, mining, forestry, fishing, and services a manufacturing.
Marketing	Promoting and selling products or services to customers, or prospective customers, is referred to as marketing.
Customer service	The ability of logistics management to satisfy users in terms of time, dependability, communication, and convenience is called the customer service.
Service	Service refers to a "non tangible product" that is not embodied in a physical good and that typically effects some change in another product, person, or institution. Contrasts with good.
Human capital	Human capital refers to the stock of knowledge and skill, embodied in an individual as a result of education, training, and experience that makes them more productive. The stock of knowledge and skill embodied in the population of an economy.
Organizational culture	The mindset of employees, including their shared beliefs, values, and goals is called the organizational culture.
Organizational control	Organizational control refers to the systematic process through which managers regulate organizational activities to make them consistent with expectations established in plans, targets, and standards of performance.
Financial control	A process in which a firm periodically compares its actual revenues, costs, and expenses with its projected ones is called financial control.
Core competency	A company's core competency are things that a firm can (alsosns) do well and that meet the following three conditions. 1. It provides customer benefits, 2. It is hard for competitors to imitate, and 3. it can be leveraged widely to many products and market. A core competency can take various forms, including technical/subject matter knowhow, a reliable process, and/or close relationships with customers and suppliers. It may also include product development or culture such as employee dedication. Modern business theories suggest that most activities that are not part of a company's core competency should be outsourced.
Balance	In banking and accountancy, the outstanding balance is the amount of money owned, (or due), that remains in a deposit account (or a loan account) at a given date, after all past remittances, payments and withdrawal have been accounted for. It can be positive (then, in

Go to **Cram101.com** for the Practice Tests for this Chapter.

the balance sheet of a firm, it is an asset) or negative (a liability).

Core	A core is the set of feasible allocations in an economy that cannot be improved upon by subset of the set of the economy's consumers (a coalition). In construction, when the force in an element is within a certain center section, the core, the element will only be under compression.
Net income	Net income is equal to the income that a firm has after subtracting costs and expenses from the total revenue. Expenses will typically include tax expense.
Motorola	The Six Sigma quality system was developed at Motorola even though it became most well known because of its use by General Electric. It was created by engineer Bill Smith, under the direction of Bob Galvin (son of founder Paul Galvin) when he was running the company.
Revenue	Revenue is a U.S. business term for the amount of money that a company receives from its activities, mostly from sales of products and/or services to customers.
Samsung	On November 30, 2005 Samsung pleaded guilty to a charge it participated in a worldwide DRAM price fixing conspiracy during 1999-2002 that damaged competition and raized PC prices.
Sony	Sony is a multinational corporation and one of the world's largest media conglomerates founded in Tokyo, Japan. One of its divisions Sony Electronics is one of the leading manufacturers of electronics, video, communications, and information technology products for the consumer and professional markets.
Board of directors	The group of individuals elected by the stockholders of a corporation to oversee its operations is a board of directors.
Corporation	A legal entity chartered by a state or the Federal government that is distinct and separate from the individuals who own it is a corporation. This separation gives the corporation unique powers which other legal entities lack.
Portfolio	In finance, a portfolio is a collection of investments held by an institution or a private individual. Holding but not always a portfolio is part of an investment and risk-limiting strategy called diversification. By owning several assets, certain types of risk (in particular specific risk) can be reduced.
Strategic intent	Strategic intent is when a firm relentlessly pursues a difficult strategic goa and concentrates its competitive actions and energies on achieving that goal.
Strategic control	Strategic control processes allow managers to evaluate a company's marketing program from a critical long-term perspective. This involves a detailed and objective analysis of a company's organization and its ability to maximize its strengths and market opportunities.
Corporate level	Corporate level refers to level at which top management directs overall strategy for the entire organization.
Tangible	Having a physical existence is referred to as the tangible. Personal property other than real estate, such as cars, boats, stocks, or other assets.
Gain	In finance, gain is a profit or an increase in value of an investment such as a stock or bond. Gain is calculated by fair market value or the proceeds from the sale of the investment minus the sum of the purchase price and all costs associated with it.
Currency crisis	Occurs when a speculative attack on the exchange value of a currency results in a sharp depreciation in the value of the currency or forces authorities to expend large volumes of international currency reserves and sharply increase interest rates to defend the prevailing exchange rate are referred to as currency crisis.
Operation	A standardized method or technique that is performed repetitively, often on different materials resulting in different finished goods is called an operation.

Standing	Standing refers to the legal requirement that anyone seeking to challenge a particular action in court must demonstrate that such action substantially affects his legitimate interests before he will be entitled to bring suit.
Credibility	The extent to which a source is perceived as having knowledge, skill, or experience relevant to a communication topic and can be trusted to give an unbiased opinion or present objective information on the issue is called credibility.
Recession	A significant decline in economic activity. In the U.S., recession is approximately defined as two successive quarters of falling GDP, as judged by NBER.
Domestic	From or in one's own country. A domestic producer is one that produces inside the home country. A domestic price is the price inside the home country. Opposite of 'foreign' or 'world.'.
Economy	The income, expenditures, and resources that affect the cost of running a business and household are called an economy.
Expense	In accounting, an expense represents an event in which an asset is used up or a liability is incurred. In terms of the accounting equation, expenses reduce owners' equity.
Stock market	An organized marketplace in which common stocks are traded. In the United States, the largest stock market is the New York Stock Exchange, on which are traded the stocks of the largest U.S. companies.
Stock	In financial terminology, stock is the capital raized by a corporation, through the issuance and sale of shares.
Fraud	Tax fraud falls into two categories: civil and criminal. Under civil fraud, the IRS may impose as a penalty of an amount equal to as much as 75 percent of the underpayment.
Medicare	Medicare refers to federal program that is financed by payroll taxes and provides for compulsory hospital insurance for senior citizens and low-cost voluntary insurance to help older Americans pay physicians' fees.
Inputs	The inputs used by a firm or an economy are the labor, raw materials, electricity and other resources it uses to produce its outputs.
WorldCom	WorldCom was the United States' second largest long distance phone company (AT&T was the largest). WorldCom grew largely by acquiring other telecommunications companies, most notably MCI Communications. It also owned the Tier 1 ISP UUNET, a major part of the Internet backbone.
Enron	Enron Corportaion's global reputation was undermined by persistent rumours of bribery and political pressure to secure contracts in Central America, South America, Africa, and the Philippines. Especially controversial was its $3 billion contract with the Maharashtra State Electricity Board in India, where it is alleged that Enron officials used political connections within the Clinton and Bush administrations to exert pressure on the board.
Allegation	An allegation is a statement of a fact by a party in a pleading, which the party claims it will prove. Allegations remain assertions without proof, only claims until they are proved.
Plea	A plea is an answer to a declaration or complaint or any material allegation of fact therein that, if untrue, would defeat the action. In criminal procedure, a plea is the matter that the accused, on his arraignment, alleges in answer to the charge against him.
Competitor	Other organizations in the same industry or type of business that provide a good or service to the same set of customers is referred to as a competitor.
Proactive	To be proactive is to act before a situation becomes a source of confrontation or crisis. It is the opposite of "retroactive," which refers to actions taken after an event.

Go to **Cram101.com** for the Practice Tests for this Chapter.

Performance appraisal	An evaluation in which the performance level of employees is measured against established standards to make decisions about promotions, compenzation, additional training, or firing is referred to as performance appraisal.
Effective communication	When the intended meaning equals the perceived meaning it is called effective communication.
Strategic vision	A strategic vision is a roadmap of a company's future-providing specifics about customer focus and technology, the product and geographic markets to be pursued, the capabilities it plans to develop, and the kind of company that management is trying to create.
Alignment	Term that refers to optimal coordination among disparate departments and divisions within a firm is referred to as alignment.
Market share	That fraction of an industry's output accounted for by an individual firm or group of firms is called market share.
Nissan	Nissan is Japan's second largest car company after Toyota. Nissan is among the top three Asian rivals of the "big three" in the US.
Shareholder	A shareholder is an individual or company (including a corporation) that legally owns one or more shares of stock in a joined stock company.
Foundation	A Foundation is a type of philanthropic organization set up by either individuals or institutions as a legal entity (either as a corporation or trust) with the purpose of distributing grants to support causes in line with the goals of the foundation.
Training and development	All attempts to improve productivity by increasing an employee's ability to perform is training and development.
Human capital investment	Any expenditure undertaken to improve the education, skills, health, or mobility of workers, with an expectation of greater productivity and thus a positive return on the investment is called human capital investment.
Knowledge base	Knowledge base refers to a database that includes decision rules for use of the data, which may be qualitative as well as quantitative.
Attribution	Under certain circumstances, the tax law applies attribution rules to assign to one taxpayer the ownership interest of another taxpayer.
Layoff	A layoff is the termination of an employee or (more commonly) a group of employees for business reasons, such as the decision that certain positions are no longer necessary.
Downturn	A decline in a stock market or economic cycle is a downturn.
Human resources	Human resources refers to the individuals within the firm, and to the portion of the firm's organization that deals with hiring, firing, training, and other personnel issues.
Information technology	Information technology refers to technology that helps companies change business by allowing them to use new methods.
Research and development	The use of resources for the deliberate discovery of new information and ways of doing things, together with the application of that information in inventing new products or processes is referred to as research and development.
PepsiCo	In many ways, PepsiCo differs from its main competitor, having three times as many employees, larger revenues, but a smaller net profit.
Intel	Intel Corporation, founded in 1968 and based in Santa Clara, California, USA, is the world's largest semiconductor company. Intel is best known for its PC microprocessors, where it maintains roughly 80% market share.

Distribution	Distribution in economics, the manner in which total output and income is distributed among individuals or factors.
Support network	A group of two or more trainees who agree to meet and discuss their progress in using learned capabilities on the job is referred to as support network.
Premium	Premium refers to the fee charged by an insurance company for an insurance policy. The rate of losses must be relatively predictable: In order to set the premium (prices) insurers must be able to estimate them accurately.
Shill	A shill is an associate of a person selling goods or services, who pretends no association to the seller and assumes the air of an enthusiastic customer.
Earnings per share	Earnings per share refers to annual profit of the corporation divided by the number of shares outstanding.
Return on sales	Return on sales refers to the percent of net income generated by each dollar of sales; computed by dividing net income before taxes by sales revenue.
Acquisition	A company's purchase of the property and obligations of another company is an acquisition.
Transparency	Transparency refers to a concept that describes a company being so open to other companies working with it that the once-solid barriers between them become see-through and electronic information is shared as if the companies were one.
Shareholder value	For a publicly traded company, shareholder value is the part of its capitalization that is equity as opposed to long-term debt. In the case of only one type of stock, this would roughly be the number of outstanding shares times current shareprice.
Stock option	A stock option is a specific type of option that uses the stock itself as an underlying instrument to determine the option's pay-off and therefore its value.
Option	A contract that gives the purchaser the option to buy or sell the underlying financial instrument at a specified price, called the exercise price or strike price, within a specific period of time.
Employee empowerment	Employee empowerment is a method of improving customer service in which workers have discretion to do what they believe is necessary, but within reason, to satisfy the customer, even if this means bending some company rules.
Empowerment	Giving employees the authority and responsibility to respond quickly to customer requests is called empowerment.
Organizational design	The structuring of workers so that they can best accomplish the firm's goals is referred to as organizational design.
Profit	Profit refers to the return to the resource entrepreneurial ability; total revenue minus total cost.
Public sector	Public sector refers to the part of the economy that contains all government entities; government.
Glass ceiling	Glass ceiling refers to a term that refers to the many barriers that can exist to thwart a woman's rise to the top of an organization; one that provides a view of the top, but a ceiling on how far a woman can go.
World Bank	The World Bank is a group of five international organizations responsible for providing finance and advice to countries for the purposes of economic development and poverty reduction, and for encouraging and safeguarding international investment.
Shell	One of the original Seven Sisters, Royal Dutch/Shell is the world's third-largest oil company by revenue, and a major player in the petrochemical industry and the solar energy business.

	Shell has six core businesses: Exploration and Production, Gas and Power, Downstream, Chemicals, Renewables, and Trading/Shipping, and operates in more than 140 countries.
Homogeneous	In the context of procurement/purchasing, homogeneous is used to describe goods that do not vary in their essential characteristic irrespective of the source of supply.
Xerox	Xerox was founded in 1906 as "The Haloid Company" manufacturing photographic paper and equipment. The company came to prominence in 1959 with the introduction of the first plain paper photocopier using the process of xerography (electrophotography) developed by Chester Carlson, the Xerox 914.
Complexity	The technical sophistication of the product and hence the amount of understanding required to use it is referred to as complexity. It is the opposite of simplicity.
Strategic plan	The formal document that presents the ways and means by which a strategic goal will be achieved is a strategic plan. A long-term flexible plan that does not regulate activities but rather outlines the means to achieve certain results, and provides the means to alter the course of action should the desired ends change.
Comprehensive	A comprehensive refers to a layout accurate in size, color, scheme, and other necessary details to show how a final ad will look. For presentation only, never for reproduction.
Growth strategy	A strategy based on investing in companies and sectors which are growing faster than their peers is a growth strategy. The benefits are usually in the form of capital gains rather than dividends.
Organizational structure	Organizational structure is the way in which the interrelated groups of an organization are constructed. From a managerial point of view the main concerns are ensuring effective communication and coordination.
Cultural values	The values that employees need to have and act on for the organization to act on the strategic values are called cultural values.
Avon	Avon is an American cosmetics, perfume and toy seller with markets in over 135 countries across the world and a sales of $7.74 billion worldwide.
General manager	A manager who is responsible for several departments that perform different functions is called general manager.
Public company	A public company is a company owned by the public rather than by a relatively few individuals. There are two different meanings for this term: (1) A company that is owned by stockholders who are members of the general public and trade shares publicly, often through a listing on a stock exchange. Ownership is open to anyone that has the money and inclination to buy shares in the company. It is differentiated from privately held companies where the shares are held by a small group of individuals, who are often members of one or a small group of families or otherwise related individuals, or other companies. The variant of this type of company in the United Kingdom and Ireland is known as a public limited compan, and (2) A government-owned corporation. This meaning of a "public company" comes from the fact that government debt is sometimes referred to as "public debt" although there are no "public bonds", government finance is sometimes called "public finance", among similar uses. This is the less-common meaning.
Productivity	Productivity refers to the total output of goods and services in a given period of time divided by work hours.
Stockholder	A stockholder is an individual or company (including a corporation) that legally owns one or more shares of stock in a joined stock company. The shareholders are the owners of a corporation. Companies listed at the stock market strive to enhance shareholder value.
Toyota	Toyota is a Japanese multinational corporation that manufactures automobiles, trucks and

Go to **Cram101.com** for the Practice Tests for this Chapter.

Go to **Cram101.com** for the Practice Tests for this Chapter.
And, **NEVER** highlight a book again!

buses. Toyota is the world's second largest automaker by sales. Toyota also provides financial services through its subsidiary, Toyota Financial Services, and participates in other lines of business.

Southwest airlines

Southwest Airlines is a low-fare airline in the United States. It is the third-largest airline in the world, by number of passengers carried, and the largest in the United States by number of passengers carried domestically.

American Express

From the early 1980s until the late 1990s, American Express was known for cutting its merchant fees (also known as a "discount rate") to fine merchants and restaurants if they only accepted American Express and no other credit or charge cards. This prompted competitors such as Visa and MasterCard to cry foul for a while, as the tactics "locked" restaurants into American Express.

Analyst

Analyst refers to a person or tool with a primary function of information analysis, generally with a more limited, practical and short term set of goals than a researcher.

Contract

A contract is a "promise" or an "agreement" that is enforced or recognized by the law. In the civil law, a contract is considered to be part of the general law of obligations.

Management	Management characterizes the process of leading and directing all or part of an organization, often a business, through the deployment and manipulation of resources. Early twentieth-century management writer Mary Parker Follett defined management as "the art of getting things done through people."
Leadership	Management merely consists of leadership applied to business situations; or in other words: management forms a sub-set of the broader process of leadership.
Management team	A management team is directly responsible for managing the day-to-day operations (and profitability) of a company.
Firm	An organization that employs resources to produce a good or service for profit and owns and operates one or more plants is referred to as a firm.
Labor market	Any arrangement that brings buyers and sellers of labor services together to agree on conditions of work and pay is called a labor market.
Market	A market is, as defined in economics, a social arrangement that allows buyers and sellers to discover information and carry out a voluntary exchange of goods or services.
Labor	People's physical and mental talents and efforts that are used to help produce goods and services are called labor.
Core competency	A company's core competency are things that a firm can (alsosns) do well and that meet the following three conditions. 1. It provides customer benefits, 2. It is hard for competitors to imitate, and 3. it can be leveraged widely to many products and market. A core competency can take various forms, including technical/subject matter knowhow, a reliable process, and/or close relationships with customers and suppliers. It may also include product development or culture such as employee dedication. Modern business theories suggest that most activities that are not part of a company's core competency should be outsourced.
Social capital	Capital that provides services to the public. Most social capital takes the form of public goods and public services.
Human capital	Human capital refers to the stock of knowledge and skill, embodied in an individual as a result of education, training, and experience that makes them more productive. The stock of knowledge and skill embodied in the population of an economy.
Capital	Capital generally refers to financial wealth, especially that used to start or maintain a business. In classical economics, capital is one of four factors of production, the others being land and labor and entrepreneurship.
Core	A core is the set of feasible allocations in an economy that cannot be improved upon by subset of the set of the economy's consumers (a coalition). In construction, when the force in an element is within a certain center section, the core, the element will only be under compression.
Organizational culture	The mindset of employees, including their shared beliefs, values, and goals is called the organizational culture.
Organizational control	Organizational control refers to the systematic process through which managers regulate organizational activities to make them consistent with expectations established in plans, targets, and standards of performance.
Avon	Avon is an American cosmetics, perfume and toy seller with markets in over 135 countries across the world and a sales of $7.74 billion worldwide.
Strategic management	A philosophy of management that links strategic planning with dayto-day decision making. Strategic management seeks a fit between an organization's external and internal environments.

Go to **Cram101.com** for the Practice Tests for this Chapter.

Entrepreneurship	The assembling of resources to produce new or improved products and technologies is referred to as entrepreneurship.
Technology	The body of knowledge and techniques that can be used to combine economic resources to produce goods and services is called technology.
Innovation	Innovation refers to the first commercially successful introduction of a new product, the use of a new method of production, or the creation of a new form of business organization.
Journal	Book of original entry, in which transactions are recorded in a general ledger system, is referred to as a journal.
Transaction value	The actual price of a product, paid or payable, used for customs valuation purposes is called transaction value.
Transaction cost	A transaction cost is a cost incurred in making an economic exchange. For example, most people, when buying or selling a stock, must pay a commission to their broker; that commission is a transaction cost of doing the stock deal.
Collaboration	Collaboration occurs when the interaction between groups is very important to goal attainment and the goals are compatible. Wherein people work together —applying both to the work of individuals as well as larger collectives and societies.
Partnership	In the common law, a partnership is a type of business entity in which partners share with each other the profits or losses of the business undertaking in which they have all invested.
Industry	A group of firms that produce identical or similar products is an industry. It is also used specifically to refer to an area of economic production focused on manufacturing which involves large amounts of capital investment before any profit can be realized, also called "heavy industry".
Toyota	Toyota is a Japanese multinational corporation that manufactures automobiles, trucks and buses. Toyota is the world's second largest automaker by sales. Toyota also provides financial services through its subsidiary, Toyota Financial Services, and participates in other lines of business.
Performance improvement	Performance improvement is the concept of measuring the output of a particular process or procedure then modifying the process or procedure in order to increase the output, increase efficiency, or increase the effectiveness of the process or procedure.
Enterprise	Enterprise refers to another name for a business organization. Other similar terms are business firm, sometimes simply business, sometimes simply firm, as well as company, and entity.
Organizational structure	Organizational structure is the way in which the interrelated groups of an organization are constructed. From a managerial point of view the main concerns are ensuring effective communication and coordination.
Strategic group	A strategic group is a concept used in strategic management that groups companies within an industry that have similar business models or similar combinations of strategies.
Complexity	The technical sophistication of the product and hence the amount of understanding required to use it is referred to as complexity. It is the opposite of simplicity.
Galbraith	Galbraith was a prolific author, producing four dozen books and over a thousand articles on various subjects. His most famous works were perhaps a popular trilogy of books on economics, "American Capitalism" (1952), "The Affluent Society (1958)", and "The New Industrial State" (1967).
Hierarchy	A system of grouping people in an organization according to rank from the top down in which all subordinate managers must report to one person is called a hierarchy.

Diversification	Investing in a collection of assets whose returns do not always move together, with the result that overall risk is lower than for individual assets is referred to as diversification.
Joint venture	Joint venture refers to an undertaking by two parties for a specific purpose and duration, taking any of several legal forms.
Microsoft	Microsoft is a multinational computer technology corporation with 2004 global annual sales of US$39.79 billion and 71,553 employees in 102 countries and regions as of July 2006. It develops, manufactures, licenses, and supports a wide range of software products for computing devices.
Exchange	The trade of things of value between buyer and seller so that each is better off after the trade is called the exchange.
Organizational strategy	The process of positioning the Organization in the competitive environment and implementing actions to compete successfully is an organizational strategy.
Harvard Business Review	Harvard Business Review is a research-based magazine written for business practitioners, it claims a high ranking business readership and enjoys the reverence of academics, executives, and management consultants. It has been the frequent publishing home for well known scholars and management thinkers.
Multinational corporations	Firms that own production facilities in two or more countries and produce and sell their products globally are referred to as multinational corporations.
Multinational corporation	An organization that manufactures and markets products in many different countries and has multinational stock ownership and multinational management is referred to as multinational corporation.
Bounded rationality	The understanding that rational decisions are very much bounded or constrained by practical constraints is referred to as bounded rationality.
Task environment	Task environment includes specific organizations, groups, and individuals that influence the organization.
Corporation	A legal entity chartered by a state or the Federal government that is distinct and separate from the individuals who own it is a corporation. This separation gives the corporation unique powers which other legal entities lack.
Economy	The income, expenditures, and resources that affect the cost of running a business and household are called an economy.
Organizational learning	Organizational learning is an area of knowledge within organizational theory that studies models and theories about the way an organization learns and adapts.
Management consulting	Management consulting refers to both the practice of helping companies to improve performance through analysis of existing business problems and development of future plans, as well as to the firms that specialize in this sort of consulting.
Accounting	A system that collects and processes financial information about an organization and reports that information to decision makers is referred to as accounting.
Service	Service refers to a "non tangible product" that is not embodied in a physical good and that typically effects some change in another product, person, or institution. Contrasts with good.
Interest	In finance and economics, interest is the price paid by a borrower for the use of a lender's money. In other words, interest is the amount of paid to "rent" money for a period of time.
Diversification	Diversification strategy is a corporate strategy that takes the organization away from both

strategy	its current markets and products, as opposed to either market or product development.
Functional structure	A type of structure in which units and departments are organized based on the activity or function that they perform is called the functional structure.
Cooperative	A business owned and controlled by the people who use it, producers, consumers, or workers with similar needs who pool their resources for mutual gain is called cooperative.
Strategic planning	The process of determining the major goals of the organization and the policies and strategies for obtaining and using resources to achieve those goals is called strategic planning.
Manufacturing	Production of goods primarily by the application of labor and capital to raw materials and other intermediate inputs, in contrast to agriculture, mining, forestry, fishing, and services a manufacturing.
Business unit	The lowest level of the company which contains the set of functions that carry a product through its life span from concept through manufacture, distribution, sales and service is a business unit.
Strategic business unit	Strategic business unit is understood as a business unit within the overall corporate identity which is distinguishable from other business because it serves a defined external market where management can conduct strategic planning in relation to products and markets. When companies become really large, they are best thought of as being composed of a number of businesses
Bottleneck	An operation where the work to be performed approaches or exceeds the capacity available to do it is a bottleneck.
Intel	Intel Corporation, founded in 1968 and based in Santa Clara, California, USA, is the world's largest semiconductor company. Intel is best known for its PC microprocessors, where it maintains roughly 80% market share.
Authority	Authority in agency law, refers to an agent's ability to affect his principal's legal relations with third parties. Also used to refer to an actor's legal power or ability to do something. In addition, sometimes used to refer to a statute, case, or other legal source that justifies a particular result.
Competitive advantage	A business is said to have a competitive advantage when its unique strengths, often based on cost, quality, time, and innovation, offer consumers a greater percieved value and there by differtiating it from its competitors.
Strategic control	Strategic control processes allow managers to evaluate a company's marketing program from a critical long-term perspective. This involves a detailed and objective analysis of a company's organization and its ability to maximize its strengths and market opportunities.
Financial control	A process in which a firm periodically compares its actual revenues, costs, and expenses with its projected ones is called financial control.
Structural change	Changes in the relative importance of different areas of an economy over time, usually measured in terms of their share of output, employment, or total spending is structural change.
Effective manager	Leader of a team that consistently achieves high performance goals is an effective manager.
Strategy implementation	Strategy implementation refers to the process of devising structures and allocating resources to enact the strategy a company has chosen.
Cost Leadership Strategy	Using a serious commitment to reducing expenses that, in turn, lowers the price of the items sold in a relatively broad array of market segments is called cost leadership strategy.

Go to **Cram101.com** for the Practice Tests for this Chapter.

Cost leadership	Organization's ability to achieve lower costs relative to competitors through productivity and efficiency improvements, elimination of waste, and tight cost control is cost leadership.
Differentiation Strategy	Differentiation strategy requires innovation and significant points of difference in product offerings, brand image, higher quality, advanced technology, or superior service in a relatively broad array of market segments.
Marketing	Promoting and selling products or services to customers, or prospective customers, is referred to as marketing.
Integrating mechanisms	Integrating mechanisms refers to mechanisms for achieving coordination between subunits within an organization.
Incentive	An incentive is any factor (financial or non-financial) that provides a motive for a particular course of action, or counts as a reason for preferring one choice to the alternatives.
Profit center	Responsibility center where the manager is accountable for revenues and costs is referred to as a profit center.
Profit	Profit refers to the return to the resource entrepreneurial ability; total revenue minus total cost.
Unrelated diversification	A business strategy in which an organization operates several businesses that are not associated with one another is unrelated diversification.
Decentralization	Decentralization is the process of redistributing decision-making closer to the point of service or action. This gives freedom to managers at lower levels of the organization to make decisions.
Host country	The country in which the parent-country organization seeks to locate or has already located a facility is a host country.
Multidomestic strategy	Emphasizing the need to be responsive to the unique conditions prevailing in different national markets is referred to as a multidomestic strategy.
Divisional structure	A divisional structure is found in diversified organizations, they contain separate divisions that are based around individual product lines or on the geographic areas of the markets being served.
Global strategy	Global strategy refers to strategy focusing on increasing profitability by reaping cost reductions from experience curve and location economies.
Transnational	Transnational focuses on the heightened interconnectivity between people all around the world and the loosening of boundaries between countries.
Transnational strategy	Plan to exploit experience-based cost and location economies, transfer core competencies with the firm, and pay attention to local responsiveness is called transnational strategy.
Acquisition	A company's purchase of the property and obligations of another company is an acquisition.
Merger	Merger refers to the combination of two firms into a single firm.
Franchising	Franchising is a method of doing business wherein a franchisor licenses trademarks and tried and proven methods of doing business to a franchisee in exchange for a recurring payment, and usually a percentage piece of gross sales or gross profits as well as the annual fees. The term " franchising " is used to describe a wide variety of business systems which may or may not fall into the legal definition provided above.
Capital expenditures	Major investments in long-term assets such as land, buildings, equipment, or research and development are referred to as capital expenditures.

Capital expenditure	A substantial expenditure that is used by a company to acquire or upgrade physical assets such as equipment, property, industrial buildings, including those which improve the quality and life of an asset is referred to as a capital expenditure.
Operation	A standardized method or technique that is performed repetitively, often on different materials resulting in different finished goods is called an operation.
Value chain	The sequence of business functions in which usefulness is added to the products or services of a company is a value chain.
Strategic alliance	Strategic alliance refers to a long-term partnership between two or more companies established to help each company build competitive market advantages.
Subcontractor	A subcontractor is an individual or in many cases a business that signs a contract to perform part or all of the obligations of another's contract. A subcontractor is hired by a general or prime contractor to perform a specific task as part of the overall project.
Contract	A contract is a "promise" or an "agreement" that is enforced or recognized by the law. In the civil law, a contract is considered to be part of the general law of obligations.
Production	The creation of finished goods and services using the factors of production: land, labor, capital, entrepreneurship, and knowledge.
Competitor	Other organizations in the same industry or type of business that provide a good or service to the same set of customers is referred to as a competitor.
Cisco Systems	While Cisco Systems was not the first company to develop and sell a router (a device that forwards computer traffic from one network to another), it did create the first commercially successful multi-protocol router to allow previously incompatible computers to communicate using different network protocols.
Outsourcing	Outsourcing refers to a production activity that was previously done inside a firm or plant that is now conducted outside that firm or plant.
Principal	In agency law, one under whose direction an agent acts and for whose benefit that agent acts is a principal.
Gain	In finance, gain is a profit or an increase in value of an investment such as a stock or bond. Gain is calculated by fair market value or the proceeds from the sale of the investment minus the sum of the purchase price and all costs associated with it.
Environmental complexity	The number of environmental components that impinge on organizational decision-making is called environmental complexity.
Stakeholder	A stakeholder is an individual or group with a vested interest in or expectation for organizational performance. Usually stakeholders can either have an effect on or are affected by an organization.
Foundation	A Foundation is a type of philanthropic organization set up by either individuals or institutions as a legal entity (either as a corporation or trust) with the purpose of distributing grants to support causes in line with the goals of the foundation.
Scope	Scope of a project is the sum total of all projects products and their requirements or features.
Economies of scope	The ability to use one resource to provide many different products and services is referred to as economies of scope.
Economies of scale	In economics, returns to scale and economies of scale are related terms that describe what happens as the scale of production increases. They are different terms and not to be used interchangeably.

Go to **Cram101.com** for the Practice Tests for this Chapter.

Product line	A group of products that are physically similar or are intended for a similar market are called the product line.
Task force	A temporary team or committee formed to solve a specific short-term problem involving several departments is the task force.
Committee	A long-lasting, sometimes permanent team in the organization structure created to deal with tasks that recur regularly is the committee.
Preference	The act of a debtor in paying or securing one or more of his creditors in a manner more favorable to them than to other creditors or to the exclusion of such other creditors is a preference. In the absence of statute, a preference is perfectly good, but to be legal it must be bona fide, and not a mere subterfuge of the debtor to secure a future benefit to himself or to prevent the application of his property to his debts.
Centralization	A structural policy in which decision-making authority is concentrated at the top of the organizational hierarchy is referred to as centralization.
Allocate	Allocate refers to the assignment of income for various tax purposes. A multistate corporation's nonbusiness income usually is distributed to the state where the nonbusiness assets are located; it is not apportioned with the rest of the entity's income.
Subsidiary	A company that is controlled by another company or corporation is a subsidiary.
Trend	Trend refers to the long-term movement of an economic variable, such as its average rate of increase or decrease over enough years to encompass several business cycles.
Market position	Market position is a measure of the position of a company or product on a market.
Expatriate	Employee sent by his or her company to live and manage operations in a different country is called an expatriate.
Business operations	Business operations are those activities involved in the running of a business for the purpose of producing value for the stakeholders. The outcome of business operations is the harvesting of value from assets owned by a business.
Restructuring	Restructuring is the corporate management term for the act of partially dismantling and reorganizing a company for the purpose of making it more efficient and therefore more profitable.
Textron	Textron today is a multi-industry company with a portfolio of familiar brands such as Bell Helicopter, E-Z-GO, Cessna Aircraft, and Greenlee, among others. With total revenues of $10 billion, and more than 37,000 employees in nearly 33 countries, Textron is headquartered in Providence, RI, USA, and currently ranked 190th on the Fortune 500 list of largest companies
Competitiveness	Competitiveness usually refers to characteristics that permit a firm to compete effectively with other firms due to low cost or superior technology, perhaps internationally.
Investment	Investment refers to spending for the production and accumulation of capital and additions to inventories. In a financial sense, buying an asset with the expectation of making a return.
Audit	An examination of the financial reports to ensure that they represent what they claim and conform with generally accepted accounting principles is referred to as audit.
Cash flow	In finance, cash flow refers to the amounts of cash being received and spent by a business during a defined period of time, sometimes tied to a specific project. Most of the time they are being used to determine gaps in the liquid position of a company.
Performance appraisal	An evaluation in which the performance level of employees is measured against established standards to make decisions about promotions, compenzation, additional training, or firing is referred to as performance appraisal.

Go to **Cram101.com** for the Practice Tests for this Chapter.
And, **NEVER** highlight a book again!

Market capitalization	Market capitalization is a business term that refers to the aggregate value of a firm's outstanding common shares. In essence, market capitalization reflects the total value of a firm's equity currently available on the market. This measure differs from equity value to the extent that a firm has outstanding stock options or other securities convertible to common shares. The size and growth of a firm's market capitalization is often one of the critical measurements of a public company's success or failure.
Revenue	Revenue is a U.S. business term for the amount of money that a company receives from its activities, mostly from sales of products and/or services to customers.
Fund	Independent accounting entity with a self-balancing set of accounts segregated for the purposes of carrying on specific activities is referred to as a fund.
Stock	In financial terminology, stock is the capital raized by a corporation, through the issuance and sale of shares.
Analyst	Analyst refers to a person or tool with a primary function of information analysis, generally with a more limited, practical and short term set of goals than a researcher.
Airbus	In 2003, for the first time in its 33-year history, Airbus delivered more jet-powered airliners than Boeing. Boeing states that the Boeing 777 has outsold its Airbus counterparts, which include the A340 family as well as the A330-300. The smaller A330-200 competes with the 767, outselling its Boeing counterpart.
Boeing	Boeing is the world's largest aircraft manufacturer by revenue. Headquartered in Chicago, Illinois, Boeing is the second-largest defense contractor in the world. In 2005, the company was the world's largest civil aircraft manufacturer in terms of value.
Bottom line	The bottom line is net income on the last line of a income statement.
Slump	A decline in performance, in a firm is a slump in sales or profits, or in a country is a slump in output or employment.
Operating profit	Operating profit is a measure of a company's earning power from ongoing operations, equal to earnings before the deduction of interest payments and income taxes.
Portfolio	In finance, a portfolio is a collection of investments held by an institution or a private individual. Holding but not always a portfolio is part of an investment and risk-limiting strategy called diversification. By owning several assets, certain types of risk (in particular specific risk) can be reduced.
Security	Security refers to a claim on the borrower future income that is sold by the borrower to the lender. A security is a type of transferable interest representing financial value.
Channel	Channel, in communications (sometimes called communications channel), refers to the medium used to convey information from a sender (or transmitter) to a receiver.
Capital market	A financial market in which long-term debt and equity instruments are traded is referred to as a capital market. The capital market includes the stock market and the bond market.
Comprehensive	A comprehensive refers to a layout accurate in size, color, scheme, and other necessary details to show how a final ad will look. For presentation only, never for reproduction.
Productivity	Productivity refers to the total output of goods and services in a given period of time divided by work hours.
Liaison	An individual who serves as a bridge between groups, tying groups together and facilitating the communication flow needed to integrate group activities is a liaison.
Integration	Economic integration refers to reducing barriers among countries to transactions and to movements of goods, capital, and labor, including harmonization of laws, regulations, and

223

standards. Integrated markets theoretically function as a unified market.

Matrix organization	Matrix organization refers to an organization in which specialists from different parts of the organization are brought together to work on specific projects but still remain part of a traditional line-and-staff structure.
Matrix structure	An organizational structure which typically crosses a functional approach with a product or service-based design, often resulting in employees having two bosses is the matrix structure.
Evaluation	The consumer's appraisal of the product or brand on important attributes is called evaluation.
Tangible	Having a physical existence is referred to as the tangible. Personal property other than real estate, such as cars, boats, stocks, or other assets.
Human resource management	The process of evaluating human resource needs, finding people to fill those needs, and getting the best work from each employee by providing the right incentives and job environment, all with the goal of meeting the needs of the firm are called human resource management.
Resource management	Resource management is the efficient and effective deployment of an organization's resources when they are needed. Such resources may include financial resources, inventory, human skills, production resources, or information technology.
Corporate level	Corporate level refers to level at which top management directs overall strategy for the entire organization.
Horizontal integration	Horizontal integration refers to production of different varieties of the same product, or different products at the same level of processing, within a single firm. This may, but need not, take place in subsidiaries in different countries.
Market development	Selling existing products to new markets is called market development.
Human resources	Human resources refers to the individuals within the firm, and to the portion of the firm's organization that deals with hiring, firing, training, and other personnel issues.
Best practice	Best practice is a management idea which asserts that there is a technique, method, process, activity, incentive or reward that is more effective at delivering a particular outcome than any other technique, method, process, etc.
Consultant	A professional that provides expert advice in a particular field or area in which customers occassionaly require this type of knowledge is a consultant.
Gold standard	The gold standard is a monetary system in which the standard economic unit of account is a fixed weight of gold.
Brand management	Brand management is the application of marketing techniques to a specific product, product line, or brand. It seeks to increase the product's perceived value to the customer and thereby increase brand franchise and brand equity.
Brand	A name, symbol, or design that identifies the goods or services of one seller or group of sellers and distinguishes them from the goods and services of competitors is a brand.
EBay	eBay manages an online auction and shopping website, where people buy and sell goods and services worldwide.
Homogeneous	In the context of procurement/purchasing, homogeneous is used to describe goods that do not vary in their essential characteristic irrespective of the source of supply.
Product development	Combinations of work teams and problem-solving teams that create new designs for products or services that will satisfy customer needs are product development teams.

Go to **Cram101.com** for the Practice Tests for this Chapter.

225

teams	
Product development	In business and engineering, new product development is the complete process of bringing a new product to market. There are two parallel aspects to this process : one involves product engineering ; the other marketing analysis. Marketers see new product development as the first stage in product life cycle management, engineers as part of Product Lifecycle Management.
Differentiated product	A firm's product that is not identical to products of other firms in the same industry is a differentiated product.
Standardized product	Standardized product refers to a product whose buyers are indifferent to the seller from whom they purchase it, as long as the price charged by all sellers is the same; a product all units of which are identical and thus are perfect substitutes.
Process improvement	Process improvement is the activity of elevating the performance of a process, especially that of a business process with regard to its goal.
Professional development	Professional development refers to vocational education with specific reference to continuing education of the person undertaking it in the area of employment, it may also provide opportunities for other career paths.
Specialist	A specialist is a trader who makes a market in one or several stocks and holds the limit order book for those stocks.
Resource allocation	Resource allocation refers to the manner in which an economy distributes its resources among the potential uses so as to produce a particular set of final goods.
Shareholder	A shareholder is an individual or company (including a corporation) that legally owns one or more shares of stock in a joined stock company.
General Motors	General Motors is the world's largest automaker. Founded in 1908, today it employs about 327,000 people around the world. With global headquarters in Detroit, it manufactures its cars and trucks in 33 countries.
DuPont	DuPont was the inventor of CFCs (along with General Motors) and the largest producer of these ozone depleting chemicals (used primarily in aerosol sprays and refrigerants) in the world, with a 25% market share in the late 1980s.
Strategic intent	Strategic intent is when a firm relentlessly pursues a difficult strategic goa and concentrates its competitive actions and energies on achieving that goal.
Drucker	Drucker as a business thinker took off in the 1940s, when his initial writings on politics and society won him access to the internal workings of General Motors, which was one of the largest companies in the world at that time. His experiences in Europe had left him fascinated with the problem of authority.
Context	The effect of the background under which a message often takes on more and richer meaning is a context. Context is especially important in cross-cultural interactions because some cultures are said to be high context or low context.
Extension	Extension refers to an out-of-court settlement in which creditors agree to allow the firm more time to meet its financial obligations. A new repayment schedule will be developed, subject to the acceptance of creditors.
Chief executive officer	A chief executive officer is the highest-ranking corporate officer or executive officer of a corporation, or agency. In closely held corporations, it is general business culture that the office chief executive officer is also the chairman of the board.
Information system	An information system is a system whether automated or manual, that comprises people, machines, and/or methods organized to collect, process, transmit, and disseminate data that

Go to **Cram101.com** for the Practice Tests for this Chapter.

represent user information.

Growth strategy	A strategy based on investing in companies and sectors which are growing faster than their peers is a growth strategy. The benefits are usually in the form of capital gains rather than dividends.
Compliance	A type of influence process where a receiver accepts the position advocated by a source to obtain favorable outcomes or to avoid punishment is the compliance.
Regulation	Regulation refers to restrictions state and federal laws place on business with regard to the conduct of its activities.
Asset	An item of property, such as land, capital, money, a share in ownership, or a claim on others for future payment, such as a bond or a bank deposit is an asset.
Eastman Chemical Company	Eastman Chemical Company is a large supplier of industrial chemicals. It was formerly the chemical division of the Eastman Kodak Company and known as Tennessee Eastman, but was spun off by Kodak in an effort by that company to reduce its operations to its "core" photographic businesses
Public company	A public company is a company owned by the public rather than by a relatively few individuals. There are two different meanings for this term: (1) A company that is owned by stockholders who are members of the general public and trade shares publicly, often through a listing on a stock exchange. Ownership is open to anyone that has the money and inclination to buy shares in the company. It is differentiated from privately held companies where the shares are held by a small group of individuals, who are often members of one or a small group of families or otherwise related individuals, or other companies. The variant of this type of company in the United Kingdom and Ireland is known as a public limited compan, and (2) A government-owned corporation. This meaning of a "public company" comes from the fact that government debt is sometimes referred to as "public debt" although there are no "public bonds", government finance is sometimes called "public finance", among similar uses. This is the less-common meaning.
Eastman Kodak	Eastman Kodak Company is an American multinational public company producing photographic materials and equipment. Long known for its wide range of photographic film products, it has focused in recent years on three main businesses: digital photography, health imaging, and printing. This company remains the largest supplier of films in the world, both for the amateur and professional markets.
Supply	Supply is the aggregate amount of any material good that can be called into being at a certain price point; it comprises one half of the equation of supply and demand. In classical economic theory, a curve representing supply is one of the factors that produce price.
Raw material	Raw material refers to a good that has not been transformed by production; a primary product.
Reorganization	Reorganization occurs, among other instances, when one corporation acquires another in a merger or acquisition, a single corporation divides into two or more entities, or a corporation makes a substantial change in its capital structure.
Product management	Product management is a function within a company dealing with the day-to-day management and welfare of a product or family of products at all stages of the product lifecycle. The product management function is responsible for defining the products in the marketing mix.
Intellectual property	In law, intellectual property is an umbrella term for various legal entitlements which attach to certain types of information, ideas, or other intangibles in their expressed form. The holder of this legal entitlement is generally entitled to exercise various exclusive rights in relation to its subject matter.
Business model	A business model is the instrument by which a business intends to generate revenue and

Go to **Cram101.com** for the Practice Tests for this Chapter.

profits. It is a summary of how a company means to serve its employees and customers, and involves both strategy (what an business intends to do) as well as an implementation.

Property
Assets defined in the broadest legal sense. Property includes the unrealized receivables of a cash basis taxpayer, but not services rendered.

Leverage
Leverage is using given resources in such a way that the potential positive or negative outcome is magnified. In finance, this generally refers to borrowing.

Consumer good
Products and services that are ultimately consumed rather than used in the production of another good are a consumer good.

Parent company
Parent company refers to the entity that has a controlling influence over another company. It may have its own operations, or it may have been set up solely for the purpose of owning the Subject Company.

Commercial bank
A firm that engages in the business of banking is a commercial bank.

Synergy
Corporate synergy occurs when corporations interact congruently. A corporate synergy refers to a financial benefit that a corporation expects to realize when it merges with or acquires another corporation.

Functional organization
Functional organization is a method of organization in which chapters and sections of a manual correspond to business functions, not specific departments or work groups.

Core business
The core business of an organization is an idealized construct intended to express that organization's "main" or "essential" activity.

Forming
The first stage of team development, where the team is formed and the objectives for the team are set is referred to as forming.

Market niche
A market niche or niche market is a focused, targetable portion of a market. By definition, then, a business that focuses on a niche market is addressing a need for a product or service that is not being addressed by mainstream providers.

Niche
In industry, a niche is a situation or an activity perfectly suited to a person. A niche can imply a working position or an area suited to a person who occupies it. Basically, a job where a person is able to succeed and thrive.

Electronic Arts
Electronic Arts is an American developer, marketer, publisher, and distributor of computer and video games. Established in 1982 by Trip Hawkins, the company was a pioneer of the early home computer games industry and was notable for promoting the designers and programmers responsible for their games.

Nintendo
Nintendo has the reputation of historically being both the oldest intact company in the video game console market and one of the most influential and well-known console manufacturers, as well as being the most dominant entity in the handheld console market.

Sony
Sony is a multinational corporation and one of the world's largest media conglomerates founded in Tokyo, Japan. One of its divisions Sony Electronics is one of the leading manufacturers of electronics, video, communications, and information technology products for the consumer and professional markets.

Hasbro
Hasbro originated with the Mr. Potato Head toy. Mr. Potato Head was the invention of George Lerner in the late 1940s. The idea was originally sold to a breakfast cereal manufacturer so that the separate parts could be distributed as cereal package premiums.

Domestic
From or in one's own country. A domestic producer is one that produces inside the home country. A domestic price is the price inside the home country. Opposite of 'foreign' or 'world.'.

Go to **Cram101.com** for the Practice Tests for this Chapter.

Total revenue | Total revenue refers to the total number of dollars received by a firm from the sale of a product; equal to the total expenditures for the product produced by the firm; equal to the quantity sold multiplied by the price at which it is sold.

233

Functional structure	A type of structure in which units and departments are organized based on the activity or function that they perform is called the functional structure.
Diversification strategy	Diversification strategy is a corporate strategy that takes the organization away from both its current markets and products, as opposed to either market or product development.
Diversification	Investing in a collection of assets whose returns do not always move together, with the result that overall risk is lower than for individual assets is referred to as diversification.
Organizational structure	Organizational structure is the way in which the interrelated groups of an organization are constructed. From a managerial point of view the main concerns are ensuring effective communication and coordination.
International strategy	Trying to create value by transferring core competencies to foreign markets where indigenous competitors lack those competencies is called international strategy.
Firm	An organization that employs resources to produce a good or service for profit and owns and operates one or more plants is referred to as a firm.
Sony	Sony is a multinational corporation and one of the world's largest media conglomerates founded in Tokyo, Japan. One of its divisions Sony Electronics is one of the leading manufacturers of electronics, video, communications, and information technology products for the consumer and professional markets.
Wall Street Journal	Dow Jones & Company was founded in 1882 by reporters Charles Dow, Edward Jones and Charles Bergstresser. Jones converted the small Customers' Afternoon Letter into The Wall Street Journal, first published in 1889, and began delivery of the Dow Jones News Service via telegraph. The Journal featured the Jones 'Average', the first of several indexes of stock and bond prices on the New York Stock Exchange.
Journal	Book of original entry, in which transactions are recorded in a general ledger system, is referred to as a journal.
International management	International management refers to the management of business operations conducted in more than one country.
Corporate governance	Corporate governance is the set of processes, customs, policies, laws and institutions affecting the way a corporation is directed, administered or controlled.
Global competition	Global competition exists when competitive conditions across national markets are linked strongly enough to form a true international market and when leading competitors compete head to head in many different countries.
Management	Management characterizes the process of leading and directing all or part of an organization, often a business, through the deployment and manipulation of resources. Early twentieth-century management writer Mary Parker Follett defined management as "the art of getting things done through people."
Service	Service refers to a "non tangible product" that is not embodied in a physical good and that typically effects some change in another product, person, or institution. Contrasts with good.
Multinational enterprise	Multinational enterprise refers to a firm, usually a corporation, that operates in two or more countries.
Social capital	Capital that provides services to the public. Most social capital takes the form of public goods and public services.
Business Week	Business Week is a business magazine published by McGraw-Hill. It was first published in 1929 under the direction of Malcolm Muir, who was serving as president of the McGraw-Hill

Go to **Cram101.com** for the Practice Tests for this Chapter.

235

	Publishing company at the time. It is considered to be the standard both in industry and among students.
Enterprise	Enterprise refers to another name for a business organization. Other similar terms are business firm, sometimes simply business, sometimes simply firm, as well as company, and entity.
Investment	Investment refers to spending for the production and accumulation of capital and additions to inventories. In a financial sense, buying an asset with the expectation of making a return.
Keiretsu	Keiretsu is a set of companies with interlocking business relationships and shareholdings. It is a type of business group.
Capital	Capital generally refers to financial wealth, especially that used to start or maintain a business. In classical economics, capital is one of four factors of production, the others being land and labor and entrepreneurship.
Business strategy	Business strategy, which refers to the aggregated operational strategies of single business firm or that of an SBU in a diversified corporation refers to the way in which a firm competes in its chosen arenas.
Business ethics	The study of what makes up good and bad conduct as related to business activities and values is business ethics.
Interest	In finance and economics, interest is the price paid by a borrower for the use of a lender's money. In other words, interest is the amount of paid to "rent" money for a period of time.
Financial management	The job of managing a firm's resources so it can meet its goals and objectives is called financial management.
Outside director	A member of the board of directors who is not an officer of the corporation is called outside director.
Strategic management	A philosophy of management that links strategic planning with dayto-day decision making. Strategic management seeks a fit between an organization's external and internal environments.
Foreign subsidiary	A company owned in a foreign country by another company is referred to as foreign subsidiary.
Management team	A management team is directly responsible for managing the day-to-day operations (and profitability) of a company.
Agency theory	The analysis of how asymmetric information problems affect economic behavior is known as agency theory.
Acquisition	A company's purchase of the property and obligations of another company is an acquisition.
Subsidiary	A company that is controlled by another company or corporation is a subsidiary.
Stock option	A stock option is a specific type of option that uses the stock itself as an underlying instrument to determine the option's pay-off and therefore its value.
Equity	Equity is the name given to the set of legal principles, in countries following the English common law tradition, which supplement strict rules of law where their application would operate harshly, so as to achieve what is sometimes referred to as "natural justice."
Option	A contract that gives the purchaser the option to buy or sell the underlying financial instrument at a specified price, called the exercise price or strike price, within a specific period of time.
Stock	In financial terminology, stock is the capital raized by a corporation, through the issuance

Go to **Cram101.com** for the Practice Tests for this Chapter.

and sale of shares.

Institutional investors	Institutional investors refers to large organizations such as pension funds, mutual funds, insurance companies, and banks that invest their own funds or the funds of others.
Shareholder	A shareholder is an individual or company (including a corporation) that legally owns one or more shares of stock in a joined stock company.
Financial analysis	Financial analysis is the analysis of the accounts and the economic prospects of a firm.
Restructuring	Restructuring is the corporate management term for the act of partially dismantling and reorganizing a company for the purpose of making it more efficient and therefore more profitable.
Poison pill	Poison pill refers to a strategy that makes a firm unattractive as a potential takeover candidate. These are attempts by a potential acquirer to obtain a control block of shares in a target company, and thereby gain control of the board and, through it, the company's management.
Divestiture	In finance and economics, divestiture is the reduction of some kind of asset, for either financial or social goals. A divestment is the opposite of an investment.
Corporation	A legal entity chartered by a state or the Federal government that is distinct and separate from the individuals who own it is a corporation. This separation gives the corporation unique powers which other legal entities lack.
Property	Assets defined in the broadest legal sense. Property includes the unrealized receivables of a cash basis taxpayer, but not services rendered.
Reorganization	Reorganization occurs, among other instances, when one corporation acquires another in a merger or acquisition, a single corporation divides into two or more entities, or a corporation makes a substantial change in its capital structure.
Bankruptcy	Bankruptcy is a legally declared inability or impairment of ability of an individual or organization to pay their creditors.
Economics	The social science dealing with the use of scarce resources to obtain the maximum satisfaction of society's virtually unlimited economic wants is an economics.
Activism	Activism, in a general sense, can be described as intentional action to bring about social or political change. This action is in support of, or opposition to, one side of an often controversial argument.
Conflict of interest	A conflict that occurs when a corporate officer or director enters into a transaction with the corporation in which he or she has a personal interest is a conflict of interest.
Composition	An out-of-court settlement in which creditors agree to accept a fractional settlement on their original claim is referred to as composition.
Leadership	Management merely consists of leadership applied to business situations; or in other words: management forms a sub-set of the broader process of leadership.
Red herring	Red herring prospectus is an initial prospectus to be submitted by a company which issues IPO. This prospectus has to be filed with SEC. It containing all the information about the company except for the offer price and the effective date, which aren't known at that time.
Committee	A long-lasting, sometimes permanent team in the organization structure created to deal with tasks that recur regularly is the committee.
Shareholder value	For a publicly traded company, shareholder value is the part of its capitalization that is equity as opposed to long-term debt. In the case of only one type of stock, this would

	roughly be the number of outstanding shares times current shareprice.
Entrepreneurship	The assembling of resources to produce new or improved products and technologies is referred to as entrepreneurship.
Industry	A group of firms that produce identical or similar products is an industry. It is also used specifically to refer to an area of economic production focused on manufacturing which involves large amounts of capital investment before any profit can be realized, also called "heavy industry".
Harvard Business Review	Harvard Business Review is a research-based magazine written for business practitioners, it claims a high ranking business readership and enjoys the reverence of academics, executives, and management consultants. It has been the frequent publishing home for well known scholars and management thinkers.
Reciprocity	An industrial buying practice in which two organizations agree to purchase each other's products and services is called reciprocity.
Diffusion	Diffusion is the process by which a new idea or new product is accepted by the market. The rate of diffusion is the speed that the new idea spreads from one consumer to the next.
Exchange	The trade of things of value between buyer and seller so that each is better off after the trade is called the exchange.
Mergers and acquisitions	The phrase mergers and acquisitions refers to the aspect of corporate finance strategy and management dealing with the merging and acquiring of different companies as well as other assets. Usually mergers occur in a friendly setting where executives from the respective companies participate in a due diligence process to ensure a successful combination of all parts.
Corporate Strategy	Corporate strategy is concerned with the firm's choice of business, markets and activities and thus it defines the overall scope and direction of the business.
Capital market	A financial market in which long-term debt and equity instruments are traded is referred to as a capital market. The capital market includes the stock market and the bond market.
Accounting	A system that collects and processes financial information about an organization and reports that information to decision makers is referred to as accounting.
Innovation	Innovation refers to the first commercially successful introduction of a new product, the use of a new method of production, or the creation of a new form of business organization.
Context	The effect of the background under which a message often takes on more and richer meaning is a context. Context is especially important in cross-cultural interactions because some cultures are said to be high context or low context.
Merger	Merger refers to the combination of two firms into a single firm.
Market	A market is, as defined in economics, a social arrangement that allows buyers and sellers to discover information and carry out a voluntary exchange of goods or services.
Financial economics	That branch of economics which analyzes how rational investors should invest their funds to attain their objectives in the best possible manner is called financial economics.
Theory of the firm	The theory of the firm consists of a number of economic theories which describe the nature of the firm (company or corporation), including its behavior and its relationship with the market.
Gainsharing	A form of group compenzation based on group or plant performance that does not become part of the employee's base salary is gainsharing.
Agency cost	An agency cost is the cost incurred by an organization that is associated with problems such

as divergent management-shareholder objectives and information asymmetry.

Contract

A contract is a "promise" or an "agreement" that is enforced or recognized by the law. In the civil law, a contract is considered to be part of the general law of obligations.

Policy

Similar to a script in that a policy can be a less than completely rational decision-making method. Involves the use of a pre-existing set of decision steps for any problem that presents itself.

Labor

People's physical and mental talents and efforts that are used to help produce goods and services are called labor.

International diversification

Achieving diversification through many different foreign investments that are influenced by a variety of factors is referred to as international diversification. By diversifying across nations whose economic cycles are not perfectly correlated, investors can typically reduce the variability of their returns.

Conglomerate merger

A conglomerate merger is whereby two companies or organizations which have no common interest and nor competitors or have or could have the same supplier or customers merger.

Transaction cost

A transaction cost is a cost incurred in making an economic exchange. For example, most people, when buying or selling a stock, must pay a commission to their broker; that commission is a transaction cost of doing the stock deal.

Collectivism

Collectivism is a term used to describe that things should be owned by the group and used for the benefit of all rather than being owned by individuals.

Conglomerate

A conglomerate is a large company that consists of divisions of often seemingly unrelated businesses.

Marketing

Promoting and selling products or services to customers, or prospective customers, is referred to as marketing.

Chief executive officer

A chief executive officer is the highest-ranking corporate officer or executive officer of a corporation, or agency. In closely held corporations, it is general business culture that the office chief executive officer is also the chairman of the board.

Corporate finance

Corporate finance is a specific area of finance dealing with the financial decisions corporations make and the tools as well as analyses used to make these decisions. The discipline as a whole may be divided among long-term and short-term decisions and techniques with the primary goal being the enhancing of corporate value by ensuring that return on capital exceeds cost of capital, without taking excessive financial risks.

Free cash flow

Cash provided by operating activities adjusted for capital expenditures and dividends paid is referred to as free cash flow.

Stockholder

A stockholder is an individual or company (including a corporation) that legally owns one or more shares of stock in a joined stock company. The shareholders are the owners of a corporation. Companies listed at the stock market strive to enhance shareholder value.

Controlling

A management function that involves determining whether or not an organization is progressing toward its goals and objectives, and taking corrective action if it is not is called controlling.

Cash flow

In finance, cash flow refers to the amounts of cash being received and spent by a business during a defined period of time, sometimes tied to a specific project. Most of the time they are being used to determine gaps in the liquid position of a company.

Takeover

A takeover in business refers to one company (the acquirer) purchasing another (the target). Such events resemble mergers, but without the formation of a new company.

Go to **Cram101.com** for the Practice Tests for this Chapter.

Compensation package	The total array of money, incentives, benefits, perquisites, and awards provided by the organization to an employee is the compensation package.
Fiscal year	A fiscal year is a 12-month period used for calculating annual ("yearly") financial reports in businesses and other organizations. In many jurisdictions, regulatory laws regarding accounting require such reports once per twelve months, but do not require that the twelve months constitute a calendar year (i.e. January to December).
Net income	Net income is equal to the income that a firm has after subtracting costs and expenses from the total revenue. Expenses will typically include tax expense.
Net sales	Gross sales less sales returns and allowances and sales discounts are referred to as net sales.
Board of directors	The group of individuals elected by the stockholders of a corporation to oversee its operations is a board of directors.
Fiduciary	Fiduciary refers to one who holds goods in trust for another or one who holds a position of trust and confidence.
Inside director	A member of the board of directors who is either an employee or stakeholder in the company is an inside director.
Incentive	An incentive is any factor (financial or non-financial) that provides a motive for a particular course of action, or counts as a reason for preferring one choice to the alternatives.
Alignment	Term that refers to optimal coordination among disparate departments and divisions within a firm is referred to as alignment.
Stakeholder	A stakeholder is an individual or group with a vested interest in or expectation for organizational performance. Usually stakeholders can either have an effect on or are affected by an organization.
Competitiveness	Competitiveness usually refers to characteristics that permit a firm to compete effectively with other firms due to low cost or superior technology, perhaps internationally.
Consideration	Consideration in contract law, a basic requirement for an enforceable agreement under traditional contract principles, defined in this text as legal value, bargained for and given in exchange for an act or promise. In corporation law, cash or property contributed to a corporation in exchange for shares, or a promise to contribute such cash or property.
Enron	Enron Corportaion's global reputation was undermined by persistent rumours of bribery and political pressure to secure contracts in Central America, South America, Africa, and the Philippines. Especially controversial was its $3 billion contract with the Maharashtra State Electricity Board in India, where it is alleged that Enron officials used political connections within the Clinton and Bush administrations to exert pressure on the board.
WorldCom	WorldCom was the United States' second largest long distance phone company (AT&T was the largest). WorldCom grew largely by acquiring other telecommunications companies, most notably MCI Communications. It also owned the Tier 1 ISP UUNET, a major part of the Internet backbone.
Agent	A person who makes economic decisions for another economic actor. A hired manager operates as an agent for a firm's owner.
Competitive advantage	A business is said to have a competitive advantage when its unique strengths, often based on cost, quality, time, and innovation, offer consumers a greater percieved value and there by diffetiating it from its competitors.
Principal	In agency law, one under whose direction an agent acts and for whose benefit that agent acts

Go to **Cram101.com** for the Practice Tests for this Chapter.

is a principal.

Specialist	A specialist is a trader who makes a market in one or several stocks and holds the limit order book for those stocks.
Separation of ownership and control	Separation of ownership and control refers to the fact that shareholders in a publicly owned corporations have little or no direct control over management decisions. This separation is generally attributed to collective action problems associated withdispersed share ownership.
Shares	Shares refer to an equity security, representing a shareholder's ownership of a corporation. Shares are one of a finite number of equal portions in the capital of a company, entitling the owner to a proportion of distributed, non-reinvested profits known as dividends and to a portion of the value of the company in case of liquidation.
Pension fund	Amounts of money put aside by corporations, nonprofit organizations, or unions to cover part of the financial needs of members when they retire is a pension fund.
Mutual fund	A mutual fund is a form of collective investment that pools money from many investors and invests the money in stocks, bonds, short-term money market instruments, and/or other securities. In a mutual fund, the fund manager trades the fund's underlying securities, realizing capital gains or loss, and collects the dividend or interest income.
Pension	A pension is a steady income given to a person (usually after retirement). Pensions are typically payments made in the form of a guaranteed annuity to a retired or disabled employee.
Fund	Independent accounting entity with a self-balancing set of accounts segregated for the purposes of carrying on specific activities is referred to as a fund.
Mitsubishi	In a statement, the Mitsubishi says that forced labor is inconsistent with the company's values, and that the various lawsuits targeting Mitsubishi are misdirected. Instead, a spokesman says the Mitsubishi of World War II is not the same Mitsubishi of today. The conglomerate also rejected a Chinese slave labor lawsuit demand by saying it bore no responsibility since it was national policy to employ Chinese laborers."
Core	A core is the set of feasible allocations in an economy that cannot be improved upon by subset of the set of the economy's consumers (a coalition). In construction, when the force in an element is within a certain center section, the core, the element will only be under compression.
Recession	A significant decline in economic activity. In the U.S., recession is approximately defined as two successive quarters of falling GDP, as judged by NBER.
Economy	The income, expenditures, and resources that affect the cost of running a business and household are called an economy.
Operating profit	Operating profit is a measure of a company's earning power from ongoing operations, equal to earnings before the deduction of interest payments and income taxes.
Profit	Profit refers to the return to the resource entrepreneurial ability; total revenue minus total cost.
Market capitalization	Market capitalization is a business term that refers to the aggregate value of a firm's outstanding common shares. In essence, market capitalization reflects the total value of a firm's equity currently available on the market. This measure differs from equity value to the extent that a firm has outstanding stock options or other securities convertible to common shares. The size and growth of a firm's market capitalization is often one of the critical measurements of a public company's success or failure.
Volkswagen	Volkswagen or VW is an automobile manufacturer based in Wolfsburg, Germany in the state of

Go to **Cram101.com** for the Practice Tests for this Chapter.

Go to **Cram101.com** for the Practice Tests for this Chapter.
And, **NEVER** highlight a book again!

Lower Saxony. It forms the core of this Group, one of the world's four largest car producers. Its German tagline is "Aus Liebe zum Automobil", which is translated as "For the love of the car" - or, For Love of the People's Cars,".

Revenue	Revenue is a U.S. business term for the amount of money that a company receives from its activities, mostly from sales of products and/or services to customers.
BMW	BMW is an independent German company and manufacturer of automobiles and motorcycles. BMW is the world's largest premium carmaker and is the parent company of the BMW MINI and Rolls-Royce car brands, and, formerly, Rover.
Premium	Premium refers to the fee charged by an insurance company for an insurance policy. The rate of losses must be relatively predictable: In order to set the premium (prices) insurers must be able to estimate them accurately.
Market share	That fraction of an industry's output accounted for by an individual firm or group of firms is called market share.
Competitor	Other organizations in the same industry or type of business that provide a good or service to the same set of customers is referred to as a competitor.
Gain	In finance, gain is a profit or an increase in value of an investment such as a stock or bond. Gain is calculated by fair market value or the proceeds from the sale of the investment minus the sum of the purchase price and all costs associated with it.
Globalization	The increasing world-wide integration of markets for goods, services and capital that attracted special attention in the late 1990s is called globalization.
Edict	Edict refers to a command or prohibition promulgated by a sovereign and having the effect of
Stock market	An organized marketplace in which common stocks are traded. In the United States, the largest stock market is the New York Stock Exchange, on which are traded the stocks of the largest U.S. companies.
Default	In finance, default occurs when a debtor has not met its legal obligations according to the debt contract, e.g. it has not made a scheduled payment, or violated a covenant (condition) of the debt contract.
Lender	Suppliers and financial institutions that lend money to companies is referred to as a lender.
Proxy	Proxy refers to a person who is authorized to vote the shares of another person. Also, the written authorization empowering a person to vote the shares of another person.
Holding	The holding is a court's determination of a matter of law based on the issue presented in the particular case. In other words: under this law, with these facts, this result.
Union	A worker association that bargains with employers over wages and working conditions is called a union.
Corporate stock	Corporate stock refers to shares of ownership in a corporation.
Insurance	Insurance refers to a system by which individuals can reduce their exposure to risk of large losses by spreading the risks among a large number of persons.
Manufacturing	Production of goods primarily by the application of labor and capital to raw materials and other intermediate inputs, in contrast to agriculture, mining, forestry, fishing, and services a manufacturing.
Toyota	Toyota is a Japanese multinational corporation that manufactures automobiles, trucks and buses. Toyota is the world's second largest automaker by sales. Toyota also provides financial services through its subsidiary, Toyota Financial Services, and participates in other lines of business.

Go to **Cram101.com** for the Practice Tests for this Chapter.

Economic problem	Economic problem refers to how to determine the use of scarce resources among competing uses. Because resources are scarce, the economy must choose what products to produce; how these products are to be produced: and for whom.
Inflation rate	The percentage increase in the price level per year is an inflation rate. Alternatively, the inflation rate is the rate of decrease in the purchasing power of money.
Devaluation	Lowering the value of a nation's currency relative to other currencies is called devaluation.
Inflation	An increase in the overall price level of an economy, usually as measured by the CPI or by the implicit price deflator is called inflation.
Arbitration	Arbitration is a form of mediation or conciliation, where the mediating party is given power by the disputant parties to settle the dispute by making a finding. In practice arbitration is generally used as a substitute for judicial systems, particularly when the judicial processes are viewed as too slow, expensive or biased. Arbitration is also used by communities which lack formal law, as a substitute for formal law.
Tactic	A short-term immediate decision that, in its totality, leads to the achievement of strategic goals is called a tactic.
Bid	A bid price is a price offered by a buyer when he/she buys a good. In the context of stock trading on a stock exchange, the bid price is the highest price a buyer of a stock is willing to pay for a share of that given stock.
Targeting	In advertizing, targeting is to select a demographic or other group of people to advertise to, and create advertisements appropriately.
Asset	An item of property, such as land, capital, money, a share in ownership, or a claim on others for future payment, such as a bond or a bank deposit is an asset.
Target firm	The firm that is being studied or benchmarked against is referred to as target firm.
Authority	Authority in agency law, refers to an agent's ability to affect his principal's legal relations with third parties. Also used to refer to an actor's legal power or ability to do something. In addition, sometimes used to refer to a statute, case, or other legal source that justifies a particular result.
Safeway	On April 18, 2005, Safeway began a 100 million dollar brand re-positioning campaign labeled "Ingredients for life". This was done in an attempt to differentiate itself from its competitors, and to increase brand involvement. Steve Burd described it as "branding the shopping experience".
Analyst	Analyst refers to a person or tool with a primary function of information analysis, generally with a more limited, practical and short term set of goals than a researcher.
Exercise price	Exercise price refers to the price at which the purchaser of an option has the right to buy or sell the underlying financial instrument. Also known as the strike price.
Balance sheet	A statement of the assets, liabilities, and net worth of a firm or individual at some given time often at the end of its "fiscal year," is referred to as a balance sheet.
Strike price	The strike price is a key variable in a derivatives contract between two parties. Where the contract requires delivery of the underlying instrument, the trade will be at the strike price, regardless of the spot price of the underlying at that time.
Balance	In banking and accountancy, the outstanding balance is the amount of money owned, (or due), that remains in a deposit account (or a loan account) at a given date, after all past remittances, payments and withdrawal have been accounted for. It can be positive (then, in the balance sheet of a firm, it is an asset) or negative (a liability).

Go to **Cram101.com** for the Practice Tests for this Chapter.

Strike	The withholding of labor services by an organized group of workers is referred to as a strike.
Microsoft	Microsoft is a multinational computer technology corporation with 2004 global annual sales of US$39.79 billion and 71,553 employees in 102 countries and regions as of July 2006. It develops, manufactures, licenses, and supports a wide range of software products for computing devices.
Internal controls	A company's policies and procedures designed to reduce the opportunity for fraud and to provide reasonable assurance that its objectives will be accomplished are internal controls.
Internal control	Internal control refers to the plan of organization and all the related methods and measures adopted within a business to safeguard its assets and enhance the accuracy and reliability of its accounting records.
Turnover	Turnover in a financial context refers to the rate at which a provider of goods cycles through its average inventory. Turnover in a human resources context refers to the characteristic of a given company or industry, relative to rate at which an employer gains and loses staff.
Short run	Short run refers to a period of time that permits an increase or decrease in current production volume with existing capacity, but one that is too short to permit enlargement of that capacity itself (eg, the building of new plants, training of additional workers, etc.).
Senior management	Senior management is generally a team of individuals at the highest level of organizational management who have the day-to-day responsibilities of managing a corporation.
Walt Disney	As the co-founder of Walt Disney Productions, Walt became one of the most well-known motion picture producers in the world. The corporation he co-founded, now known as The Walt Disney Company, today has annual revenues of approximately US $30 billion.
Disney	Disney is one of the largest media and entertainment corporations in the world. Founded on October 16, 1923 by brothers Walt and Roy Disney as a small animation studio, today it is one of the largest Hollywood studios and also owns nine theme parks and several television networks, including the American Broadcasting Company (ABC).
Stock exchange	A stock exchange is a corporation or mutual organization which provides facilities for stock brokers and traders, to trade company stocks and other securities.
Chief financial officer	Chief financial officer refers to executive responsible for overseeing the financial operations of an organization.
Operation	A standardized method or technique that is performed repetitively, often on different materials resulting in different finished goods is called an operation.
Evaluation	The consumer's appraisal of the product or brand on important attributes is called evaluation.
Transparency	Transparency refers to a concept that describes a company being so open to other companies working with it that the once-solid barriers between them become see-through and electronic information is shared as if the companies were one.
Senior executive	Senior executive means a chief executive officer, chief operating officer, chief financial officer and anyone in charge of a principal business unit or function.
Proxy statement	Proxy statement refers to a document that fully describes the matter for which the proxy is being solicited, who is soliciting the proxy, and any other pertinent information.
Disclosure	Disclosure means the giving out of information, either voluntarily or to be in compliance with legal regulations or workplace rules.

Go to **Cram101.com** for the Practice Tests for this Chapter.

253

General Electric	In 1876, Thomas Alva Edison opened a new laboratory in Menlo Park, New Jersey. Out of the laboratory was to come perhaps the most famous invention of all—a successful development of the incandescent electric lamp. By 1890, Edison had organized his various businesses into the Edison General Electric Company.
Buyout	A buyout is an investment transaction by which the entire or a controlling part of the stock of a company is sold. A firm buysout the stake of the company to strengthen its influence on the company's decision making body. A buyout can take the forms of a leveraged buyout or a management buyout.
Securities and exchange commission	Securities and exchange commission refers to U.S. government agency that determines the financial statements that public companies must provide to stockholders and the measurement rules that they must use in producing those statements.
Security	Security refers to a claim on the borrower future income that is sold by the borrower to the lender. A security is a type of transferable interest representing financial value.
Investment portfolio	An investment portfolio is an aggregate of investments, such as stocks, bonds, real estate, arts or even fine wines. What distinguishes an investment portfolio from net worth is that some asset classes are not considered investments.
Portfolio	In finance, a portfolio is a collection of investments held by an institution or a private individual. Holding but not always a portfolio is part of an investment and risk-limiting strategy called diversification. By owning several assets, certain types of risk (in particular specific risk) can be reduced.
Issued shares	Issued shares refer to the number of shares that a corporation has sold to its shareholders. This may be equal to or less than the number of shares a company is authorized to issue.
Product line	A group of products that are physically similar or are intended for a similar market are called the product line.
Optimum	Optimum refers to the best. Usually refers to a most preferred choice by consumers subject to a budget constraint or a profit maximizing choice by firms or industry subject to a technological constraint.
Financial institution	A financial institution acts as an agent that provides financial services for its clients. Financial institutions generally fall under financial regulation from a government authority.
Compliance	A type of influence process where a receiver accepts the position advocated by a source to obtain favorable outcomes or to avoid punishment is the compliance.
Smart card	A stored-value card that contains a computer chip that allows it to be loaded with digital cash from the owner's bank account whenever needed is called a smart card.
Credit	Credit refers to a recording as positive in the balance of payments, any transaction that gives rise to a payment into the country, such as an export, the sale of an asset, or borrowing from abroad.
Net present value	Net present value is a standard method in finance of capital budgeting – the planning of long-term investments. Using this method a potential investment project should be undertaken if the present value of all cash inflows minus the present value of all cash outflows (which equals the net present value) is greater than zero.
Present value	The value today of a stream of payments and/or receipts over time in the future and/or the past, converted to the present using an interest rate. If X_t is the amount in period t and r the interest rate, then present value at time t=0 is $V = ?T\ /t$.
Anticipation	In finance, anticipation is where debts are paid off early, generally in order to pay less interest.

Go to **Cram101.com** for the Practice Tests for this Chapter.

Dividend	Amount of corporate profits paid out for each share of stock is referred to as dividend.
Welfare	Welfare refers to the economic well being of an individual, group, or economy. For individuals, it is conceptualized by a utility function. For groups, including countries and the world, it is a tricky philosophical concept, since individuals fare differently.
Managerial revolution	Burham's concept of managerial revolution stated that as control of large businesses moved from the original owners to professional managers, society's new governing class would be not the traditional possessors of wealth-but those who have the professional expertise to manage and to lead, large organizations.
Public corporation	A corporation formed to meet a specific governmental or political purpose is referred to as public corporation.
Entrepreneur	The owner/operator. The person who organizes, manages, and assumes the risks of a firm, taking a new idea or a new product and turning it into a successful business is an entrepreneur.
Holder	A person in possession of a document of title or an instrument payable or indorsed to him, his order, or to bearer is a holder.
Residual	Residual payments can refer to an ongoing stream of payments in respect of the completion of past achievements.
Expense	In accounting, an expense represents an event in which an asset is used up or a liability is incurred. In terms of the accounting equation, expenses reduce owners' equity.
Diversified portfolio	Diversified portfolio refers to a portfolio that includes a variety of assets whose prices are not likely all to change together. In international economics, this usually means holding assets denominated in different currencies.
Closing	The finalization of a real estate sales transaction that passes title to the property from the seller to the buyer is referred to as a closing. Closing is a sales term which refers to the process of making a sale. It refers to reaching the final step, which may be an exchange of money or acquiring a signature.
Effective manager	Leader of a team that consistently achieves high performance goals is an effective manager.
Layoff	A layoff is the termination of an employee or (more commonly) a group of employees for business reasons, such as the decision that certain positions are no longer necessary.
Publicity	Publicity refers to any information about an individual, product, or organization that's distributed to the public through the media and that's not paid for or controlled by the seller.

Corporate governance	Corporate governance is the set of processes, customs, policies, laws and institutions affecting the way a corporation is directed, administered or controlled.
Corporation	A legal entity chartered by a state or the Federal government that is distinct and separate from the individuals who own it is a corporation. This separation gives the corporation unique powers which other legal entities lack.
Market	A market is, as defined in economics, a social arrangement that allows buyers and sellers to discover information and carry out a voluntary exchange of goods or services.
Strategic management	A philosophy of management that links strategic planning with dayto-day decision making. Strategic management seeks a fit between an organization's external and internal environments.
Management	Management characterizes the process of leading and directing all or part of an organization, often a business, through the deployment and manipulation of resources. Early twentieth-century management writer Mary Parker Follett defined management as "the art of getting things done through people."
Sony	Sony is a multinational corporation and one of the world's largest media conglomerates founded in Tokyo, Japan. One of its divisions Sony Electronics is one of the leading manufacturers of electronics, video, communications, and information technology products for the consumer and professional markets.
Fund	Independent accounting entity with a self-balancing set of accounts segregated for the purposes of carrying on specific activities is referred to as a fund.
Bottom line	The bottom line is net income on the last line of a income statement.
Strategic alliance	Strategic alliance refers to a long-term partnership between two or more companies established to help each company build competitive market advantages.
Logistics	Those activities that focus on getting the right amount of the right products to the right place at the right time at the lowest possible cost is referred to as logistics.
Marketing	Promoting and selling products or services to customers, or prospective customers, is referred to as marketing.
Outbound	Communications originating inside an organization and destined for customers, prospects, or other people outside the organization are called outbound.
Service	Service refers to a "non tangible product" that is not embodied in a physical good and that typically effects some change in another product, person, or institution. Contrasts with good.
Layout	Layout refers to the physical arrangement of the various parts of an advertisement including the headline, subheads, illustrations, body copy, and any identifying marks.
Economies of scale	In economics, returns to scale and economies of scale are related terms that describe what happens as the scale of production increases. They are different terms and not to be used interchangeably.
Economy	The income, expenditures, and resources that affect the cost of running a business and household are called an economy.
Insolvency	Insolvency is a financial condition experienced by a person or business entity when their assets no longer exceed their liabilities or when the person or entity can no longer meet its debt obligations when they come due.
Asset	An item of property, such as land, capital, money, a share in ownership, or a claim on others for future payment, such as a bond or a bank deposit is an asset.

Go to **Cram101.com** for the Practice Tests for this Chapter.

Go to **Cram101.com** for the Practice Tests for this Chapter.
And, **NEVER** highlight a book again!

Bid	A bid price is a price offered by a buyer when he/she buys a good. In the context of stock trading on a stock exchange, the bid price is the highest price a buyer of a stock is willing to pay for a share of that given stock.
Television network	Television network refers to the provider of news and programming to a series of affiliated local television stations.
General Electric	In 1876, Thomas Alva Edison opened a new laboratory in Menlo Park, New Jersey. Out of the laboratory was to come perhaps the most famous invention of all—a successful development of the incandescent electric lamp. By 1890, Edison had organized his various businesses into the Edison General Electric Company.
Excess capacity	Excess capacity refers to plant resources that are underused when imperfectly competitive firms produce less output than that associated with purely competitive firms, who by definiation, are achieving minimum average total cost.
Market share	That fraction of an industry's output accounted for by an individual firm or group of firms is called market share.
Acquisition	A company's purchase of the property and obligations of another company is an acquisition.
Operation	A standardized method or technique that is performed repetitively, often on different materials resulting in different finished goods is called an operation.
Cooperative	A business owned and controlled by the people who use it, producers, consumers, or workers with similar needs who pool their resources for mutual gain is called cooperative.
Firm	An organization that employs resources to produce a good or service for profit and owns and operates one or more plants is referred to as a firm.
Competitive advantage	A business is said to have a competitive advantage when its unique strengths, often based on cost, quality, time, and innovation, offer consumers a greater percieved value and there by differtiating it from its competitors.
Gain	In finance, gain is a profit or an increase in value of an investment such as a stock or bond. Gain is calculated by fair market value or the proceeds from the sale of the investment minus the sum of the purchase price and all costs associated with it.
Technology	The body of knowledge and techniques that can be used to combine economic resources to produce goods and services is called technology.
Industry	A group of firms that produce identical or similar products is an industry. It is also used specifically to refer to an area of economic production focused on manufacturing which involves large amounts of capital investment before any profit can be realized, also called "heavy industry".
Information technology	Information technology refers to technology that helps companies change business by allowing them to use new methods.
Productivity	Productivity refers to the total output of goods and services in a given period of time divided by work hours.
Leadership	Management merely consists of leadership applied to business situations; or in other words: management forms a sub-set of the broader process of leadership.
Venture capital	Venture capital is capital provided by outside investors for financing of new, growing or struggling businesses. Venture capital investments generally are high risk investments but offer the potential for above average returns.
Partnership	In the common law, a partnership is a type of business entity in which partners share with each other the profits or losses of the business undertaking in which they have all invested.

Go to **Cram101.com** for the Practice Tests for this Chapter.

Investment	Investment refers to spending for the production and accumulation of capital and additions to inventories. In a financial sense, buying an asset with the expectation of making a return.
Innovation	Innovation refers to the first commercially successful introduction of a new product, the use of a new method of production, or the creation of a new form of business organization.
Capital	Capital generally refers to financial wealth, especially that used to start or maintain a business. In classical economics, capital is one of four factors of production, the others being land and labor and entrepreneurship.
Intel	Intel Corporation, founded in 1968 and based in Santa Clara, California, USA, is the world's largest semiconductor company. Intel is best known for its PC microprocessors, where it maintains roughly 80% market share.
Enterprise	Enterprise refers to another name for a business organization. Other similar terms are business firm, sometimes simply business, sometimes simply firm, as well as company, and entity.
Interest	In finance and economics, interest is the price paid by a borrower for the use of a lender's money. In other words, interest is the amount of paid to "rent" money for a period of time.
Revenue	Revenue is a U.S. business term for the amount of money that a company receives from its activities, mostly from sales of products and/or services to customers.
Air France	Air France took over the Dutch company KLM in May 2004, resulting in the creation of Air France -KLM. Air France -KLM is the largest airline company in the world in terms of operating revenues, and the third-largest in the world in terms of passengers-kilometers.
Swap	In finance a swap is a derivative, where two counterparties exchange one stream of cash flows against another stream. These streams are called the legs of the swap. The cash flows are calculated over a notional principal amount. Swaps are often used to hedge certain risks, for instance interest rate risk. Another use is speculation.
American Airlines	American Airlines developed from a conglomeration of about 82 small airlines through a series of corporate acquisitions and reorganizations: initially, the name American Airways was used as a common brand by a number of independent air carriers. American Airlines is the largest airline in the world in terms of total passengers transported and fleet size, and the second-largest airline in the world.
British Airways	British Airways is the largest airline of the United Kingdom. It is also one of the largest airlines in the world, with the greatest number of flights from Europe to North America. Its main bases are London Heathrow (LHR) and London Gatwick (LGW).
Purchasing	Purchasing refers to the function in a firm that searches for quality material resources, finds the best suppliers, and negotiates the best price for goods and services.
Lufthansa	Lufthansa is a founding member of Star Alliance, the largest airline alliance in the world. The Lufthansa Group operates more than 400 aircraft and employs nearly 100,000 people world-wide.
Buying power	The dollar amount available to purchase securities on margin is buying power. The amount is calculated by adding the cash held in the brokerage accounts and the amount that could be spent if securities were fully margined to their limit. If an investor uses their buying power, they are purchasing securities on credit.
Boeing	Boeing is the world's largest aircraft manufacturer by revenue. Headquartered in Chicago, Illinois, Boeing is the second-largest defense contractor in the world. In 2005, the company was the world's largest civil aircraft manufacturer in terms of value.
Points	Loan origination fees that may be deductible as interest by a buyer of property. A seller of

Go to **Cram101.com** for the Practice Tests for this Chapter.

property who pays points reduces the selling price by the amount of the points paid for the buyer.

Users	Users refer to people in the organization who actually use the product or service purchased by the buying center.
Wireless communication	Wireless communication refers to a method of communication that uses low-powered radio waves to transmit data between devices. The term refers to communication without cables or cords, chiefly using radio frequency and infrared waves. Common uses include the various communications defined by the IrDA, the wireless networking of computers and cellular mobile phones.
Competitiveness	Competitiveness usually refers to characteristics that permit a firm to compete effectively with other firms due to low cost or superior technology, perhaps internationally.
Consolidation	The combination of two or more firms, generally of equal size and market power, to form an entirely new entity is a consolidation.
Insurance	Insurance refers to a system by which individuals can reduce their exposure to risk of large losses by spreading the risks among a large number of persons.
Joint venture	Joint venture refers to an undertaking by two parties for a specific purpose and duration, taking any of several legal forms.
Privatization	A process in which investment bankers take companies that were previously owned by the government to the public markets is referred to as privatization.
Conglomerate	A conglomerate is a large company that consists of divisions of often seemingly unrelated businesses.
Market testing	Market testing refers to exposing actual products to prospective consumers under realistic purchase conditions to see if they will buy.
Proprietary	Proprietary indicates that a party, or proprietor, exercises private ownership, control or use over an item of property, usually to the exclusion of other parties. Where a party, holds or claims proprietary interests in relation to certain types of property (eg. a creative literary work, or software), that property may also be the subject of intellectual property law (eg. copyright or patents).
Credit	Credit refers to a recording as positive in the balance of payments, any transaction that gives rise to a payment into the country, such as an export, the sale of an asset, or borrowing from abroad.
Foreign direct investment	Foreign direct investment refers to the buying of permanent property and businesses in foreign nations.
Direct investment	Direct investment refers to a domestic firm actually investing in and owning a foreign subsidiary or division.
Financial institution	A financial institution acts as an agent that provides financial services for its clients. Financial institutions generally fall under financial regulation from a government authority.
Sears	Before the Sears catalog, farmers typically bought supplies (often at very high prices) from local general stores. Sears took advantage of this by publishing his catalog with clearly stated prices, so that consumers could know what he was selling and at what price, and order and obtain them conveniently. The catalog business soon grew quickly.
Forming	The first stage of team development, where the team is formed and the objectives for the team are set is referred to as forming.
Control system	A control system is a device or set of devices that manage the behavior of other devices.

Go to **Cram101.com** for the Practice Tests for this Chapter.

Some devices or systems are not controllable. A control system is an interconnection of components connected or related in such a manner as to command, direct, or regulate itself or another system.

Globalization	The increasing world-wide integration of markets for goods, services and capital that attracted special attention in the late 1990s is called globalization.
Competitor	Other organizations in the same industry or type of business that provide a good or service to the same set of customers is referred to as a competitor.
Foundation	A Foundation is a type of philanthropic organization set up by either individuals or institutions as a legal entity (either as a corporation or trust) with the purpose of distributing grants to support causes in line with the goals of the foundation.
Leverage	Leverage is using given resources in such a way that the potential positive or negative outcome is magnified. In finance, this generally refers to borrowing.
Lockheed Martin	Lockheed Martin is the world's largest defense contractor (by defense revenue). As of 2005, 95% of revenues came from the U.S. Department of Defense, other U.S. federal government agencies, and foreign military customers.
General Motors	General Motors is the world's largest automaker. Founded in 1908, today it employs about 327,000 people around the world. With global headquarters in Detroit, it manufactures its cars and trucks in 33 countries.
Collaboration	Collaboration occurs when the interaction between groups is very important to goal attainment and the goals are compatible. Wherein people work together —applying both to the work of individuals as well as larger collectives and societies.
Distribution	Distribution in economics, the manner in which total output and income is distributed among individuals or factors.
Toyota	Toyota is a Japanese multinational corporation that manufactures automobiles, trucks and buses. Toyota is the world's second largest automaker by sales. Toyota also provides financial services through its subsidiary, Toyota Financial Services, and participates in other lines of business.
Honda	With more than 14 million internal combustion engines built each year, Honda is the largest engine-maker in the world. In 2004, the company began to produce diesel motors, which were both very quiet whilst not requiring particulate filters to pass pollution standards. It is arguable, however, that the foundation of their success is the motorcycle division.
Brand	A name, symbol, or design that identifies the goods or services of one seller or group of sellers and distinguishes them from the goods and services of competitors is a brand.
Equity	Equity is the name given to the set of legal principles, in countries following the English common law tradition, which supplement strict rules of law where their application would operate harshly, so as to achieve what is sometimes referred to as "natural justice."
Tacit knowledge	Knowledge that has not been articulated. Tacit knowledge is often subconscious and relatively difficult to communicate to other people. Tacit knowledge consists often of habits and culture that we do not recognize in ourselves.
Entrepreneur	The owner/operator. The person who organizes, manages, and assumes the risks of a firm, taking a new idea or a new product and turning it into a successful business is an entrepreneur.
Big Business	Big business is usually used as a pejorative reference to the significant economic and political power which large and powerful corporations (especially multinational corporations), are capable of wielding.

Go to **Cram101.com** for the Practice Tests for this Chapter.

Premium	Premium refers to the fee charged by an insurance company for an insurance policy. The rate of losses must be relatively predictable: In order to set the premium (prices) insurers must be able to estimate them accurately.
Yahoo	Yahoo is an American computer services company. It operates an Internet portal, the Yahoo Directory and a host of other services including the popular Yahoo Mail. Yahoo is the most visited website on the Internet today with more than 400 million unique users. The global network of Yahoo! websites received 3.4 billion page views per day on average as of October 2005.
Stock	In financial terminology, stock is the capital raized by a corporation, through the issuance and sale of shares.
BellSouth	BellSouth is currently the only "Baby Bell" that does not operate pay telephones. By 2003, the payphone operation was discontinued because it had become too unprofitable, most likely due to the increased availability of cell phones. Cincinnati Bell has taken their place for payphones in northern BellSouth territory; independents have set in further south.
Verizon	Verizon a Dow 30 company, is a broadband and telecommunications provider. The acquisition of GTE by Bell Atlantic, on June 30, 2000, which formed Verizon, was among the largest mergers in United States business history. Verizon, with MCI, is currently the second largest telecommunications company in the United States.
Comcast	Comcast Corporation based in Philadelphia, Pennsylvania, is the largest cable company and the largest broadband (second overall) Internet service provider in the United States. They develop broadband cable networks and are involved in electronic retailing and television programming content.
Regulatory agency	Regulatory agency refers to an agency, commission, or board established by the Federal government or a state government to regulates businesses in the public interest.
Discount	The difference between the face value of a bond and its selling price, when a bond is sold for less than its face value it's referred to as a discount.
DIRECTV	DirecTV was launched in 1994 by General Motors subsidiary Hughes Electronics. It was the first high-powered direct broadcast satellite service in the world. Digital Equipment Corporation provided the customer-care out of their existing technical support center in Colorado Springs, Colorado.
Qwest	Qwest is a large telecommunications carrier. Qwest provides local service in 14 western U.S. states. Qwest provides voice, backbone data services, and digital television in some areas. It operates in three segments: Wireline Services, Wireless Services, and Other Services.
Analyst	Analyst refers to a person or tool with a primary function of information analysis, generally with a more limited, practical and short term set of goals than a researcher.
Switching costs	Switching costs is a term used in microeconomics, strategic management, and marketing to describe any impediment to a customer's changing of suppliers. In many markets, consumers are forced to incur costs when switching from one supplier to another. These costs are called switching costs and can come in many different shapes.

Go to **Cram101.com** for the Practice Tests for this Chapter.
And, **NEVER** highlight a book again!

Strategic alliance	Strategic alliance refers to a long-term partnership between two or more companies established to help each company build competitive market advantages.
Cooperative	A business owned and controlled by the people who use it, producers, consumers, or workers with similar needs who pool their resources for mutual gain is called cooperative.
Firm	An organization that employs resources to produce a good or service for profit and owns and operates one or more plants is referred to as a firm.
Service	Service refers to a "non tangible product" that is not embodied in a physical good and that typically effects some change in another product, person, or institution. Contrasts with good.
Diversification strategy	Diversification strategy is a corporate strategy that takes the organization away from both its current markets and products, as opposed to either market or product development.
Multinational enterprise	Multinational enterprise refers to a firm, usually a corporation, that operates in two or more countries.
Internationa-ization	Internationalization refers to another term for fragmentation. Used by Grossman and Helpman.
Strategic management	A philosophy of management that links strategic planning with dayto-day decision making. Strategic management seeks a fit between an organization's external and internal environments.
Diversification	Investing in a collection of assets whose returns do not always move together, with the result that overall risk is lower than for individual assets is referred to as diversification.
Enterprise	Enterprise refers to another name for a business organization. Other similar terms are business firm, sometimes simply business, sometimes simply firm, as well as company, and entity.
Management	Management characterizes the process of leading and directing all or part of an organization, often a business, through the deployment and manipulation of resources. Early twentieth-century management writer Mary Parker Follett defined management as "the art of getting things done through people."
Valuation	In finance, valuation is the process of estimating the market value of a financial asset or liability. They can be done on assets (for example, investments in marketable securities such as stocks, options, business enterprises, or intangible assets such as patents and trademarks) or on liabilities (e.g., Bonds issued by a company).
Journal	Book of original entry, in which transactions are recorded in a general ledger system, is referred to as a journal.
Market	A market is, as defined in economics, a social arrangement that allows buyers and sellers to discover information and carry out a voluntary exchange of goods or services.
Multinational corporations	Firms that own production facilities in two or more countries and produce and sell their products globally are referred to as multinational corporations.
Multinational corporation	An organization that manufactures and markets products in many different countries and has multinational stock ownership and multinational management is referred to as multinational corporation.
Corporation	A legal entity chartered by a state or the Federal government that is distinct and separate from the individuals who own it is a corporation. This separation gives the corporation unique powers which other legal entities lack.

Go to **Cram101.com** for the Practice Tests for this Chapter.

International management	International management refers to the management of business operations conducted in more than one country.
Evaluation	The consumer's appraisal of the product or brand on important attributes is called evaluation.
Subsidiary	A company that is controlled by another company or corporation is a subsidiary.
Innovation	Innovation refers to the first commercially successful introduction of a new product, the use of a new method of production, or the creation of a new form of business organization.
Marketing	Promoting and selling products or services to customers, or prospective customers, is referred to as marketing.
Industry	A group of firms that produce identical or similar products is an industry. It is also used specifically to refer to an area of economic production focused on manufacturing which involves large amounts of capital investment before any profit can be realized, also called "heavy industry".
Economy	The income, expenditures, and resources that affect the cost of running a business and household are called an economy.
Context	The effect of the background under which a message often takes on more and richer meaning is a context. Context is especially important in cross-cultural interactions because some cultures are said to be high context or low context.
Asset	An item of property, such as land, capital, money, a share in ownership, or a claim on others for future payment, such as a bond or a bank deposit is an asset.
Wall Street Journal	Dow Jones & Company was founded in 1882 by reporters Charles Dow, Edward Jones and Charles Bergstresser. Jones converted the small Customers' Afternoon Letter into The Wall Street Journal, first published in 1889, and began delivery of the Dow Jones News Service via telegraph. The Journal featured the Jones 'Average', the first of several indexes of stock and bond prices on the New York Stock Exchange.
Business Week	Business Week is a business magazine published by McGraw-Hill. It was first published in 1929 under the direction of Malcolm Muir, who was serving as president of the McGraw-Hill Publishing company at the time. It is considered to be the standard both in industry and among students.
Leadership	Management merely consists of leadership applied to business situations; or in other words: management forms a sub-set of the broader process of leadership.
International diversification	Achieving diversification through many different foreign investments that are influenced by a variety of factors is referred to as international diversification. By diversifying across nations whose economic cycles are not perfectly correlated, investors can typically reduce the variability of their returns.
Management team	A management team is directly responsible for managing the day-to-day operations (and profitability) of a company.
Manufacturing	Production of goods primarily by the application of labor and capital to raw materials and other intermediate inputs, in contrast to agriculture, mining, forestry, fishing, and services a manufacturing.
Competitive advantage	A business is said to have a competitive advantage when its unique strengths, often based on cost, quality, time, and innovation, offer consumers a greater percieved value and there by differtiating it from its competitors.
Contingency theory	Any theory that presupposes that there is no theory or method for operating a business that can be applied in all instances is referred to as a contingency theory.

Go to **Cram101.com** for the Practice Tests for this Chapter.

Business strategy	Business strategy, which refers to the aggregated operational strategies of single business firm or that of an SBU in a diversified corporation refers to the way in which a firm competes in its chosen arenas.
Strategic choice	Strategic choice refers to an organization's strategy; the ways an organization will attempt to fulfill its mission and achieve its long-term goals.
Human resources	Human resources refers to the individuals within the firm, and to the portion of the firm's organization that deals with hiring, firing, training, and other personnel issues.
Alignment	Term that refers to optimal coordination among disparate departments and divisions within a firm is referred to as alignment.
International Business	International business refers to any firm that engages in international trade or investment.
Emerging market	The term emerging market is commonly used to describe business and market activity in industrializing or emerging regions of the world.
Conglomerate	A conglomerate is a large company that consists of divisions of often seemingly unrelated businesses.
Foreign direct investment	Foreign direct investment refers to the buying of permanent property and businesses in foreign nations.
Direct investment	Direct investment refers to a domestic firm actually investing in and owning a foreign subsidiary or division.
Emerging markets	The term emerging markets is commonly used to describe business and market activity in industrializing or emerging regions of the world. It is sometimes loosely used as a replacement for emerging economies, but really signifies a business phenomenon that is not fully described by or constrained to geography or economic strength; such countries are considered to be in a transitional phase between developing and developed status.
Systematic risk	Movements in a stock portfolio's value that are attributable to macroeconomic forces affecting all firms in an economy, rather than factors specific to an individual firm are referred to as systematic risk.
Transparency	Transparency refers to a concept that describes a company being so open to other companies working with it that the once-solid barriers between them become see-through and electronic information is shared as if the companies were one.
Corruption	The unauthorized use of public office for private gain. The most common forms of corruption are bribery, extortion, and the misuse of inside information.
Investment	Investment refers to spending for the production and accumulation of capital and additions to inventories. In a financial sense, buying an asset with the expectation of making a return.
Exchange	The trade of things of value between buyer and seller so that each is better off after the trade is called the exchange.
Policy	Similar to a script in that a policy can be a less than completely rational decision-making method. Involves the use of a pre-existing set of decision steps for any problem that presents itself.
Currency union	A group of countries that agree to peg their exchange rates and to coordinate their monetary policies so as to avoid the need for currency realignments is called a currency union.
Expatriate	Employee sent by his or her company to live and manage operations in a different country is called an expatriate.
Union	A worker association that bargains with employers over wages and working conditions is called

Go to **Cram101.com** for the Practice Tests for this Chapter.

	a union.
Political economy	Early name for the discipline of economics. A field within economics encompassing several alternatives to neoclassical economics, including Marxist economics. Also called radical political economy.
Privatization	A process in which investment bankers take companies that were previously owned by the government to the public markets is referred to as privatization.
Big Business	Big business is usually used as a pejorative reference to the significant economic and political power which large and powerful corporations (especially multinational corporations), are capable of wielding.
Integration	Economic integration refers to reducing barriers among countries to transactions and to movements of goods, capital, and labor, including harmonization of laws, regulations, and standards. Integrated markets theoretically function as a unified market.
Harvard Business Review	Harvard Business Review is a research-based magazine written for business practitioners, it claims a high ranking business readership and enjoys the reverence of academics, executives, and management consultants. It has been the frequent publishing home for well known scholars and management thinkers.
Strategic trade policy	Strategic trade policy refers to the use of trade policies, including tariffs, subsidies, and even export subsidies, in a context of imperfect competition and/or increasing returns, to alter the outcome of international competition in a country.
Management development	The process of training and educating employees to become good managers and then monitoring the progress of their managerial skills over time is management development.
Mergers and acquisitions	The phrase mergers and acquisitions refers to the aspect of corporate finance strategy and management dealing with the merging and acquiring of different companies as well as other assets. Usually mergers occur in a friendly setting where executives from the respective companies participate in a due diligence process to ensure a successful combination of all parts.
Acquisition	A company's purchase of the property and obligations of another company is an acquisition.
Merger	Merger refers to the combination of two firms into a single firm.
Wage	The payment for the service of a unit of labor, per unit time. In trade theory, it is the only payment to labor, usually unskilled labor. In empirical work, wage data may exclude other compenzation, which must be added to get the total cost of employment.
Extension	Extension refers to an out-of-court settlement in which creditors agree to allow the firm more time to meet its financial obligations. A new repayment schedule will be developed, subject to the acceptance of creditors.
Organizational routines	Recognizable, recurring patterns of activity inside an organization are called organizational routines.
Global strategy	Global strategy refers to strategy focusing on increasing profitability by reaping cost reductions from experience curve and location economies.
Globalization	The increasing world-wide integration of markets for goods, services and capital that attracted special attention in the late 1990s is called globalization.
New economy	New economy, this term was used in the late 1990's to suggest that globalization and/or innovations in information technology had changed the way that the world economy works.
Accounting	A system that collects and processes financial information about an organization and reports that information to decision makers is referred to as accounting.

Go to **Cram101.com** for the Practice Tests for this Chapter.

Keiretsu	Keiretsu is a set of companies with interlocking business relationships and shareholdings. It is a type of business group.
Trend	Trend refers to the long-term movement of an economic variable, such as its average rate of increase or decrease over enough years to encompass several business cycles.
Joint venture	Joint venture refers to an undertaking by two parties for a specific purpose and duration, taking any of several legal forms.
Transnational	Transnational focuses on the heightened interconnectivity between people all around the world and the loosening of boundaries between countries.
Consideration	Consideration in contract law, a basic requirement for an enforceable agreement under traditional contract principles, defined in this text as legal value, bargained for and given in exchange for an act or promise. In corporation law, cash or property contributed to a corporation in exchange for shares, or a promise to contribute such cash or property.
Technology	The body of knowledge and techniques that can be used to combine economic resources to produce goods and services is called technology.
Export	In economics, an export is any good or commodity, shipped or otherwise transported out of a country, province, town to another part of the world in a legitimate fashion, typically for use in trade or sale.
Entrepreneurship	The assembling of resources to produce new or improved products and technologies is referred to as entrepreneurship.
Supply chain	Supply chain refers to the flow of goods, services, and information from the initial sources of materials and services to the delivery of products to consumers.
Licensing	Licensing is a form of strategic alliance which involves the sale of a right to use certain proprietary knowledge (so called intellectual property) in a defined way.
Supply	Supply is the aggregate amount of any material good that can be called into being at a certain price point; it comprises one half of the equation of supply and demand. In classical economic theory, a curve representing supply is one of the factors that produce price.
Wholly owned subsidiary	A subsidiary in which the firm owns 100 percent of the stock is a wholly owned subsidiary.
Partnership	In the common law, a partnership is a type of business entity in which partners share with each other the profits or losses of the business undertaking in which they have all invested.
Operation	A standardized method or technique that is performed repetitively, often on different materials resulting in different finished goods is called an operation.
Option	A contract that gives the purchaser the option to buy or sell the underlying financial instrument at a specified price, called the exercise price or strike price, within a specific period of time.
Brand	A name, symbol, or design that identifies the goods or services of one seller or group of sellers and distinguishes them from the goods and services of competitors is a brand.
Foundation	A Foundation is a type of philanthropic organization set up by either individuals or institutions as a legal entity (either as a corporation or trust) with the purpose of distributing grants to support causes in line with the goals of the foundation.
Case study	A case study is a particular method of qualitative research. Rather than using large samples and following a rigid protocol to examine a limited number of variables, case study methods involve an in-depth, longitudinal examination of a single instance or event: a case. They provide a systematic way of looking at events, collecting data, analyzing information, and

Go to Cram101.com for the Practice Tests for this Chapter.

reporting the results.

Market opportunities	Market opportunities refer to areas where a company believes there are favorable demand trends, needs, and/or wants that are not being satisfied, and where it can compete effectively.
Incentive	An incentive is any factor (financial or non-financial) that provides a motive for a particular course of action, or counts as a reason for preferring one choice to the alternatives.
Motorola	The Six Sigma quality system was developed at Motorola even though it became most well known because of its use by General Electric. It was created by engineer Bill Smith, under the direction of Bob Galvin (son of founder Paul Galvin) when he was running the company.
Buyer	A buyer refers to a role in the buying center with formal authority and responsibility to select the supplier and negotiate the terms of the contract.
Revenue	Revenue is a U.S. business term for the amount of money that a company receives from its activities, mostly from sales of products and/or services to customers.
Contract	A contract is a "promise" or an "agreement" that is enforced or recognized by the law. In the civil law, a contract is considered to be part of the general law of obligations.
Fraud	Tax fraud falls into two categories: civil and criminal. Under civil fraud, the IRS may impose as a penalty of an amount equal to as much as 75 percent of the underpayment.
Fund	Independent accounting entity with a self-balancing set of accounts segregated for the purposes of carrying on specific activities is referred to as a fund.
Compensatory damages	Damages received or paid by the taxpayer can be classified as compensatory damages or as punitive damages. Compensatory damages are those paid to compensate one for harm caused by another.
Punitive damages	Damages received or paid by the taxpayer can be classified as compensatory damages or as punitive damages. Punitive damages are those awarded to punish the defendant for gross negligence or the intentional infliction of harm. Such damages are includible.
Compensatory	Damages that will compensate a part for direct losses due to an injury suffered are referred to as compensatory .
Punitive	Damages designed to punish flagrant wrongdoers and to deter them and others from engaging in similar conduct in the future are called punitive.
Damages	The sum of money recoverable by a plaintiff who has received a judgment in a civil case is called damages.
International strategy	Trying to create value by transferring core competencies to foreign markets where indigenous competitors lack those competencies is called international strategy.
World Trade Organization	The World Trade Organization is an international, multilateral organization, which sets the rules for the global trading system and resolves disputes between its member states, all of whom are signatories to its approximately 30 agreements.
International trade	The export of goods and services from a country and the import of goods and services into a country is referred to as the international trade.
Production	The creation of finished goods and services using the factors of production: land, labor, capital, entrepreneurship, and knowledge.
Labor	People's physical and mental talents and efforts that are used to help produce goods and services are called labor.

Go to **Cram101.com** for the Practice Tests for this Chapter.

Consumer market	All the individuals or households that want goods and services for personal consumption or use are a consumer market.
Internal control	Internal control refers to the plan of organization and all the related methods and measures adopted within a business to safeguard its assets and enhance the accuracy and reliability of its accounting records.
Competitiveness	Competitiveness usually refers to characteristics that permit a firm to compete effectively with other firms due to low cost or superior technology, perhaps internationally.
Host country	The country in which the parent-country organization seeks to locate or has already located a facility is a host country.
Inverse relationship	The relationship between two variables that change in opposite directions, for example, product price and quantity demanded is an inverse relationship.
Exporter	A firm that sells its product in another country is an exporter.
General Motors	General Motors is the world's largest automaker. Founded in 1908, today it employs about 327,000 people around the world. With global headquarters in Detroit, it manufactures its cars and trucks in 33 countries.
Regulation	Regulation refers to restrictions state and federal laws place on business with regard to the conduct of its activities.
Toyota	Toyota is a Japanese multinational corporation that manufactures automobiles, trucks and buses. Toyota is the world's second largest automaker by sales. Toyota also provides financial services through its subsidiary, Toyota Financial Services, and participates in other lines of business.
Forming	The first stage of team development, where the team is formed and the objectives for the team are set is referred to as forming.
Product life cycle	Product life cycle refers to a series of phases in a product's sales and cash flows over time; these phases, in order of occurrence, are introductory, growth, maturity, and decline.
Economies of scale	In economics, returns to scale and economies of scale are related terms that describe what happens as the scale of production increases. They are different terms and not to be used interchangeably.
Factors of production	Economic resources: land, capital, labor, and entrepreneurial ability are called factors of production.
Multidomestic strategy	Emphasizing the need to be responsive to the unique conditions prevailing in different national markets is referred to as a multidomestic strategy.
Business unit	The lowest level of the company which contains the set of functions that carry a product through its life span from concept through manufacture, distribution, sales and service is a business unit.
Competitive Strategy	An outline of how a business intends to compete with other firms in the same industry is called competitive strategy.
Standardization	Standardization, in the context related to technologies and industries, is the process of establishing a technical standard among competing entities in a market, where this will bring benefits without hurting competition.
Transnational strategy	Plan to exploit experience-based cost and location economies, transfer core competencies with the firm, and pay attention to local responsiveness is called transnational strategy.
Product line	A group of products that are physically similar or are intended for a similar market are called the product line.

Go to **Cram101.com** for the Practice Tests for this Chapter.

Greenfield venture	The most risky type of direct investment, whereby a company builds a subsidiary from scratch in a foreign country is referred to as the greenfield venture.
Exporting	Selling products to another country is called exporting.
Gain	In finance, gain is a profit or an increase in value of an investment such as a stock or bond. Gain is calculated by fair market value or the proceeds from the sale of the investment minus the sum of the purchase price and all costs associated with it.
Scope	Scope of a project is the sum total of all projects products and their requirements or features.
Economies of scope	The ability to use one resource to provide many different products and services is referred to as economies of scope.
Political risk	Refers to the many different actions of people, subgroups, and whole countries that have the potential to affect the financial status of a firm is called political risk.
Economic risk	The likelihood that events, including economic mismanagement, will cause drastic changes in a country's business environment that adversely affects the profit and other goals of a particular business enterprise is referred to as economic risk.
Trade barrier	An artificial disincentive to export and/or import, such as a tariff, quota, or other NTB is called a trade barrier.
Distribution	Distribution in economics, the manner in which total output and income is distributed among individuals or factors.
Intellectual property rights	Intellectual property rights, such as patents, copyrights, trademarks, trade secrets, trade names, and domain names are very valuable business assets. Federal and state laws protect intellectual property rights from misappropriation and infringement.
Intellectual property right	Intellectual property right refers to the right to control and derive the benefits from something one has invented, discovered, or created.
Intellectual property	In law, intellectual property is an umbrella term for various legal entitlements which attach to certain types of information, ideas, or other intangibles in their expressed form. The holder of this legal entitlement is generally entitled to exercise various exclusive rights in relation to its subject matter.
Property rights	Bundle of legal rights over the use to which a resource is put and over the use made of any income that may be derived from that resource are referred to as property rights.
Property	Assets defined in the broadest legal sense. Property includes the unrealized receivables of a cash basis taxpayer, but not services rendered.
Interest	In finance and economics, interest is the price paid by a borrower for the use of a lender's money. In other words, interest is the amount of paid to "rent" money for a period of time.
Inventory	Tangible property held for sale in the normal course of business or used in producing goods or services for sale is an inventory.
Market share	That fraction of an industry's output accounted for by an individual firm or group of firms is called market share.
Customs	Customs is an authority or agency in a country responsible for collecting customs duties and for controlling the flow of people, animals and goods (including personal effects and hazardous items) in and out of the country.
Trademark	A distinctive word, name, symbol, device, or combination thereof, which enables consumers to identify favored products or services and which may find protection under state or federal law is a trademark.

Go to **Cram101.com** for the Practice Tests for this Chapter.

Trademark infringement	Trademark infringement refers to unauthorized use of another's mark. The holder may recover damages and other remedies from the infringer.
Hasbro	Hasbro originated with the Mr. Potato Head toy. Mr. Potato Head was the invention of George Lerner in the late 1940s. The idea was originally sold to a breakfast cereal manufacturer so that the separate parts could be distributed as cereal package premiums.
Microsoft	Microsoft is a multinational computer technology corporation with 2004 global annual sales of US$39.79 billion and 71,553 employees in 102 countries and regions as of July 2006. It develops, manufactures, licenses, and supports a wide range of software products for computing devices.
Profit	Profit refers to the return to the resource entrepreneurial ability; total revenue minus total cost.
Transaction cost	A transaction cost is a cost incurred in making an economic exchange. For example, most people, when buying or selling a stock, must pay a commission to their broker; that commission is a transaction cost of doing the stock deal.
Forbes	David Churbuck founded online Forbes in 1996. The site drew attention when it uncovered Stephen Glass' journalistic fraud in The New Republic in 1998, a scoop that gave credibility to internet journalism.
Capital	Capital generally refers to financial wealth, especially that used to start or maintain a business. In classical economics, capital is one of four factors of production, the others being land and labor and entrepreneurship.
Complexity	The technical sophistication of the product and hence the amount of understanding required to use it is referred to as complexity. It is the opposite of simplicity.
Authority	Authority in agency law, refers to an agent's ability to affect his principal's legal relations with third parties. Also used to refer to an actor's legal power or ability to do something. In addition, sometimes used to refer to a statute, case, or other legal source that justifies a particular result.
Recession	A significant decline in economic activity. In the U.S., recession is approximately defined as two successive quarters of falling GDP, as judged by NBER.
Domestic	From or in one's own country. A domestic producer is one that produces inside the home country. A domestic price is the price inside the home country. Opposite of 'foreign' or 'world.'.
Competitor	Other organizations in the same industry or type of business that provide a good or service to the same set of customers is referred to as a competitor.
Research and development	The use of resources for the deliberate discovery of new information and ways of doing things, together with the application of that information in inventing new products or processes is referred to as research and development.
Developed country	A developed country is one that enjoys a relatively high standard of living derived through an industrialized, diversified economy. Countries with a very high Human Development Index are generally considered developed countries.
Asea Brown Boveri	Asea Brown Boveri, is a multinational corporation headquartered in Zürich, Switzerland, operating mainly in the power and automation technology areas. It operates in around 100 countries, with about 104,000 employees.
Reorganization	Reorganization occurs, among other instances, when one corporation acquires another in a merger or acquisition, a single corporation divides into two or more entities, or a corporation makes a substantial change in its capital structure.

Go to **Cram101.com** for the Practice Tests for this Chapter.

Go to **Cram101.com** for the Practice Tests for this Chapter.
And, **NEVER** highlight a book again!

Litigation	The process of bringing, maintaining, and defending a lawsuit is litigation.
Liability	A liability is a present obligation of the enterprise arizing from past events, the settlement of which is expected to result in an outflow from the enterprise of resources embodying economic benefits.
Stock market	An organized marketplace in which common stocks are traded. In the United States, the largest stock market is the New York Stock Exchange, on which are traded the stocks of the largest U.S. companies.
Stock	In financial terminology, stock is the capital raized by a corporation, through the issuance and sale of shares.
Core business	The core business of an organization is an idealized construct intended to express that organization's "main" or "essential" activity.
Core	A core is the set of feasible allocations in an economy that cannot be improved upon by subset of the set of the economy's consumers (a coalition). In construction, when the force in an element is within a certain center section, the core, the element will only be under compression.
Core competency	A company's core competency are things that a firm can (alsosns) do well and that meet the following three conditions. 1. It provides customer benefits, 2. It is hard for competitors to imitate, and 3. it can be leveraged widely to many products and market. A core competency can take various forms, including technical/subject matter knowhow, a reliable process, and/or close relationships with customers and suppliers. It may also include product development or culture such as employee dedication. Modern business theories suggest that most activities that are not part of a company's core competency should be outsourced.
Synergy	Corporate synergy occurs when corporations interact congruently. A corporate synergy refers to a financial benefit that a corporation expects to realize when it merges with or acquires another corporation.
Labor market	Any arrangement that brings buyers and sellers of labor services together to agree on conditions of work and pay is called a labor market.
Monopoly	A monopoly is defined as a persistent market situation where there is only one provider of a kind of product or service.
Information system	An information system is a system whether automated or manual, that comprises people, machines, and/or methods organized to collect, process, transmit, and disseminate data that represent user information.
Greenfield investment	In foreign investment, direct investment in new facilities or the expansion of existing facilities is Greenfield investment.
Market development	Selling existing products to new markets is called market development.
Tactic	A short-term immediate decision that, in its totality, leads to the achievement of strategic goals is called a tactic.
Lockheed Martin	Lockheed Martin is the world's largest defense contractor (by defense revenue). As of 2005, 95% of revenues came from the U.S. Department of Defense, other U.S. federal government agencies, and foreign military customers.
Airbus	In 2003, for the first time in its 33-year history, Airbus delivered more jet-powered airliners than Boeing. Boeing states that the Boeing 777 has outsold its Airbus counterparts, which include the A340 family as well as the A330-300. The smaller A330-200 competes with the 767, outselling its Boeing counterpart.

Go to **Cram101.com** for the Practice Tests for this Chapter.

Boeing	Boeing is the world's largest aircraft manufacturer by revenue. Headquartered in Chicago, Illinois, Boeing is the second-largest defense contractor in the world. In 2005, the company was the world's largest civil aircraft manufacturer in terms of value.
Nissan	Nissan is Japan's second largest car company after Toyota. Nissan is among the top three Asian rivals of the "big three" in the US.
Honda	With more than 14 million internal combustion engines built each year, Honda is the largest engine-maker in the world. In 2004, the company began to produce diesel motors, which were both very quiet whilst not requiring particulate filters to pass pollution standards. It is arguable, however, that the foundation of their success is the motorcycle division.
Corporate culture	The whole collection of beliefs, values, and behaviors of a firm that send messages to those within and outside the company about how business is done is the corporate culture.
Nestle	Nestle is the world's biggest food and beverage company. In the 1860s, a pharmacist, developed a food for babies who were unable to be breastfed. His first success was a premature infant who could not tolerate his own mother's milk nor any of the usual substitutes. The value of the new product was quickly recognized when his new formula saved the child's life.
Consultant	A professional that provides expert advice in a particular field or area in which customers occassionaly require this type of knowledge is a consultant.
Negotiation	Negotiation is the process whereby interested parties resolve disputes, agree upon courses of action, bargain for individual or collective advantage, and/or attempt to craft outcomes which serve their mutual interests.
Trust	An arrangement in which shareholders of independent firms agree to give up their stock in exchange for trust certificates that entitle them to a share of the trust's common profits.
Free trade	Free trade refers to a situation in which there are no artificial barriers to trade, such as tariffs and quotas. Usually used, often only implicitly, with frictionless trade, so that it implies that there are no barriers to trade of any kind.
Debt financing	Obtaining financing by borrowing money is debt financing.
Cost Leadership Strategy	Using a serious commitment to reducing expenses that, in turn, lowers the price of the items sold in a relatively broad array of market segments is called cost leadership strategy.
Differentiation Strategy	Differentiation strategy requires innovation and significant points of difference in product offerings, brand image, higher quality, advanced technology, or superior service in a relatively broad array of market segments.
Cost leadership	Organization's ability to achieve lower costs relative to competitors through productivity and efficiency improvements, elimination of waste, and tight cost control is cost leadership.
License	A license in the sphere of Intellectual Property Rights (IPR) is a document, contract or agreement giving permission or the 'right' to a legally-definable entity to do something (such as manufacture a product or to use a service), or to apply something (such as a trademark), with the objective of achieving commercial gain.
Exchange rate	Exchange rate refers to the price at which one country's currency trades for another, typically on the exchange market.
Currency exchange rate	The rate between two currencies that specifies how much one country's currency is worth expressed in terms of the other country's currency is the currency exchange rate.
Administration	Administration refers to the management and direction of the affairs of governments and institutions; a collective term for all policymaking officials of a government; the execution and implementation of public policy.

Euro	The common currency of a subset of the countries of the EU, adopted January 1, 1999 is called euro.
Licensee	A person lawfully on land in possession of another for purposes unconnected with the business interests of the possessor is referred to as the licensee.
International firm	International firm refers to those firms who have responded to stiff competition domestically by expanding their sales abroad. They may start a production facility overseas and send some of their managers, who report to a global division, to that country.
Caterpillar	Caterpillar is a United States based corporation headquartered in Peoria, Illinois. Caterpillar is "the world's largest manufacturer of construction and mining equipment, diesel and natural gas engines, and industrial gas turbines."
International Harvester	International Harvester was an American corporation based in Chicago that produced a multitude of agricultural machinery and vehicles. In 1924, International Harvester introduced the Farmall tractor, a smaller general-purpose tractor, to fend off competition from the Ford Motor Company's Fordson tractors. The Farmall was the first tractor in the United States to incorporate a tricycle-like design (or row-crop front axle), which could be used on tall crops such as cotton and corn.
Expense	In accounting, an expense represents an event in which an asset is used up or a liability is incurred. In terms of the accounting equation, expenses reduce owners' equity.
Tariff	A tax imposed by a nation on an imported good is called a tariff.
Advertising	Advertising refers to paid, nonpersonal communication through various media by organizations and individuals who are in some way identified in the advertising message.
Petition	A petition is a request to an authority, most commonly a government official or public entity. In the colloquial sense, a petition is a document addressed to some official and signed by numerous individuals.
North American Free Trade Agreement	A 1993 agreement establishing, over a 15-year period, a free trade zone composed of Canada, Mexico, and the United States is referred to as the North American Free Trade Agreement.
Retaliation	The use of an increased trade barrier in response to another country increasing its trade barrier, either as a way of undoing the adverse effects of the latter's action or of punishing it is retaliation.
Aid	Assistance provided by countries and by international institutions such as the World Bank to developing countries in the form of monetary grants, loans at low interest rates, in kind, or a combination of these is called aid. Aid can also refer to assistance of any type rendered to benefit some group or individual.
Estate	An estate is the totality of the legal rights, interests, entitlements and obligations attaching to property. In the context of wills and probate, it refers to the totality of the property which the deceased owned or in which some interest was held.
Agent	A person who makes economic decisions for another economic actor. A hired manager operates as an agent for a firm's owner.
Comprehensive	A comprehensive refers to a layout accurate in size, color, scheme, and other necessary details to show how a final ad will look. For presentation only, never for reproduction.
Entrepreneur	The owner/operator. The person who organizes, manages, and assumes the risks of a firm, taking a new idea or a new product and turning it into a successful business is an entrepreneur.
Fixture	Fixture refers to a thing that was originally personal property and that has been actually or

	constructively affixed to the soil itself or to some structure legally a part of the land.
Profit margin	Profit margin is a measure of profitability. It is calculated using a formula and written as a percentage or a number. Profit margin = Net income before tax and interest / Revenue.
Margin	A deposit by a buyer in stocks with a seller or a stockbroker, as security to cover fluctuations in the market in reference to stocks that the buyer has purchased but for which he has not paid is a margin. Commodities are also traded on margin.
Venture capital	Venture capital is capital provided by outside investors for financing of new, growing or struggling businesses. Venture capital investments generally are high risk investments but offer the potential for above average returns.
Venture capital firm	A financial intermediary that pools the resources of its partners and uses the funds to help entrepreneurs start up new businesses is referred to as a venture capital firm.
Driving force	The key external pressure that will shape the future for an organization is a driving force. The driving force in an industry are the main underlying causes of changing industry and competitive conditions.
Michael Dell	Michael Dell is the founder of Dell, Inc., the world's largest computer manufacturer which revolutionized the home computer industry.
Proactive	To be proactive is to act before a situation becomes a source of confrontation or crisis. It is the opposite of "retroactive," which refers to actions taken after an event.
Creative destruction	The hypothesis that the creation of new products and production methods simultaneously destroys the market power of existing monopolies is referred to as creative destruction.
Business model	A business model is the instrument by which a business intends to generate revenue and profits. It is a summary of how a company means to serve its employees and customers, and involves both strategy (what an business intends to do) as well as an implementation.
Social entrepreneur-hip	Social entrepreneurship is the act of recognizing a social problem and useing traditional entrepreneurial principles to organize, create, and manage a venture to make social change.
Private sector	The households and business firms of the economy are referred to as private sector.
Public sector	Public sector refers to the part of the economy that contains all government entities; government.
Public policy	Decision making by government. Governments are constantly concerned about what they should or should not do. And whatever they do or do not do is public policy. public program All those activities designed to implement a public policy; often this calls for the creation of organizations, public agencies, and bureaus.
Drucker	Drucker as a business thinker took off in the 1940s, when his initial writings on politics and society won him access to the internal workings of General Motors, which was one of the largest companies in the world at that time. His experiences in Europe had left him fascinated with the problem of authority.
Productivity	Productivity refers to the total output of goods and services in a given period of time divided by work hours.
Human capital	Human capital refers to the stock of knowledge and skill, embodied in an individual as a result of education, training, and experience that makes them more productive. The stock of knowledge and skill embodied in the population of an economy.
Patent	The legal right to the proceeds from and control over the use of an invented product or process, granted for a fixed period of time, usually 20 years. Patent is one form of

Go to **Cram101.com** for the Practice Tests for this Chapter.

	intellectual property that is subject of the TRIPS agreement.
Shareholder	A shareholder is an individual or company (including a corporation) that legally owns one or more shares of stock in a joined stock company.
Apple Computer	Apple Computer has been a major player in the evolution of personal computing since its founding in 1976. The Apple II microcomputer, introduced in 1977, was a hit with home users.
Users	Users refer to people in the organization who actually use the product or service purchased by the buying center.
Market position	Market position is a measure of the position of a company or product on a market.
Credit	Credit refers to a recording as positive in the balance of payments, any transaction that gives rise to a payment into the country, such as an export, the sale of an asset, or borrowing from abroad.
Economic development	Increase in the economic standard of living of a country's population, normally accomplished by increasing its stocks of physical and human capital and improving its technology is an economic development.
Balance	In banking and accountancy, the outstanding balance is the amount of money owned, (or due), that remains in a deposit account (or a loan account) at a given date, after all past remittances, payments and withdrawal have been accounted for. It can be positive (then, in the balance sheet of a firm, it is an asset) or negative (a liability).
Product development	In business and engineering, new product development is the complete process of bringing a new product to market. There are two parallel aspects to this process : one involves product engineering ; the other marketing analysis. Marketers see new product development as the first stage in product life cycle management, engineers as part of Product Lifecycle Management.
New product development	New product development is the complete process of bringing a new product to market. There are two parallel aspects to this process : one involves product engineering ; the other marketing analysis.
Knowledge base	Knowledge base refers to a database that includes decision rules for use of the data, which may be qualitative as well as quantitative.
Commercializ-tion	Promoting a product to distributors and retailers to get wide distribution and developing strong advertising and sales campaigns to generate and maintain interest in the product among distributors and consumers is commercialization.
Product champion	A person who is able and willing to cut red tape and move the program forward is called product champion.
Corporate Strategy	Corporate strategy is concerned with the firm's choice of business, markets and activities and thus it defines the overall scope and direction of the business.
Ford Motor Company	Ford Motor Company introduced methods for large-scale manufacturing of cars, and large-scale management of an industrial workforce, especially elaborately engineered manufacturing sequences typified by the moving assembly lines. Henry Ford's combination of highly efficient factories, highly paid workers, and low prices revolutionized manufacturing and came to be known around the world as Fordism by 1914.
Ford	Ford is an American company that manufactures and sells automobiles worldwide. Ford introduced methods for large-scale manufacturing of cars, and large-scale management of an industrial workforce, especially elaborately engineered manufacturing sequences typified by the moving assembly lines.
Functional	A type of structure in which units and departments are organized based on the activity or

Go to **Cram101.com** for the Practice Tests for this Chapter.

Go to **Cram101.com** for the Practice Tests for this Chapter.
And, **NEVER** highlight a book again!

structure	function that they perform is called the functional structure.
Organizational structure	Organizational structure is the way in which the interrelated groups of an organization are constructed. From a managerial point of view the main concerns are ensuring effective communication and coordination.
Product development teams	Combinations of work teams and problem-solving teams that create new designs for products or services that will satisfy customer needs are product development teams.
Product innovations	Innovations that introduce new goods or services to better meet customer needs are product innovations.
Product innovation	The development and sale of a new or improved product is a product innovation. Production of a new product on a commercial basis.
Preparation	Preparation refers to usually the first stage in the creative process. It includes education and formal training.
Organizational politics	Organizational politics occurs when power sources and influence tactics are used to serve personal goals or motives.
Time orientation	The extent to which members of a culture adopt a long term versus a short term outlook on work is time orientation.
Strategic intent	Strategic intent is when a firm relentlessly pursues a difficult strategic goa and concentrates its competitive actions and energies on achieving that goal.
Effective communication	When the intended meaning equals the perceived meaning it is called effective communication.
Product design	Product Design is defined as the idea generation, concept development, testing and manufacturing or implementation of a physical object or service. It is possibly the evolution of former discipline name - Industrial Design.
Competitive market	A market in which no buyer or seller has market power is called a competitive market.
Social capital	Capital that provides services to the public. Most social capital takes the form of public goods and public services.
Lease	A contract for the possession and use of land or other property, including goods, on one side, and a recompense of rent or other income on the other is the lease.
Targeting	In advertizing, targeting is to select a demographic or other group of people to advertise to, and create advertisements appropriately.
Leverage	Leverage is using given resources in such a way that the potential positive or negative outcome is magnified. In finance, this generally refers to borrowing.
Cisco Systems	While Cisco Systems was not the first company to develop and sell a router (a device that forwards computer traffic from one network to another), it did create the first commercially successful multi-protocol router to allow previously incompatible computers to communicate using different network protocols.
Collaboration	Collaboration occurs when the interaction between groups is very important to goal attainment and the goals are compatible. Wherein people work together —applying both to the work of individuals as well as larger collectives and societies.
Customer contact	Customer contact refers to a characteristic of services that notes that customers tend to be more involved in the production of services than they are in manufactured goods.

Go to **Cram101.com** for the Practice Tests for this Chapter.

Commodity	Could refer to any good, but in trade a commodity is usually a raw material or primary product that enters into international trade, such as metals or basic agricultural products.
Strategic goal	A strategic goal is a broad statement of where an organization wants to be in the future; pertains to the organization as a whole rather than to specific divisions or departments.
Capital market	A financial market in which long-term debt and equity instruments are traded is referred to as a capital market. The capital market includes the stock market and the bond market.
Market value	Market value refers to the price of an asset agreed on between a willing buyer and a willing seller; the price an asset could demand if it is sold on the open market.
Novartis	Novartis was created in 1996 from the merger of Ciba-Geigy and Sandoz Laboratories, both Swiss companies with long individual histories. At the time of the merger, it was the largest corporate merger in history.
Strategic control	Strategic control processes allow managers to evaluate a company's marketing program from a critical long-term perspective. This involves a detailed and objective analysis of a company's organization and its ability to maximize its strengths and market opportunities.
Financial control	A process in which a firm periodically compares its actual revenues, costs, and expenses with its projected ones is called financial control.
Venture capitalists	Venture capitalists refer to individuals or companies that invest in new businesses in exchange for partial ownership of those businesses.
Rate of return	A rate of return is a comparison of the money earned (or lost) on an investment to the amount of money invested.
Food and Drug Administration	The Food and Drug Administration is an agency of the United States Department of Health and Human Services and is responsible for regulating food (human and animal), dietary supplements, drugs (human and animal), cosmetics, medical devices (human and animal) and radiation emitting devices (including non-medical devices), biologics, and blood products in the United States.
Pfizer	Pfizer is the world's largest pharmaceutical company based in New York City. It produces the number-one selling drug Lipitor (atorvastatin, used to lower blood cholesterol).
Analyst	Analyst refers to a person or tool with a primary function of information analysis, generally with a more limited, practical and short term set of goals than a researcher.
Trial	An examination before a competent tribunal, according to the law of the land, of the facts or law put in issue in a cause, for the purpose of determining such issue is a trial. When the court hears and determines any issue of fact or law for the purpose of determining the rights of the parties, it may be considered a trial.
Controlling	A management function that involves determining whether or not an organization is progressing toward its goals and objectives, and taking corrective action if it is not is called controlling.
Controlling interest	A firm has a controlling interest in another business entity when it owns more than 50 percent of that entity's voting stock.
Holding	The holding is a court's determination of a matter of law based on the issue presented in the particular case. In other words: under this law, with these facts, this result.
Portfolio	In finance, a portfolio is a collection of investments held by an institution or a private individual. Holding but not always a portfolio is part of an investment and risk-limiting strategy called diversification. By owning several assets, certain types of risk (in particular specific risk) can be reduced.

Go to **Cram101.com** for the Practice Tests for this Chapter.

Initial public offering	Firms in the process of becoming publicly traded companies will issue shares of stock using an initial public offering, which is merely the process of selling stock for the first time to interested investors.
Investment banker	Investment banker refers to a financial organization that specializes in selling primary offerings of securities. Investment bankers can also perform other financial functions, such as advising clients, negotiating mergers and takeovers, and selling secondary offerings.
Economic growth	Economic growth refers to the increase over time in the capacity of an economy to produce goods and services and to improve the well-being of its citizens.
Process innovations	Innovations introducing into operations new and better ways of doing things are called process innovations. Nominations in this category must have made significant achievements in reducing environmental impacts of manufacturing processes, including the acquisition and refinement of materials used by the transportation industries in their products
Process innovation	The development and use of new or improved production or distribution methods is called process innovation. It is an approach in business process reengineering by which radical changes are made through innovations.
Economic problem	Economic problem refers to how to determine the use of scarce resources among competing uses. Because resources are scarce, the economy must choose what products to produce; how these products are to be produced: and for whom.
Stakeholder	A stakeholder is an individual or group with a vested interest in or expectation for organizational performance. Usually stakeholders can either have an effect on or are affected by an organization.
Brief	Brief refers to a statement of a party's case or legal arguments, usually prepared by an attorney. Also used to make legal arguments before appellate courts.
Fringe benefits	The rewards other than wages that employees receive from their employers and that include pensions, medical and dental insurance, paid vacations, and sick leaves are referred to as fringe benefits.
Fringe benefit	Benefits such as sick-leave pay, vacation pay, pension plans, and health plans that represent additional compenzation to employees beyond base wages is a fringe benefit.
Closing	The finalization of a real estate sales transaction that passes title to the property from the seller to the buyer is referred to as a closing. Closing is a sales term which refers to the process of making a sale. It refers to reaching the final step, which may be an exchange of money or acquiring a signature.
Shares	Shares refer to an equity security, representing a shareholder's ownership of a corporation. Shares are one of a finite number of equal portions in the capital of a company, entitling the owner to a proportion of distributed, non-reinvested profits known as dividends and to a portion of the value of the company in case of liquidation.
Internal environment	Variables that are under some degree of control by organizational members is the internal enviroment. Internal environment scans are conducted to identify an organization's internal capabilities, performance levels, strengths, and weaknesses.
Small business	Small business refers to a business that is independently owned and operated, is not dominant in its field of operation, and meets certain standards of size in terms of employees or annual receipts.
Affiliates	Local television stations that are associated with a major network are called affiliates. Affiliates agree to preempt time during specified hours for programming provided by the network and carry the advertising contained in the program.

Go to **Cram101.com** for the Practice Tests for this Chapter.

Organizational learning	Organizational learning is an area of knowledge within organizational theory that studies models and theories about the way an organization learns and adapts.
Knowledge management	Sharing, organizing and disseminating information in the simplest and most relevant way possible for the users of the information is a knowledge management.
General Electric	In 1876, Thomas Alva Edison opened a new laboratory in Menlo Park, New Jersey. Out of the laboratory was to come perhaps the most famous invention of all—a successful development of the incandescent electric lamp. By 1890, Edison had organized his various businesses into the Edison General Electric Company.
Vendor	A person who sells property to a vendee is a vendor. The words vendor and vendee are more commonly applied to the seller and purchaser of real estate, and the words seller and buyer are more commonly applied to the seller and purchaser of personal property.
Interdependence	The extent to which departments depend on each other for resources or materials to accomplish their tasks is referred to as interdependence.
Empowerment	Giving employees the authority and responsibility to respond quickly to customer requests is called empowerment.
Paradox	As used in economics, paradox means something unexpected, rather than the more extreme normal meaning of something seemingly impossible. Some paradoxes are just theoretical results that go against what one thinks of as normal.
Dysfunctional conflict	Conflict that is responsible for hindering group performance is dysfunctional conflict.
Sun Microsystems	Sun Microsystems is most well known for its Unix systems, which have a reputation for system stability and a consistent design philosophy.
Sponsorship	When the advertiser assumes responsibility for the production and usually the content of a television program as well as the advertising that appears within it, we have sponsorship.

Go to **Cram101.com** for the Practice Tests for this Chapter.